IS YOUR GOD
GOOD?

Searching for Why We Suffer

Dave Jackson

CASTLE
ROCK
CREATIVE

Champaign, Illinois 61822

Published by Castle Rock Creative
Champaign, Illinois 61822

ISBN: 978-1-7372401-1-2

Cover Design: Julian Jackson

Printed in the United States of America

For a complete listing of
books by Dave and Neta Jackson visit
www.daveneta.com
www.riskinggrace.com
www.trailblazerbooks.com

Endorsements

Theologians, Pastors, Philosophers, Therapists

Dave Jackson takes on perhaps the greatest single obstacle to faith in the Christian God—the widespread occurrence of seemingly unfair and senseless suffering. He does not downplay the seriousness of the problem or offer simplistic solutions. Suffering is often random and not always deserved. Nor does he dodge the difficulty of certain biblical texts that portray God as the agent of evils but emphatically urges readers to consider Jesus Christ as the definitive revelation of God that corrects these all-too-human ancient, albeit "biblical" misconceptions of God's moral character. Jackson makes good use of personal anecdotes taken from years of experience as a pastor, writer, teacher, and Army National Guard member to offer a very readable, knowledgeable, and practically wise Christian approach to the problem of God and human suffering.

—John R. Schneider,
Professor Emeritus of Theology,
Calvin University

How can we believe that God is perfectly good when so many prayers go unanswered, when so much pain and evil is allowed to take place, and when Scripture sometimes depicts him as a violent nationalistic warrior deity? In *Is Your God Good?*, Jackson boldly addresses these and other objections to the goodness of God, providing insightful and informed responses at every turn. Everyone who is concerned with the character of God and the problem of evil would benefit from this work.

—Greg Boyd, author, theologian, and
Teaching Pastor, Woodland Hills Church,
Maplewood, Minnesota

When it comes to the core Christian belief that "God is good all the time," the American Church is confused and divided, especially on the question of suffering and the sovereignty of God. This leaves the door open for many to assume that church-goers worship a deity who intends and causes harm. The strength of Jackson's *Is Your God*

Good is his willingness to step on toes to address this most complex of theological questions, and in a way understandable by regular folks. His approach is unapologetically gospel-centered, looking to Christ to ultimately clarify the nature of God. For all who long to believe that God is indeed good all of the time and that "if it isn't good, it isn't God," here is a book that offers both comfort and confidence.

—Julia Pferdehirt, LPC, author of *Soul Mending*
and other books on mental and spiritual health

As a pastor, I can think of dozens of conversations I've had with people who were struggling with the very questions Jackson addresses. I wish I'd had a resource like this to give them. This book is thoughtful and accessible for anyone wrestling with some of the hard questions of faith, especially when it comes to understanding the heart of God and how God engages with humanity.

—Scott Keebles, Lead Pastor,
Copper Creek Church, Champaign, Illinois

Jackson has written a very engaging and easy to read survey of various views on God and suffering. He does not hesitate to proclaim his unwavering belief in God's innate goodness in the face of difficult Scripture passages and hard-to-explain life situations. Whether you agree with every one of Jackson's conclusions or not, this book will be helpful to you if you are struggling with unhelpful messages you may have received in the midst of your suffering. May it guide you deeper into the arms of our eternally loving God.

—X. Nader Sahyouni, DMin, LCPC, author of
Anxiety Transformed, Prayer that Brings Enduring Change

Is Your God Good? Searching for Why We Suffer does crucial work. Some of that work is conceptual. We subscribe to theological ideas and to ways of reading Scripture that deliver spoiled products when we suffer. Jackson names these ideas and ways and offers better alternatives. Some of the work is pastoral. By naming his own experience with suffering, Jackson makes it safe for readers to explore how their own suffering has been excused, denied, ignored, or even justified in the name of God. There are no final answers here, but if honest, productive engagement is what you are looking for, I highly recommend *Is Your God Good?*

—Gregory A. Clark, Ph.D.,
Professor of Philosophy, North Park University

If I praise God for the good in my life and believe God is in control, how do I not also believe I am being punished or it is my fault when bad things happen? With well documented historical references, *Is Your God Good?* provides a powerful foundation for understanding that God's role in our lives always comes from a place of love. One of the biggest gifts Jackson highlights is the ongoing revelatory nature of God's teachings. Rather than condemning past scholars or perspectives, he notes that they were based on what had been revealed and what the authors could understand at the time. When tragedies occur, we are compassionately made aware of our own beliefs and given permission to grieve, question wrong or limited teachings, doubt, experience anger, and not know everything, while holding onto God's love and support as we heal.

—Ruth Lipschutz, LCSW, ACSW

In this present, disorienting political moment, where $60 Bibles incorporate the U.S. Constitution and "God Bless America," Jackson's book, *Is Your God Good?* could not be more timely. While the Word of God has always had a history of being misused, today's Christ-followers (particularly the emerging generations) are disillusioned by the present American-brand of Christianity that has propagated all kinds of violence and human suffering in the name of God. In the face of such jaw-dropping displays of Christian nationalism like the January 6th insurrection, young believers have all but dismissed the Bible as dangerously archaic. Jackson's read is a labor-of-love, helping "set the record straight" on the irrefutable goodness of God via a remarkable survey of some of the Bible's most difficult texts and narratives, and in a way accessible to all ages. Furthermore, Jackson's discussion ranges from the cosmic and philosophical to the on-the-ground practical. I cannot overstate the contribution this book can make to the health and renewal of a Church in crisis.

—Dr. Craig Wong
Executive Director, New College Berkeley

For all who cry, "Why?"

CONTENTS

God did not wait until the Israelites were fully convinced of his sovereignty to begin revealing himself as other than violent and retributive. He began immediately to correct their misconceptions, but it wasn't until he came as Jesus to live among us that the full goodness of his character was revealed.

Jesus' disciples expected a violent Messiah to throw off the Romans. But political revolution was not his purpose. He did not come to "tune up" old ideas, getting people to obey Mosaic Law more strictly. With the authority and the character of the "I AM," he introduced a New Covenant with new ethics and goals.

Much suffering stems from unmitigated evil, in which God cannot have been involved. The ultimate example is Satan's rebellion. Passages, such as the man born blind, are poor translations, suggesting God planned it. Some scriptures that sound like threats from God may have been warnings of natural consequences.

Proving the literal details of the Creation and Flood stories reveals the absurdity of insisting all Scripture is inerrant. But Paul already told us, "For now we see only . . . in part." Did the Bible's authors see only in part, also? Thankfully, Jesus brings us corrections to—not contradictions within—our understanding of God.

The Book of Job is the most extended examination of suffering in the Bible, and it is based on two common premises believed by both ancient and many modern people: (1) God micromanages all events. (2) God primarily blesses those who please him and vents his wrath on those who displease him. However, . . .

Many read God's response to Job as a put down, but God may have had a deeper purpose by revealing to Job things in the universe about which Job had little understanding. Job responded, "My ears had heard of you but now my eyes have seen you," relieving him of his two great errors about the sources of suffering.

We also may need a "magical mystery tour." Imbedded in the evolutionary beauty of the universe are many events we might call "natural disasters." But without them, we couldn't exist. Grasping this complex requisite reveals *why* God allows complications such as freewill that characterize us as humans rather than robots.

The *past, present,* and *future*—time moves in one direction at a constant pace, right? No, reality is bigger. Our plans are *finite;* defined by our perception of time, but God's purposes are *infinite.* Without predestining everything, God can adjust to any possibility, allowing humans freewill while still achieving his purposes.

Satan's rebellion against God resulted in a cosmic battle that includes human warfare. Satan doesn't care who wins because he's not fighting for one side or the other; he's only interested in pitting us against each other. Forced to face people around my church with a gun rather than God's Word, I withdrew from the Army.

The "penal substitutionary" theory that *God's anger* required death for our sins is not the only way to understand Christ's Atonement. In *The Lion, the Witch, and the Wardrobe,* C.S. Lewis portrays the *"Christus victor"* or "ransom theory" (favored by the early church), in which Satan is the one demanding our death.

Judgment exposes behavior as good or evil, also revealing our unfaithfulness to God and our harm to others. Full repentance relieves suffering far more than does punishment. Facing the truth and turning from sin is essential to spend eternity with God and one another. But it's not required to follow Satan and his minions.

Jesus' miracles transformed history. And we can recognize more miracles when we note that *all* good gifts are from him. But though God is sovereign, he has not *chosen* to micromanage *all* events and rarely thwarts human freewill. Still, he welcomes our prayers and speaks if we listen. Those are also miracles.

God's discipline might not be easy, but it doesn't harm, destroy, or kill. Instead, it heals and strengthens. Hebrews 12 speaks of a father's *love* and a sports analogy of strengthening weak limbs. Jesus' analogy of the vine and branches in John 15 does not mean branches are "cut off" but cleaned and lifted up.

Redemptive suffering is different from other kinds. By suffering while spreading the Gospel or in someone else's place, we do not replace Christ's work on the Cross, but we share in Christ's suffering by joining the fight against Satan. While God does not cause it, he gives us a degree of agency to embrace the risk or not.

After reviewing the assumptions of bad theology that characterize God as violent and retributive, we are free to embrace his goodness by joining Jesus' sacrificial mission to free all of humanity from Satan's claims and influence. We can resist evil, pray, not fear, embrace change, practice thanksgiving, live by faith, and sing!

A selective list of books on suffering or issues related to the bad theology that cause people to doubt the goodness of God from authors: Gregory Boyd, Jerry Bridges, Paul Copan, Bart Ehrman, Timothy Keller, Peter Kreeft, C.S. Lewis, Thomas Joy Oord, J.B. Phillips, Paul David Tripp, and Philip Yancey.

Introduction

My heart is not proud, O LORD, my eyes are
not haughty; I do not concern myself with great
matters or things too difficult for me.
But I have stilled and quieted my soul; like a weaned child
with its mother, like a weaned child is my soul within me.
. . . Put your hope in the LORD both now and forevermore.

—*Psalm 131, by David*

THE PROBLEM IS, WHEN IT COMES TO SUFFERING, we are all involved in great matters too difficult for us to fully understand. If we could leave them alone, as the psalmist advises, we would.

But we can't! We wonder if God causes suffering—or at least doesn't care enough to stop it. Might God be more intent on executing specific plans than avoiding collateral damage? Is suffering always traceable to someone's sin? "Who sinned, this man or his parents?" asked the disciples about the man born blind—the same presumption made by Job and his friends.

The reason we can't help but ask these questions goes beyond the demands of our own suffering to include the wrong answers we have received from others, even wrong answers believed by some ancient biblical characters. Answers that characterize God as so much harsher than Jesus Christ, as though we're supposed to amalgamate two different deities.

To unravel this dilemma, we need to revisit the earliest characterization of God's attributes as portrayed through the stories of Noah's flood, God's interaction with Abraham, Isaac, and Jacob, the Israelites' Exodus and sojourn in the wilderness, the Law given through Moses, and the conquest of Canaan. In those reports, God was said to either bless or curse people based on their behavior;

1

God was willing to annihilate his enemies and even encourage his followers to conduct genocide.

If from those stories we believe—even subconsciously—that God proved his sovereignty through violence, control, and retribution, where does that leave us? When we suffer or see others suffer, do we think God is behind it all? Such a view differs so sharply from who God showed himself to be when he dwelt among us as Jesus Christ that we are compelled to ask: *Why this big difference?*

That contradiction doesn't work for a lot of people. Research by the Barna Group shows that the percentage of agnostics and atheists among the Gen Z population is 174 percent higher than among Boomers.[1] Even among older people, I just spoke to a friend who grew up in the church, who said, "Hey, Dave, you know that book you're working on? Well, I *don't* believe God is good! Not anymore. Not after what's happening in the Middle East." But it wasn't only that, and she's not alone. People of all ages, and maybe you're among them, have a hard time believing that a good God would allow so much evil or suffering in the world.

In this book we'll dig into the arc of Scripture's narratives. Only in its full sweep do we begin to see how God's character was initially misunderstood and why he did not redact those early characterizations. Instead, God began to make known his true character until, in the promised Messiah, we find the full revelation of himself as *truly good,* a God of unfathomable love. The implications may not explain all suffering, but we'll be less inclined to blame God.

This search for why we suffer discloses four important theses:

1. **Biblical inspiration**. We cannot equate the descriptions of God's character recorded by the prophets of old with God's immeasurably more perfect self-revelation through the words, actions, and attitudes God exhibited as Immanuel, God with us in Jesus Christ. If any disparity appears, we must embrace the more perfect revelation of God's love in Jesus, and humbly

---

1. Barna Group, "Atheism Doubles Among Generation Z," 2018, https://www.barna.com/research/atheism-doubles-among-generation-z/.

accept that the ideas we gathered from other sources, even the patriarchs, may not have conveyed the full picture.

2. **Humans were made in the image of God**. And therefore, God honors our ability to make choices. We may not understand all their consequences or be free from all pressures, but God will not violate our agency to choose. God invites, explains, appeals, warns, scolds, even disciplines. But he does not coerce or lobotomize us. Even though numerous biblical passages affirm this truth, we often overlook the implications of God's gift of freewill for ourselves and others, hoping—even praying—that God would intervene in ways that would violate someone's freewill.

3. **God's purpose**. God operates inconceivably beyond our experience of the passage of time. Before the creation of the universe, he had a purpose for humanity and for each of us. But we tend to envision the *way* God pursues his purposes according to how we humans execute our plans by micromanaging everything over which we have sufficient power. Our plans are *finite*; but God's purposes are *infinite*. God doesn't need to control everything to achieve his purposes. Even in the context of an active cosmic war, God is not surprised by Satan's attacks, the seemingly random dangers in nature, or the consequences of human freewill. Therefore, God does not need to micromanage the universe. Instead, Scripture documents God's adjustments *and* willingness to embrace us as partners in achieving his purposes. When we fail (or don't listen), God never leaves us, but forgives and adjusts.

4. **God does not gaslight**. God never asks us to deny the reality of suffering by calling it "good." Instead, God respects the sincere seeker's ability to "Taste and see that the Lord is good," as the psalmist said. And Jesus reminded us, "If you, then, though you are evil, know how to give good gifts to your children, how much more will your Father in heaven give good gifts to those who ask him!" We *can* recognize what's good and not good, and that means we don't have to deny our suffering.

As you will discover as you read, I am not qualified to address the topic of suffering based on my personal experience of suffering in any intense manner. Yes, I've had cancer, undergone open-heart surgery, and nearly lost my sight. And at my age, I can keep pace with other seniors swapping tales of daily aches and pains or contemplating this life's approaching close. But all of that is very different from people who have lost a child, endured years of excruciating pain from disease or wounds or faced constant discrimination, abuse, enslavement, poverty, or hopelessness. Nor have I endured war, famine, persecution, homelessness, or a major natural disaster. My suffering has been rather pedestrian.

However, I care about and am deeply moved by people who have suffered far more than I have and feel compelled to make some sense out of what's happened to them. I am also someone who recognizes the profound and undeserved grace I've received to escape such suffering, to the point that I can empathize with a friend who struggled with why he should thank God for *his* food when the same God has not fed the nine million people who die of starvation each year—perhaps a form of survivor syndrome—until he pretty much gave up on God.

So, I wrestle with all of this in the context of a God who I experience as active, who I believe speaks personally to me (when I'll listen), and who on more than one occasion saved me from death.

Nevertheless, if you are looking for *the* fits-all answer for why we suffer, I'll save you some time: I don't know! Some suffering involves mysteries I don't understand, and neither do far greater thinkers who have tackled this subject over the centuries. But I'm convinced there are some very popular as well as some very ancient answers that confuse us and compound our suffering by causing us to conclude that the God we want to believe is *good* is neither good nor trustworthy if we apply the logical consequences of those traditional answers. Those answers imply that our suffering is what we deserve, and we should therefore just embrace it.

C.S. Lewis, the renowned twentieth-century author of *The Chronicles of Narnia* and nonfiction works of Christian apologetics such as *Mere Christianity* said, "Pain insists upon being attended to. God whispers to us in our pleasures, speaks in our consciences, but shouts in our pains. It is his megaphone to rouse a deaf world."[2] But if misguided Christians translate God's *shouts* as: "I control all things, including causing you to suffer," "It's your fault—your sin and lack of faith," or even "I don't care about human pain," then that bad theology will drive people away from the church and any trust they may have had in a good God.

There are several kinds of suffering and several sources of suffering. They are not the same. Some people wrongly blame God, and some wrongly blame the victim, even if they are the victim. But both indictments separate us from the love of God and his promise to be with us always. Nothing can make suffering worse than to face it alone! But we don't have to.

So, join me in this search to clear out some false answers—some bad theology, if you will—and identify some other answers that, while not comprehensive, are at least more understandable. Then we can *be still and quiet our souls like a weaned child with its mother and put our hope in the LORD both now and forevermore*, leaving what mysteries remain in the hands of our good God.

Discussion Questions

1. How might our view of God's character impact our presumptions about why there is so much suffering in the world?
2. What are some implications of the idea that "Our plans are *finite*; but God's purposes are *infinite*"?
3. Why might some people not distinguish between different kinds of suffering and different sources of suffering?

---

2. C.S. Lewis, *The Problem of Pain*, (New York: Macmillan, 1962), 93.

Chapter 1
What Is the Weight that Stifles Faith?

"I can't breathe. I can't breathe. I can't breathe!
I can't breathe. I can't breathe. I can't breathe!
I can't breathe. I can't breathe. I can't breathe!
I can't breathe. I can't breathe. I can't breathe!
I can't breathe. I can't . . ."

> —*George Floyd, crying for mercy twenty-seven times over nine minutes while a Minneapolis police officer pinned him to the street with a knee compressing his neck until he died, May 25, 2020.*

WHY DIDN'T DEREK CHAUVIN'S FELLOW OFFICERS pull their supervisor off the already subdued and handcuffed George Floyd? Why didn't several bystanders take their own lives into their hands and charge Derek Chauvin to knock him off Floyd? Why didn't a voice from heaven boom, "This is my son, whom I love; *GET OFF HIS NECK!*"[1]

There were so many ways God could have stepped in to save George Floyd's life. So, why didn't he?

---

1. More than once, God spoke from heaven in an audible voice, saying, "This is my son, whom I love . . ." [See Jesus' baptism (Matt. 3:17) and on the Mount of Transfiguration (Luke 9:35) where God validated Jesus' divinity]. Scripture also reports other instances (e.g., 1 Kings 19:13; Ezra 12; 22; 30; John 12:28; 2 Pet. 1:17 etc.). So, God could have used the first two phrases regarding George Floyd. After all, Floyd was a child of God and God did love him. I also believe God never intended Chauvin to murder him.

Or why didn't God intervene to spare my dear friend Jan and her husband, Jerral, from the years they and their little Jimmy suffered after he was born with Hurler Syndrome, a rare birth defect resulting from a missing gene that eventually leads to severe deformities and a terrifying death before age ten, often from respiratory failure.[2] (*"I can't breathe!"*)

The horror of struggling to get a diagnosis, the incompetence and ignorance of some medical professionals, and physicians reluctant to try new treatments to ease the symptoms was all more than any family should have to endure. But their most bewildering discovery was that both parents must carry the recessive gene before the disease manifests. So how could Jan and Jerral, who were both strong Christians, have been confident that God had *led* them together? Had God tricked them? As she put it, "How could I have found 'Mr. Right,' and this have happened to us?" Is it God's will that *any* baby be brought into this world . . . *to suffer*?

Jan has a lot to teach me about managing suffering, but the details of her son's battle for life and the alternative medical treatments she found helpful are her story to tell.[3] I don't need to give you more details of her family's suffering just to grab your attention because, if you're reading this book out of more than mere curiosity, you already know something about suffering, and you, too, are already asking, *Why?*

Our hearts rightly break over Jimmy's tragedy as well as sweeping historical events like the genocide of indigenous people, the inhumane greed of slavery, the Holocaust, the Black Death, or the back-and-forth blood and torture of the Reformation. All such suffering seems to be the risk of humankind—perhaps of all cre-

---

2. While there is still no cure for Hurler syndrome, treatment now exists to extend life that involves weekly IV enzyme replacement therapy (ERT), bone marrow transplant, and various surgeries to reverse damage the disease has already caused. https://www.chop.edu/stories/bone-marrow-transplant-treat-hurler-syndrome-josie-s-story.

3. I have summarized Jimmy's experience from the forthcoming book by Jan Rogers Wimberley, *The Unprejudiced Mind: A Personal and Upfront Journey and Fight for Life.* For publication information, email naturalguru@startmail.com.

ation—and we can't help but ask, "Why doesn't God stop it? Does he not care? Is he not powerful enough? Why? *Why? WHY?*"

When Jesus said, "In this world you will have trouble. But take heart! I have overcome the world" (John 16:33), some of us may think he was encouraging us to not become discouraged by everyday challenges. But that is not the context. Jesus was speaking of real persecution, even martyrdom. When enslaved people in this country sang "Soon-a will be done-a / With the trouble of the world / Goin' home to live with God,"[4] they were in effect asking, *Why?* and grasping for the faith to survive beatings, rapes, and their families being ripped apart.

But there is another kind of suffering that is also real.

The Accumulation of Trauma

Suffering is always personal and subjective. That's because suffering often results from more than a single shock. It can also be the accumulation of the presenting trauma on top of previous unhealed hits that churn in your chest until the sorrow and grief weigh so heavily on your neck you can't grab a breath . . . and it goes on and on. This can even happen when you are not the direct recipient of trauma if your vicarious experience of someone else's ordeal triggers you personally.

In the past, I often thought some people just needed to buck up and quit whining if they claimed they were "suffering" over setbacks to their plans or slights from others or privileges they lost that were never there for other people in the first place. I thought calling such challenges *suffering* demeaned people who truly suffer, and perhaps it does. However, sometimes what may appear to others like common or small troubles, might actually be the last straw in a whole string of things that pushes someone over the edge. That weight on your neck from which you cannot seem to rise might be genuine suffering even if you're not a refugee from gang violence in Central America who is fleeing with three small

---

4. Originally sung by enslaved African Americans, Mahalia Jackson made it famous in the 1959 film, "Imitation of Life," in addition to later recordings. Sinead O'Connor revived it in support of the Black Lives Matter movement in her October 2020 single.

children. Even if you haven't battled the pain of terminal cancer for months on end that no opioid can dampen. Even if no tsunami has wiped out your town and most of your family and neighbors. Even if your whole country has not been reduced to rubble by the war of a tyrant. Even if you're not caught in a sexually abusive relationship no one else seems to believe or understand. Even if social and political chaos has buried you under total despair. While these are the kinds of trauma that characterize classic suffering, they are not the only things.

I am not someone who has experienced suffering of that more devastating kind. Perhaps the closest I came was in 2005 when I endured five eye surgeries over several months in an effort to save the vision in my left eye after a macular hole had developed. I agonized and wondered *why* and prayed harder than I'd ever prayed, while I went legally blind in that eye . . . until finally, Norm Blair, a brother in Christ and one of the finest retinal surgeons in the country, succeeded in stopping the cascading deterioration, and I regained close to 20/30 corrected vision in that eye. I thank God that no problems developed in my right eye.

But two months after those surgeries, I was diagnosed with papillary thyroid carcinoma—thyroid cancer. Thankfully, it was detected very early, and a thyroidectomy and one round of radiation (an I-131 treatment) was prescribed. After over eighteen years of monitoring, I've been declared cancer-free. That event did not involve any significant pain or fear because, from the outset, I was assured it was quite treatable and easily monitored. While I technically *am* a "cancer-survivor," I don't feel like I deserve that "purple heart" like so many people who've endured horrible pain under a protracted threat of death.

A few months later, I had open-heart surgery to repair a mitral valve prolapse that was leaking backwards close to 60 percent of the blood of each heartbeat. Again, my cardiologist had been monitoring me for several years, and we were anticipating this. The pain, though significant for a few days, was not overwhelming, and within two weeks I was walking five miles a day and feeling better than before the surgery.

Despite feeling as if my whole body was falling apart during that thirteen-month stretch, I felt more grateful for God's protection through good medical care than I felt like I was truly suffering—except for my eye trauma. It terrified me that I might go blind in both eyes.

Interminable Stress

Like so many people, the last few years have included a build-up of small and large stressors that can push anyone to the breaking point. You may have heard of the Holmes-Rahe Life Stress Inventory.[5] It lists and assigns scores to forty-three typical events in one's life that can produce stress, suggesting that a total score of 300 points or more projects an 80 percent chance of a health breakdown in the next two years.

After several years of careful consideration, my wife, Neta, and I decided it was time to downsize our home in the Chicago area and look for a smaller place on one floor so we wouldn't have to climb stairs ten to twelve times a day. In the fall of 2019, we found the ideal condo 150 miles south in Champaign, near our daughter and her family. We put our home on the market and bought the condo, certain our home would sell quickly. But it was five nail-biting months later before it sold at considerably less than our realtor promised we could get. And we moved to Champaign just seven days before the governor shut the State down because of COVID.

Not long thereafter, Neta's older sister, Pegge, died at the age of 82, sad but not unanticipated. However, three months later her daughter, who'd been Pegge's caretaker, also died. Her death was tragically and shockingly unexpected.

Events like . . .

- Death of a close family member
- Major change in living conditions

---

5. The Holmes-Rahe Stress Inventory, https://www.stress.org/holmes-rahe-stress-inventory.

- Change in residence
- Major change in church

. . . along with several other life experiences on the Holmes-Rahe Life Stress Inventory brought my score to 345. But that list doesn't take into account several other things I experienced as far more stressful. For instance, although the list identifies "Change in residence" as a stressor, leaving our neighborhood of forty-seven years with all our roots, friends, church, and other familiarities while not being able to go to a new church in person for months or make new friends and have people over for dinner because of the pandemic was one of the most stressful experiences—a far higher score than just moving into a new house.

That doesn't even begin to consider the ever-present threat of contracting COVID. At our age, the threat was and remains real: We lost thirteen friends and acquaintances to the pandemic—their names are written on a white board beside my desk—and we were shocked to learn that more people in the United States died from COVID (1,127,152) than died in the Civil War and WW II *combined* (1,060,399)![6] Also, ever since our move, Neta made daily calls to her life-long girlfriend who was dying of cancer. Before her friend passed, Neta went out to Seattle twice to visit her. I got to tag along with her once. It was a great visit, but her friend's excruciating pain, especially in her final months, weighed heavily on both of us. Yes, the Bible says, "People are destined to die once" (Heb. 9:27). We all know that, but why is it so often excruciatingly painful? Why, why does God allow all that pain?

Overlay our isolation and challenges with one of the craziest times in our country's history with all the lies, shootings, blatant racism, attacks on our government, war, and so many people

---

6. U.S. COVID deaths: https://covid19.who.int/region/amro/country/us. Civil War deaths (655,000) and WW II deaths (405,399): https://en.wikipedia.org/wiki/United_States_military_casualties_of_war. Some people scoff at this comparison, claiming the COVID numbers include numerous people who might have died soon anyway due to their underlying conditions. I find that comparison as ridiculous as saying a train wreck where 100 died actually only killed 70 because 30 people might have lived if they hadn't had heart issues, strokes, or were weakened by cancer.

11

IS YOUR GOD GOOD?

leaving the faith for un-Christian "Christian nationalism," and there's been very little in this old world to hold on to. "In this world you *will* have trouble!" Jesus had said. And that is so true even if it doesn't add up to martyrdom. Even though the thing we *need* most during such times of pain is relationships with others, too often the thing we *do* most is stare at our phones, sipping on more of the world's traumas through the news feed or toxic social media.

Still, just like my hesitation to claim the status of "cancer-survivor" or "veteran" (when I never faced deadly combat), I hesitate to say, "I've been suffering." I'm not a refugee or a victim of domestic violence, and yet we are all human, and everybody has a breaking point. So, if the stress of the last few years has pushed you near the edge, you *have* been suffering, and you know it, even if you've maintained a stiff upper lip.

So, where was God?

Even if your life feels particularly blessed right now, you may be grieving other people's suffering that still causes you to ask: "Why do they have to go through that? Where is God?" You are not alone if those questions erode your faith in God's goodness . . . or even God's existence!

Trying to Make Sense of It All

The subject of suffering is laced throughout the Bible—describing other people's suffering, Christ's suffering, telling us that we can expect suffering, helping us endure it, noting that God can transform suffering into good, and promising that one day suffering will cease.

For centuries, theologians and scholars have wrestled with the overarching question: "Where is God when it hurts?"[7] Many of those efforts have addressed certain aspects, such as: Is God in control? Is God punishing us? But far too many ignore other biblical principles, cosmic contradictions that nullify our prayers, and obvious realities about our universe that suggest clues as to why

---

7. The title my friend Philip Yancey gave his book on the subject: Philip Yancey, *Where Is God When It Hurts?* (Grand Rapids, MI, Zondervan, 2002).

12

we suffer. And some theories about human suffering are based on a faulty image of God and a myopic view of God's creation.

In the end (spoiler), I don't think there *is* a simple, concise answer. The words of songwriter Jim Croegaert's, "Alabama Skies,"[8] say it all: "And I don't understand so much of what I've seen / How it comes out of nowhere and changes everything." But Croegaert goes on to affirm that, nevertheless, there are revelations even in the midst of our greatest trauma that assure us we are held "in the arms of God." Seeing that truth is not a matter of rehearsing cheap clichés or cranking up more blind trust . . . which can only go so far. But I think there are some unconsidered insights that give us enough peace to renew trust in our good God.

The Weight of Shallow Answers

Research by the Barna Group into trends regarding faith shows that Gen Z, Gen X, Millennials, and Boomers collectively say their top barrier to faith is: "I have a hard time believing that a good God would allow so much evil or suffering in the world."[9] This research was compiled in 2018, and I seriously doubt that the numbers have improved since the COVID pandemic, the vitriol in our political arena, and our increasing experience of the seriousness of climate change. Far too many have given up on finding a relationship with a good God. Lurking just under the surface is the multitude of believers who are also troubled by rampant evil and suffering but cope by stuffing their questions or by reciting the old clichés they know don't satisfy. If we are alarmed that "Atheism has doubled among Gen Z," as the research shows, then we should be even more concerned about all of us who are holding onto our faith by our fingernails.

---

8. Jim Croegaert, "Alabama Skies," on *The Sky Above These Clouds*, 2021. This song was in response to a woman who had lost her sister and her grandkids in a sudden tornado during the spring of 2011.

9. "Atheism Doubles Among Generation Z," Jan 24, 2018. https://www. barna.com/research/atheism-doubles-among-generation-z/. (Boomers— born 1946 to1964, Gen X—born 1965 to 1983, Millennials—born 1984 to 1998, and Gen Z—born 1999 to 2015.)

Discussion Questions

1. How does the accumulation of trauma tend to stifle our faith?
2. How were you affected by people who died of COVID?
3. Name three platitudes people tend to offer in times of suffering. What does each imply about the character of God?
4. Describe a time—is you can—when, either during or after a traumatic period, you had a sense that you were nevertheless held in the arms of God? Take a few moments to verbalize your thanks to God for that care.

Chapter 2
Is Everything an "Act of God"?

"From the smallest thing to the greatest thing, good and evil, happy and sad, pagan and Christian, pain and pleasure—God governs . . . 'all things' includ[ing] the fall of sparrows (Matt. 10:29), the rolling of dice (Prov. 16:33), the slaughter of his people (Ps. 44:11), the decisions of kings (Prov. 21:1), the failing of sight (Exod. 4:11), the sickness of children (2 Sam. 12:15), the loss and gain of money (1 Sam. 2:7), the suffering of saints (1 Pet. 4:19), the completion of travel plans (James 4:15), the persecution of Christians (Heb. 12:4-7), the repentance of souls (2 Tim. 2:25), the gift of faith (Phil. 1:29), the pursuit of holiness (Phil. 3:12-13), the growth of believers (Heb. 6:3), the giving of life and the taking in death (1 Sam. 2:6), and the crucifixion of his Son (Acts 4:27-28)."

—*John Piper, "Why I Do Not Say, 'God Did Not Cause the Calamity . . .'?" in commenting on the 9/11 terrorist attacks on the United States.*[1]

W HY WOULD A RENOWNED BIBLE TEACHER and pastor, chancellor of a seminary, and author of more than fifty books declare in so many words that God *did cause* a cell of terrorists to attack the

---

1. John Piper, "Why I Do Not Say, 'God Did Not Cause the Calamity, but He Can Use It for Good.,'" article on his *Desiring God* website, Sept. 17, 2001, https://www.desiringgod.org/articles/why-i-do-not-say-god-did-not-cause-the-calamity-but-he-can-use-it-for-good.

United States and destroy the Twin Towers, fly another airliner into the Pentagon, and crash a fourth plane full of passengers into a field, collectively killing thousands?

The answer is: *Because he had to!*

That is, he had to in order to remain consistent with how he understands God. One could point out that some of his biblical referances only assert God's awareness of and care for the "sparrow that falls to the ground," and doesn't say God caused it, but there are plenty of other passages, particularly in the Old Testament, where the authors, such as the Prophet Amos, said things like, "When disaster comes to a city has not the Lord caused it?" (Amos 3:6). Those writers assert God's control over and therefore the ultimate cause of all events, good and bad, small and large.

And many of us—if we have not jettisoned our belief in God entirely—buy into that understanding to some degree, often far more than we realize. It is, after all, where the idea comes from when we refer to an unavoidable tragedy as being "an act of God." Business contracts include that phrase to give one party or the other a reprieve if "an act of God" prevents them from fulfilling their obligation. Many insurance policies become void if a disaster is declared "an act of God," meaning no one else is responsible.

Texts of Terror

If you believe God micromanages every event and detail of the cosmos—good or bad, small or large—it follows that God is ultimately responsible for all pain and suffering. And what supports that conclusion? Are you brave enough to review the Old Testament record? It's admittedly quite troubling. In fact, it's so ghastly most of us cringe and close our eyes to it, or, if we have to face it, we excuse its seriousness as a one-off or an instance when the people were so evil they deserved annihilation (which sets us up to take that approach when our enemies get bad enough).

However, the relevant Old Testament references are not rare or confined to the most extreme events. Instead, they constitute a gruesome and extensive *pattern* that unquestionably qualify as war crimes, crimes against humanity, genocide, and physical and sexual abuse. All attributed to God's will, God's acts, God's threats, or God's decreed punishments. Sound harsh? Well, take courage, there may be an explanation that reveals our good God in a very different light. But first we need to deal with how seriously distorted our view of God may be. So, take a deep breath and read as many of these "Texts of Terror" as you can stomach, looking up the sources if you choose.

- God is said to have directly annihilated nearly the whole human race in the Genesis Flood (Gen. 6—8) and all the inhabitants of the cities of Sodom and Gomorrah except for Lot and his two daughters (Gen. 19).
- God is said to have slain the first born of each Egyptian family as well as Pharaoh's army (Exod. 11:4-6; 15:3-6).
- After Moses received the Ten Commandments on Mount Sinai, he came down to find the Israelites worshiping a golden calf. At that point, God is said to have been so angry he ordered the Levites to strap on swords and "Go back and forth through the camp from one end to the other, each killing his brother and friend and neighbor." Once they had slain about three thousand of their own sons and brothers, Moses claimed God "has blessed you this day" (Exod. 32:27-29).
- Though the Ten Commandments God gave to the Israelites doesn't include specific consequences for their violation, much of the rest of the Law of Moses (ultimately attributed to God) does include penalties. Death was the *required* consequence for murder (Num. 35:33), kidnapping (Exod. 21:16), adultery (Lev. 20:10), homosexuality (Lev. 20:13), incest (Lev. 20:11, 14), bestiality (Lev. 20:15–16), fornication (Lev. 21:9), and rebellious children (Deut. 21:18-21).
- When the Israelites complained too much in the wilderness, the Lord is said to have slain 14,700 of them with a plague (Num. 16:42-49).
- As the Israelites prepared to enter the "Promised Land," Moses instructed them: "When the Lord your God brings you into the land you are entering to possess and drives out before you many nations—the Hittites, Girgashites, Amorites, Canaanites, Perizzites, Hivites and Jebusites,

seven nations larger and stronger than you—and when the Lord your God has delivered them over to you and you have defeated them, then you must destroy them totally. Make no treaty with them, and show them no mercy" (Deut. 7:1-2).

- "The Lord said to Moses, 'Take vengeance on the Midianites . . . .' [So, the Israelites] fought against Midian, as the Lord commanded Moses, and killed every man . . ." and woman. But Moses allowed them to "save for yourselves every girl who has never slept with a man." (See Num. 31:1-18.) By the way, the Midianites were descendants of Abraham, and therefore related to the Israelites (Gen. 25:1-6).

- "In the cities of the nations the Lord your God is giving you as an inheritance, do not leave alive anything that breathes. Completely destroy them—the Hittites, Amorites, Canaanites, Perizzites, Hivites and Jebusites—as the Lord your God has commanded you" (Deut. 20:16-17). Greg Boyd, theologian and senior pastor of Woodland Hills Church in St. Paul, Minnesota, notes that "We find variations of this frightful command being given or carried out *thirty-seven times* in the Old Testament."[2]

- David was praised and glorified for having slain *tens of thousands* (1 Sam. 18:7-8).

- For stealing Bathsheba and murdering her husband Uriah, the Prophet Nathan claimed as the Lord's word to David: "Before your very eyes I will take your wives and give them to one who is close to you, and he will sleep with your wives in broad daylight" (2 Sam. 12:11). Really? Rape eight women in public? David's sin wasn't their fault!

- Later, when Israel was under threat of attack by Babylon, the prophet Ezekiel said it was because of idolatry and claimed God wouldn't even spare those who had been innocent of any idolatry. "This is what the Lord says: I am against you [Israel]. I will draw my sword from its sheath and cut off

---

2. Boyd, Gregory A., *Cross Vision* (Minneapolis, Fortress Press, 2017), 9.

from you both the righteous and the wicked. . . . everyone from south to north" (Ezek. 21:3-4).

- Greg Boyd points out: "Other passages depict Yahweh declaring that, as judgment for the Israelites' rebellion, parents would have to witness their babies being dashed to the ground, while pregnant women would have their unborn babies ripped out of their wombs. (See Hosea 13:8-16; Isa. 13:16.) And perhaps the bloodiest of all are the Old Testament's portraits of Yahweh causing parents to 'eat their children' and children to 'eat their parents.' (See Exod. 5:9–10; Lev. 26:28–29; Jer. 19:7, 9; Lam. 2:20.)"[3]

If you have been raised in church or have otherwise studied the Bible, you may have been familiar with those events (though Sunday school lessons often sanitized the grisly details). And you may never have reviewed the list all at once. Still, how did you justify them? Did a preacher use the occasion to instruct you on how irredeemably sinful the people were? "Something had to be done to stamp out their idolatry!" Or was the passage presented to scare *you* into repentance like Jonathan Edwards' 18th Century sermon, "Sinners in the Hands of an Angry God"?

The God that holds you over the pit of hell, much as one holds a spider, or some loathsome insect over the fire, abhors you, and is dreadfully provoked: his wrath towards you burns like fire; he looks upon you as worthy of nothing else, but to be cast into the fire. . . . It is the wrath of the infinite God.[4]

And having heard those stories, how did they mold your ethics? Did they lead you to justify war? Tolerate wars of annihilation? How about the genocide of indigenous people on land our ancestors wanted? Capital punishment? Slavery? If you are a par-

---

3. Boyd, Gregory A., *Cross Vision* (Minneapolis, Fortress Press, 2017), 15.
4. Jonathan Edwards, "Sinners in the Hands of an Angry God" (preached July 8, 1741). https://www.blueletterbible.org/Comm/edwards_jonathan/Sermons/Sinners.cfm.

ent, you know that sometimes our kids can *get on our last nerve*, but I hope you never seriously entertained stoning them to death as prescribed in (Deut. 21:18-21).

How have you dealt with the images of God as portrayed in those Texts of Terror? Have you refused to dwell on them like the three monkeys: "see no evil, hear no evil, speak no evil"? Have you blamed those viewpoints on another "dispensation" when God had to be that harsh to whip his people into shape? And if you subscribe to that explanation, how did *that* work out?

One consequence is that many people have rejected any serious belief in God because if that's God's character, one might fear him, but who would want to worship him?

But "God Is Good . . ."

In the Black church, when someone says, "God is good . . ." the traditional response is, "All the time." Then the original speaker says, "And all the time . . ." and everyone affirms, "God is good."

So, how did this whole family of Christians—millions of them from numerous denominations over a dozen generations—come to the resolute conviction that God is good when their personal history mirrors those Old Testament characterizations in the outrageous, sustained persecution from the very people who introduced them to the Christian Gospel? They certainly didn't come to believe that God is good because their oppressors demonstrated God's goodness to them in any consistent manner. So, their belief in the goodness of God was *despite* the gruesome Old Testament reports that described God's character in terms as horrific as their own experience.

Neta and I have been closely involved with African American brothers and sisters—often in the context of the black church—for much of our fifty-eight years of marriage. And we have grown in our conviction that they have much to teach us about this mystery, even though—like other traditions—bad theology has sometimes muddied the waters of understanding.

If God is in control of everything in the sense that everything happens for a reason—God's reason—how can we say God is good? If God controls everything, then that also must include . . .

All those Old Testament reports, the persecution of Christians, the Holy Wars, the torture and murder surrounding the Reformation, the genocide of indigenous people, the death of two million kidnapped Africans on the Middle Passage along with hundreds of years of enslavement and beatings and lynchings, the World Wars including the murder of six million Jews and some two hundred thousand Japanese killed by U.S. atomic bombs, twenty million Russians killed under Stalin, and the forty million who died under Mao. And of course, there were the thousands who died in the 9/11 attacks.

That litany barely scratches the surface of the known death and destruction perpetrated by humans on one another throughout human history.

And what about all the plagues and natural disasters? When the death toll following the 7.8 magnitude earthquake in Turkey approached fifty thousand, I wondered if it was the deadliest earthquake ever recorded. No! My memory is too short. In 2010, 316,000 died in the Port-au-Prince, Haiti, quake. And the earthquake recorded as most powerful in modern times was the Valdivia quake that struck Chile in 1960. It registered at 9.5 magnitude. Much earlier, in 1556, in Shaanxi, China, 830,000 were estimated to have died from a quake. In addition, there have been innumerable accidents, birth defects, diseases, tornadoes, hurricanes, floods, famines . . . and the list goes on and on—death and destruction, often made worse by human neglect, greed, and inhumanity, but still labeled "natural disasters."

Whether administered by nature or by humans, all this suffering has impacted billions of truly innocent people. No, not necessarily "sinless" people, but people—many just children and infants—who had no responsibility for their own suffering and death.

How could a *good* God be the cause of all that?

Now, please forgive me for having dragged you through that depressing review when all you had to do was tune into your daily news feed. But anyone who claims that God controls all things from the smallest to the greatest and that therefore everything happens for *his* reason is trying to get you to bury your

21

head in the sand and offers no comfort to the victims of such a horrendous history.

But if God *is* good, what's going on?

Discussion Questions

1. Where do you think the idea that God "is in control of everything" came from?
2. What was your reaction to reading a partial list of the "Texts of Terror"? Did it change your mind about the character of God? Why or why not?
3. How might embracing the "Texts of Terror" as representative of God's character have affected policies Christians have supported through the centuries?

Chapter 3

What Didn't the Patriarchs Know?

Among the gods there is none like you, Lord;
no deeds can compare with yours.
All the nations you have made
will come and worship before you, Lord;
they will bring glory to your name.
For you are great and do marvelous deeds;
you alone are God.

—Psalm 86:8-10, a prayer of David

WORKING ON A BOOK LIKE THIS AND SEARCHING such imponderables as why we suffer is scary, at least it has been to me. What was I risking? Was my faith at stake? It would have been so much easier to avoid the hard questions and simply accept the answers others have offered without sifting through them. And in sharing with you what I've found, I am not presenting it as dogma that you must accept or force on others. But I can assure you that neither the search nor the results destroyed my faith in Jesus. In fact, it's much stronger.

I encourage you with this same hope—that your sincere search will bring you to a place of more peace where you no longer need to close your eyes to those hard, scary questions or hold them at arm's length. John tells us that when Jesus appeared to the gathered disciples, fearfully hiding in that locked room after his crucifixion, he twice said, "Peace be with you!" Then, a week later when they were again together, he said, "Peace be with you!" a third time. (See John 20:19, 21, 26.) They were hiding out of fear of the authorities who had crucified Jesus. But I'm sure they were also still reeling with questions about what was happening—the reports from the women, the reports of the empty tomb, the reports from the disciples traveling to Emmaus—and the recollection of the times Jesus had foretold his death and resurrection. They may have argued over exactly what he had said and what it now meant.

Rather than destroying their faith, the process forged a stronger faith. Earlier in Jesus' ministry, there had been times when his followers fell away (John 6:66; Matt. 26:31), but not as a result of sincere searching. There is no record that any of the eleven lost their faith in the tumult of questions following his crucifixion and resurrection.

An unexamined faith is a weak faith, and a faith that fears doubt is built on sand, not on the rock of Christ Jesus. Biblical mysteries can be troubling, as is the search for why we suffer, because it inevitably raises the question: If God cares and is all powerful, why doesn't he stop the suffering? There are many things we may never fully answer concerning that question. However, if we really want to know more, God will help us understand as much as we can receive, and he can do it without us losing our faith . . . or our minds. When things simply don't make sense according to what we've been told, we can doubt and should doubt and explore our questions with sincerity and prayer. This is because the opposite of faith is not doubt but certainty. Don't forget that Jesus did not reject Thomas for doubting the most crucial aspect of the Christian faith—Jesus' resurrection. Only *after* Jesus showed Thomas his wounded hands and side—thereby giving Thomas a little more information—did Jesus say, "Stop doubting and believe" (John 20:27).

Take heart and trust Jesus' promise: "Ask and it will be given to you; seek and you will find; knock and the door will be opened to you. For everyone who asks receives; the one who seeks finds; and to the one who knocks, the door will be opened" (Matt. 7:7-8). It's a pledge that extends to far more than material provisions. I believe it includes a promise of greater faith for everyone who sincerely asks, seeks, and knocks.

Why Didn't God "Tell All" in the First Place?

Believing that God will respond when we ask, seek, and knock doesn't mean he will or can give us a comprehensive answer in 140 characters or less like an X post (or Twitter post). Do you think he could have explained to Moses *how* he created the universe *in a way Moses could have comprehended*? Perhaps at the time, it was enough to simply tell Moses that he *had* created the universe. But some may insist, even if God didn't reveal everything about himself as he made himself known to the patriarchs, certainly he must have taken care to avoid any misleading impressions. Perhaps. But I'm suggesting that whether we are talking about the Creation story or God being characterized as violent and retributive, the facts from that era may be . . .

- Incomplete because no initial summary could cover the whole subject.
- Distorted because Old Testament authors were not robots and inevitably wove some of their own cultural understandings into their work.
- Unrevised because even the Old Testaments prophets who tried to offer correctives were often ignored.
- Redeemed only when updated by the incarnation of God in Jesus Christ.

This does not cancel the promise that "All Scripture is God-breathed and is useful for teaching, rebuking, correcting and training in righteousness, so that the servant of God may be thoroughly equipped for every good work" (2 Tim. 3:16-17), which is a cornerstone passage for belief in the inspiration of Scripture. Everything in the Bible is there for a reason inspired by God. But that doesn't mean some initial misunderstandings didn't need correcting by later revelation through the character and work of Jesus Christ, or as the writer to the Hebrews said, "In the past God spoke to our ancestors through the prophets at many times and in various ways, but in these last days he has spoken to us by his Son, . . . the radiance of God's glory and *the exact representation of his being"* (Heb. 1:1-3, emphasis added). If we had to wait for Jesus, the exact representation of God, then it follows that what came before *wasn't* complete.

For some, this is a challenging concept, particularly for those who were taught to believe in a theory known as the "verbal plenary inspiration of Scripture." We will come back to this question in Chapter 4, but first, let's look at how God presented himself to ancient people as Scripture reports it.

God's Self-Revelation

In Genesis 3:8, 9, we are told that after the first humans chose to disobey God, they "heard the sound of the LORD God as he was walking in the garden in the cool of the day, and they hid from the LORD God among the trees of the garden. But the LORD God called to the man, 'Where are you?'" Their decision to hide suggests God visited these people on a regular basis—perhaps daily—during which he shared himself with them. After all, why "had God said, 'Let us make mankind in our image, in our likeness" (Gen.1:26) unless he desired to relate to them?

But because of their rebellion, the closeness of God's relationship with humanity as a whole was broken.

After that, God did continue to reach out and communicate to receptive individuals like Abel, Enoch, Noah, and Job. But what was happening to much of the rest of society? Genesis 6:1, 5-6 says, "When human beings began to increase in number on the earth . . .. The Lord saw how great the wickedness of the human race had become and that every inclination of the thoughts of the human heart was only evil all the time. The Lord regretted that he had made human beings on the earth, and his heart was deeply troubled." After that follows the story of the flood, wiping out all civilization, but through which only Noah and his family survived.

Ten generations are named in the Bible between Noah and Abraham—taking roughly 400 years—with virtually no record of any spiritual life among the inhabitants other than that they kept a genealogy. In other words, from the time God interacted with Noah to the time he called Abraham, there is no recorded corporate communion with God, no prophets to teach the people, no spiritual instruction, no correction of ideas or concepts, no visions, no reported acts of God other than scattering the people of Babel by confusing their languages.

As the human population grew, many early cultures believed in divine beings. Perhaps some of their notions were distorted versions of ideas passed down about the God of Noah. But most were infused with invented gods they thought more or less controlled natural events and human fortune, focusing on the cause, deterrence, and meaning of those phenomena. The "gods" brought the weather, blessed or cursed the crops, caused fertility or infertility, and provided victory or defeat in battle—all depending on whether the gods were happy or angry or whether the gods of their enemies were weaker or stronger. This characterization of the ancient religions of many cultures coincides with archaeological evidence as well as biblical descriptions. With no intentional pursuit of a relationship with the true God, human presumptions concerning God's nature became garbled, distorted, and often fragmented into many gods.

Such conditions were largely true in Abraham's Mesopotamian environment in Ur, up through Harran, and down into Canaan. But because of Abraham's personal relationship with God, he had a different awareness, as did his offspring, Isaac and Jacob. Nevertheless, the spiritual understanding of the patriarchs may not have been as sanitized as we sometimes imagine. Abraham's father, Terah, worshiped idols (Josh. 24:2). One might speculate that the reason Terah did not accompany Abraham down to Canaan was because he did not recognize the validity of Abraham's God. Years later, after Jacob returned to Harran and married Rachel, Rachel stole the idols from her father's house and took them with her as they traveled back to Canaan. Idolatry was the cultural milieu out of which Abraham came.

Yes, Abraham did hear and respond to God's call to go to the Promised Land, and he exercised unprecedented trust in God concerning his son, Isaac. But where did he get the idea God wanted him to sacrifice his son . . . just like so many of the surrounding pagan gods demanded? Fortunately, God put a stop to it, even though Abraham interpreted the whole event as a test *from* God, but . . . we'll come back to that in Chapter 4.[1] Nevertheless, Abraham exercised genuine faith in God at many other points during his life. Because the Book of Hebrews includes Abraham in the "Hall of Fame" for his faith (Heb. 11:8-12), one might think Abraham's spirit would have been transformed, and yet his character sometimes fell below that of the surrounding pagans. For instance, he pimped his wife *twice* to ensure his own safety, a behavior deplored by both of the polytheistic rulers on which he pulled this trick (Gen. 12:10-20; 20:1-18). As for Isaac and Jacob (despite his having wrestled with God), the whole clan was tragically dysfunctional, morally not very reformed by their encounters with a good God . . . except for Jacob's next to youngest son, Joseph. His communion with God in the form of dreams ultimately resulted in expressions of Godly character.

However, in terms of the patriarchs, God points out in Exodus 6:3, "I appeared to Abraham, to Isaac and to Jacob as God Almighty, but by my name the Lord, I did not make myself fully known to them." So, they clearly did not have a *full* understanding of the character of God.

And then these people through whom God would bless the whole world experienced another pagan cultural emersion when, at Joseph's invitation, Jacob took the whole Israelite tribe—some sixty-six people—down to Egypt to escape a famine. They ended up staying 430 years, much of the time as slaves. They succeeded in maintaining a small measure of cultural integrity as evidenced by the existence of recognized "elders" (Exod. 4:29) and an organized team of underground midwives to prevent the Egyptians from exterminating all the male babies (Exod. 1:15-21).[2] But their

---

1. Even though Genesis (traditionally written by Moses) says *God* told Abraham to sacrifice his son, to Abraham's credit, he apparently never believed he would have to follow through. To his servants, he said, "Stay here with the donkey while I and the boy go over there. We will worship and then *we will come back* to you" (Gen. 22:5, emphasis added). And later when Isaac asked where the lamb was, Abraham answered, "God himself will provide the lamb for the burnt offering, my son" (v. 8).

2. The Children of Israel did enjoy some degree of cultural insulation by living in the "ghetto" of Goshen, where the Egyptians avoided them because they were shepherds (until they were enslaved), and the Egyptians detested shepherds (Gen. 46:34).

freedom to worship and pass on the rudiments of their faith was so severely curtailed that Moses' first and only demand of Pharaoh was simply to let the Israelites take a three-day journey into the wilderness to offer sacrifices to the Lord (Exod. 5:1-4). In short, Pharaoh's response was, "No breaks, get back to work!" It was a heavy oppression! Think of enslaved Africans and their descendants in this country for the last 400 years. Whisps of their indigenous tribal religions survived, but most of it was snuffed out or got mixed with western religion. The same undoubtedly happened to the Israelites.

When God initiated their Exodus from Egypt, this religious confusion and spiritual ignorance was the state of the people he wished to woo. What was the first thing they needed to know about him? "God said to Moses, 'I AM WHO I AM'; and He said, 'Thus you shall say to the sons of Israel, "I AM has sent me to you"' (Exod. 3:14). Later, "God also said to Moses, 'I am the LORD. I appeared to Abraham, to Isaac and to Jacob as God Almighty [Hebrew El-Shaddai], but by my name the LORD [Hebrew Yahweh] I did not make myself fully known to them'" (Exod. 6:2-3). Most English Bibles translate the name El-Shaddai as "God Almighty." However, a more accurate translation might be, "The God who is more than enough," While Yahweh is best translated "The self-existent, eternal God."

The significance of this distinction cannot be overstated. If El-Shaddai meant God Almighty as we have commonly read it to mean, then as little as the Hebrews may have known about him, he was "the greatest," and there was no need for them to be convinced of that. On the other hand, if their name for God meant "The God who is more than enough," they might have felt El-Shaddai may have been good enough for Abraham, Isaac, and Jacob, but they were in much worse trouble under bondage to the greatest nation on earth with its mighty war machine and all its powerful gods. If that was their understanding, then it was monumental news to learn their God was Yahweh, "The self-existent, eternal God," who is unquestionably "The Greatest." Our English Bibles give the reverse impression when they translate the earlier name to mean "God Almighty," when in fact, the new name, "I AM the

Lord," claims the highest power and authority for the God of the Hebrews.

Of course, God had not changed. The great "I am the Lord (*Yahweh*)" was the *El-Shaddai* "the God who was more than enough" as Abraham, Isaac, and Jacob had experienced him. He functioned for them, perhaps from their perspective in the same way other tribes had personal gods, but they did not know him as the "self-existent, eternal God," the almighty creator of the universe.[3] And that was the *new* news!

But how might God have shown himself to be the great I AM? How might he have delivered that message in a way the people could understand and would believe, given their historical environment and experience? The people saw Moses as a mighty wizard, more powerful than any of Egypt's magicians (Exod. 7—8), but that didn't mean they knew or trusted God. And while they had plenty of incentive to flee Egypt when Moses' dramatic plagues convinced Pharaoh to release them, it didn't take long before they were clamoring to return to Egypt (Num. 14:1-4). God repeated eleven times that his actions in freeing the Israelites from bondage in Egypt proved, "I am the Lord."[4]

How long and what would it take to truly convince them of the care and presence of the great I AM?

Our God Is Greater

Chris Tomlin's song, "Our God," says: *Our God is greater, our God is stronger / God You are higher than any other.*[5] It amplifies the affirmations in David's prayer quoted at the beginning of this chap-

---

3. Some may point out that in Genesis 2, the term *Yahweh-Elohim* is used to refer to God. This "retrofitting" of *Yahweh*, if it was that, may have had more to do with Moses' role in writing the Pentateuch. What is clear from Exodus 6:2-3 is that by the time of Abraham, Isaac, and Jacob, the concept of God as *Yahweh* was unfamiliar. And therefore "God also said to Moses, 'I am the Lord. I appeared to [them] as [*El-Shaddai*], but by my name the Lord [*Yahweh*] I did not make myself fully known to them.'" If *Yahweh* was known earlier, it had been forgotten. And that was the spiritual condition of the Children of Israel at the time of the Exodus.

4. See Exod. 6:2, 6, 7, 8, 29; 7:5, 17; 10:2; 12:12; 14:4, 18.

5. Chris Tomlin, "Our God," Capitol Christian Music Group, Capitol CMG Publishing, 2010.

ter. And those affirmations are true, but in the ancient world where a god's greatness was proved by military might and control over natural phenomena, what would convince the Israelites (or their enemies, for that matter) that their *Yahweh* was indeed the greatest, the I AM?

When Moses confronted Pharaoh to convince him to free the Israelites, he relayed these words from God: "By now I could have stretched out my hand and struck you and your people with a plague that would have wiped you off the earth. But I have raised you up [i.e., spared you] for this very purpose, that I might show you my power and that my name might be proclaimed in all the earth" (Exod. 9:15, 16). John Piper crassly says, "The point of the Exodus was to make a worldwide reputation for God."[6] Yes, but I think we'll see in the next chapter that God's need to establish himself as the great I AM was far more strategic than a mere ego trip. He had an even higher motive for rescuing the Israelites.

The Long Lesson

Convincing the Israelites that God was the only I AM was not complete with the Exodus. Very little time passed in the wilderness before they ended up forging a Golden Calf.[7] God was so angry that Moses believed he contemplated destroying them for regressing to idol worship, and "Moses sought the favor of the Lord his God. . . .

> "LORD," he said, "why should your anger burn against your people, whom you brought out of Egypt with great power and a mighty hand? Why should the Egyptians say, 'It was with evil intent that he brought them out, to kill them in the

---

6. John Piper, "The Pleasure of God in His Name," an article on his *Desiring God* website, Feb. 15, 1987, https://www.desiringgod.org/messages/the-pleasure-of-god-in-his-name.

7. If there were any uncertainty as to how deeply the Israelites were influenced by the pagan cultures around them and in their history, here is one more piece of evidence: The very first thing they did when the great "I AM" did not perform as they expected was to build an idol, possibly in the form of the Egyptian bull god, Apis. One might say, "You can take the people out of Egypt, but it is hard to take Egypt out of the people."

mountains and to wipe them off the face of the earth'? Turn from your fierce anger; relent and do not bring disaster on your people. Remember your servants Abraham, Isaac and Israel, to whom you swore by your own self: 'I will make your descendants as numerous as the stars in the sky and I will give your descendants all this land I promised them, and it will be their inheritance forever.'" Then the LORD relented and did not bring on his people the disaster he had threatened (Exod. 32:11-14).

Forty years later, when Hebrew spies were reconning the City of Jericho before the Israelites crossed the Jordan to invade the Promised Land, Rahab befriended them and confirmed the reputation that their God was gaining: "Our hearts melted in fear and everyone's courage failed because of you, for the LORD your God is God in heaven above and on earth below" (Josh. 2:11). And when those same spies went back across the Jordan to face Joshua, they said, "The LORD has surely given the whole land into our hands; all the people are melting in fear because of us" (v. 24).

In David's prayer asking God to let him build the temple, he appealed to God's reputation by reminding God that Israel was "the one nation on earth that God went out to redeem as a people for himself, and to make a name for himself" (2 Sam. 7:23).

Unfortunately, God's efforts to convince the people of his presence, care, and provision as the one and only great I AM was not accomplished by punishing their rebellion in the wilderness, defeating their enemies, giving them a land "flowing with milk and honey," sending down fire to consume a sacrifice (1 Kings 18:20-40), controlling the weather to end a drought (1 Kings 18:41—19:21), or giving them a king in place of their direct reliance on him (1 Sam. 8—15). In spite of all these and many other wonderful deeds, in spite of the first commandment: "You shall have no other gods before me," or the specific reminder in Leviticus 18:3 that "You must not do as they do in Egypt, where you used to live, and you must not do as they do in the land of Canaan, where I am bringing you," the people continually turned to the false gods of the surrounding peoples. God's objective of establishing himself as the great I AM, their one true God, was not yet done.

Prophets called them back to faithfulness, and the altars to false gods were torn down. But then they were rebuilt with the next wicked king or rebellious movement. This cycle continued for some seven hundred years until the Jews returned from the Babylonian Exile in 538 BC. Finally, as most scholars agree, the Jews never returned to idolatry. In fulfillment of Micah's prophecy, "In the last days . . . all the nations may walk in the name of their gods, but we will walk in the name of the LORD [*Yahweh*] our God for ever and ever" (Mic. 4:1, 5).

God's reputation as the great I AM was finally secured, but at a very high price in terms of the people's misunderstandings about certain aspects of his character. The people were learning to value God's lovingkindness (Num. 14:18), patience (Ps. 103:8), and readiness to forgive (Ps. 86:5). But they also remembered him as a violent God they hoped would come as the messiah king to wage war on their oppressors and punish all evil doers . . . including those among themselves who failed to keep the Law as the Pharisees and teachers demanded. God's progressive revelation of himself would not be complete until he came to earth in the person of Jesus Christ. Unfortunately, many of us still expect God to behave toward us in violent and retributive ways and therefore blame him more quickly as the source of our suffering than any other cause.

Discussion Questions

1. What do you think of the statement, "The opposite of faith is not doubt but certainty"?
2. What do you make of the observation that for the 400 years between Noah and Abraham "there is no recorded corporate communion with God, no prophets to teach the people, no spiritual instruction, no correction of ideas or concepts, no visions, no reported acts of God

other than scattering the people of Babel by confusing their languages"?

3. What are the most disturbing concepts seemingly embraced by the Patriarchs? How have you dealt with them?

Chapter 4

Why Did God Tolerate Cultural Assumptions?

He had no beauty or majesty to attract us to him,
*   nothing in his appearance that we should desire him.*
He was despised and rejected by mankind,
*   a man of suffering, and familiar with pain.*
Like one from whom people hide their faces
*   he was despised, and we held him in low esteem.*
. . . We considered him punished by God,
*   Stricken by him, and afflicted.*

—Isaiah 53:2-4

W HEN GOD CAME TO EARTH AS JESUS to live among the people
    through whom he chose to introduce himself to the whole
world, their expectations were so off base that they didn't even
recognize him. They couldn't even identify him after one of their
most highly revered prophets had told them what to expect. Why?

It may have been because, in his great love for his people, God
had tolerated their cultural presumptions of his character in order
to firmly establish his relationship with them.

Greg Boyd, the senior pastor of Woodland Hills Church in St.
Paul, Minnesota, tells the story of a missionary couple who went to
a remote community in Africa that was, at the time, unfamiliar with
Christianity. These missionaries were appalled to discover that the
tribe practiced the ancient ritual of female circumcision, in which
the genitalia of young girls were partially cut away in an attempt

to ensure their virginity and reinforce male rights over women.[1] To the outsiders, this ordeal seemed so barbaric they could hardly contain their outrage. But they knew any confrontation over a cultural practice that had endured for hundreds of years would sabotage their efforts to share the Gospel of Christ and probably end their welcome in the village. Wisely, they decided they first had to gain the trust of the people. As a compromise, they chose to provide sanitary surgical knives, pain medication, and antiseptics to make the procedure as safe as possible.

Their approach worked as the tribe grew to appreciate their advice and how it reduced infections and the mortality rate among the girls. Finally, after about three years, as the missionaries continued to teach about God's love, they were able to suggest and then show that there was a better way to love their young girls until the practice of female circumcision died out.

However, if anyone had recorded the activity of that missionary couple *before* the old practice ended, it would have appeared as though they not only tolerated the barbaric ritual but actually promoted it.[2]

This anecdote is a profound example of how much God loves us—so much that he was willing to be misunderstood, to have his reputation besmirched, in order to speak to us *in a way we could understand*. And that last phrase is the key: *in a way we could understand*! When God called Abraham, it was not simply to relate to him as an isolated individual; God promised to make him the father of a great nation and furthermore, through his descendants, all nations on earth would be blessed (Gen. 22:17-18). By the time of the Exodus, the decedents of Abraham constituted a vast multitude that needed to be convinced that *Yahweh* was the LORD al-

---

1. While we may imagine this practice to be a tragic remnant of a bygone era, more than 200 million girls and women live with the consequences of Female Genital Mutilation (FGM), and it is estimated that every ten seconds another girl is mutilated. See: Leyla Hussein, "Every few seconds, a girl's genitals are cut in Africa. I was one of those girls," May 12, 2023, https://www.cnn.com/2023/05/12/opinions/female-genital-mutilation-african-girls-hussein.

2. Gregory A. Boyd, *Cross Vision* (Minneapolis, MN: Fortress Press, 2017, 2018), 83-84. Also in a message: "[Suffering] Happens," Woodland Hills Church, St. Paul, MN, Mar. 13,2011.

mighty and not just some private or even regional god. As we saw in the last chapter, it took hundreds of years before the Jews as a people fully embraced that truth, so deep was the suspicion that, maybe, when they thought they needed a stronger god, they could try some other gods.

For instance, by the time the Israelites arrived in semi-arid Canaan, they would have had very few farming skills—when to plant, what to plant, how to plant. They had come from the lush delta of the Nile where they were not even farmers but construction slaves. Then they spent forty years wandering around in the wilderness. What did they know about farming in this new land other than that the locals were the ones who knew how to make it "flow with milk and honey" (Exod. 3:8)? If the local people said you had to sacrifice to Baal or Asherah to enjoy fertility, well, maybe they were right. Maybe those were the real regional superheroes they, as newcomers, should worship.

People so easily want a superhero—the bigger, the badder, the better!

Looking for a Superhero

Even today, we fantasize about being rescued by a superhero. According to Statista Research Department, Marvel and DC films are among the highest grossing superhero franchises, bringing in billions of dollars annually.[3] We want someone to defeat the bad guys, rescue us from disaster, and make us safe. Is it any wonder that the Israelites were looking for the same thing, perhaps looking so hard they applied the common wisdom of attributing any "success" they experienced to God's direct actions on their behalf and any disaster to his anger toward them even if those violent events came from other sources?

Their escape from Egypt and the destruction of Pharoah's army was understood as God's rescue. Their infighting after worshiping the Golden Calf, when they killed each other—3,000 brothers against brothers, fathers against sons—certainly seemed like

---

3. Statista Research Department, Jan. 5, 2023, https://www.statista.com/topics/4741/superhero-movies/#topicOverview.

the vindictive punishment from an angry God. When the earth opened up and all Korah's men and associates (at least 250) fell into the abyss and died after rebelling against Moses—again, they assumed it must have been God's anger. Following that, a large number of the people blamed Moses, and lo and behold, 14,700 of them died of a plague (Num. 16). Whether the violence was against Israel's enemies as they conquered Canaan or seemingly against rebellious Israelites, it made no difference. God was seen as an angry and violent superhero in each case!

I have no reason to doubt the basic events recorded in the Old Testament such as the Israelites' miraculous escape from Egypt, their crossing the Red Sea, God's provision of water and food in the wasteland, or the healing from venomous snakes, and sandals and clothes that lasted the duration of their sojourn. Neither do I doubt the tragedies that befell the people during those forty years in the wilderness.

But what if—spoiler alert, so you know where I'm going with this—what if most of the violence attributed to *Yahweh*, whether visited on Israel's enemies or as "punishment" for rebellious Israelites, was what the people *expected* to see from any God claiming to be I AM the LORD Almighty? While all the acts of grace and kindness and forgiveness and second chances were the true and direct deeds of *Yahweh*? I'm talking about all the good things that coincide with the character and ministry of Jesus. Think of the parallels: the God who came proclaiming good news to the poor, release to the captives, letting the oppressed go free, who fed five thousand in the desert near Galilee and later another four thousand people north of there, healed the sick wherever he went, raised the dead, forgave sinners, and even absorbed Satan's most violent attack against all humanity by turning it into good on the Cross!

Scripture assures us that "in all things God works for the good of those who love him, who have been called according to his purpose" (Rom. 8:28), which summarizes what happened when Joseph confronted his brothers who had almost killed him before selling him into slavery in Egypt. He said, "You intended to harm me, but God intended it for good to accomplish what is now being done, the saving of many lives [from famine]" (Gen. 50:20).

The problem is, even in that passage, some people assume God engineered the whole thing, meaning God was the author of the brothers' evil scheme. But that's not what the text says. What God "intended" as a means of saving Joseph's extended family from starvation can be seen as an adjustment that circumvented the *brothers'* evil actions. God could have saved them from the famine by various means, but once the brothers made their move (or because God knew what they were going to do before they did it), God used Joseph's high position in Egypt as a perfect way to save them.

God is never the author of evil! As 1 John 1:5 says, "This is the message we have heard from him [Jesus] and declare to you: God is light; in him there is no darkness at all." James is even more emphatic: "God cannot be tempted by evil, nor does he tempt anyone" (James 1:13). So, God didn't create the plan to sell Joseph into slavery in Egypt, and he didn't put that evil idea in the minds of the brothers. In fact, according to Jesus, *it is Satan* who "comes only to steal and kill and destroy" (John 10:10). We shouldn't assume God initiates evil, even when he transforms and brings good out of it. Evil comes through many channels, but never from God.

However, the Old Testament doesn't always make a clear distinction between how those ancient people—and many of us—assume God acts (like the pagan gods) to administer suffering and death anytime it serves his plans in contrast to a more complete picture of God's true nature. There are hints of this distinction even in the Old Testament, and there are prophecies that herald this correction. Finally, there is Jesus who came revising many old expectations, images, and laws, and who the New Testament declares "is the image of the invisible God" in whom "God was pleased to have *all his fullness* dwell in him" (Col. 1:15, 19, emphasis added).

So, if Jesus is the more perfect and complete picture of God's true character, perhaps much of the violence and suffering the Old Testament writers attributed to God corresponded more to the people's expectations than to God's true character. This misunderstanding is not unlike the initial assumptions that African tribe may have had regarding the support the missionaries showed toward female circumcision.

Alarming Implications for "Inspiration"

If you haven't realized it yet, my theory about how God was misunderstood in ancient times raises serious implications for the theory of the "verbal plenary inspiration" of Scripture, which allows for the authors of Scripture to write in their unique *style*, but insists the results were without error. This view variously says God insured that "Every word, word form, and word placement found in the Bible's original manuscripts was divinely and intentionally written"[4] without error. This theory would require any mistaken comment or even any lie told by a biblical character to be redacted from the final text or identified as an error—"footnoted," so to speak—so no misunderstanding was communicated.

Therefore, if Abraham believed God told him to sacrifice his son, Isaac, as Moses apparently recorded some 400 years *after* the event, then, according to this theory, that is exactly what happened. And it was not Abraham's mistaken presumption based on the typical expectations of regional gods, even though God stopped Abraham from following through with such a heathen sacrifice. According to rigid theories of inspiration, since Abraham's initial understanding *wasn't* disavowed in the text itself, God must have said it. And we are expected to just shut our eyes to the fact that the mere suggestion of such a barbaric event is totally inconsistent with the character of God *as revealed in Jesus*.[5]

The English word *inspiration* is derived from the Latin, *inspiratio*, referring to the act of breathing in. It occurs only twice in Scripture as *inspiration*, and that only in older translations like the King James Version where Job 32:8 says, "But there is a spirit in man: And the inspiration of the Almighty giveth them understanding," and in 2 Timothy 3:16, which says, "All scripture is given by inspi-

---

4. "What is verbal plenary inspiration," *Got Questions*, https://www.gotquestions.org/verbal-plenary-inspiration.html.
5. Some see this event as a prophetic picture of Jesus (the ram in the bush) who died for our sins. And in a way it does. However, there's nothing in the story about substitutionary atonement for sin—not Abraham's, Isaac's, or anyone else's sin. Genesis 22 begins, "God tested Abraham" regarding whether Abraham believed God would fulfill the promise to make him the father of many nations if he was asked to sacrifice his only son. If God actually ordered that event, maybe it taught Abraham something about himself, but God already knew the answer.

ration of God, and is profitable for doctrine, for reproof, for correction, for instruction in righteousness." In both cases newer translations more accurately say: "the breath of the Almighty" and "All Scripture is God-breathed . . .." In neither case does the concept of God breathing his message into the hearts of the writers eliminate the possibility that they could sometimes blur God's intent.

The comprehensiveness of a rigid theory of inspiration—that everything in the original manuscripts was precisely accurate—is based on the words, "*All* Scripture," as well as certain New Testament texts where Paul used a detail from an Old Testament quotation to make a point. (See Gal. 3:16.) Or even Jesus' statement in Matthew 5:18, "For truly I tell you, until heaven and earth disappear, not the smallest letter, not the least stroke of a pen, will by any means disappear from the Law until everything is accomplished."

But it's unlikely Jesus' statement was a declaration concerning biblical inerrancy. Rather, in context, it was about his ministry: "Do not think that I have come to abolish the Law or the Prophets. I have not come to abolish them, but to fulfill them" (v. 17), and indeed, his advent and ministry accomplished and fulfilled much—correcting false interpretations of the Law and even repealing parts of it.

The claim that everything in the Bible happened precisely as presented in our current English translations invites controversies that distract from the core messages in Scriptures. Were there six literal days for Creation a few thousand years ago or does the Bible tell us *that* God created the universe in six poetic segments, metaphorically called "days," and we are left to explore through science *how* and *when*? If the Creation story is to be taken literally, which version is correct: Genesis 1 or 2? After Jesus' crucifixion, did the women spread the word about the empty tomb or not (compare Luke 24:9 with Mark 16:8)? There are numerous such issues—some trivial or easily explained, others more significant. But does fighting over those matters do anything other than give the adherents bragging rights while allowing them to identify who they are against? Psalm 19 portrays the whole revelation from God in much broader strokes than to pin truth on individual words that may have been subject to human assumptions.

After noting that his faith is based on the person of Jesus Christ, Greg Boyd said Jesus frequently quoted the Old Testament, thereby demonstrating his conviction that it was the inspired Word of God. Therefore, "I'm going to affirm that the Bible is the inspired Word of God on the authority of Jesus." But . . .

> I'm not going to affirm that the Bible is the inspired Word of God because it fits someone's standard of what a perfect book is supposed to look like. I'm not going to believe in the Bible because I think it's completely free of all inaccuracies, completely free of all human elements, completely free of all errors. No! I believe the Bible on the authority of Jesus.[6]

The whole Bible *is* "God-breathed" to tell us who God is, his love for us, and to give us instructions for how to find and relate to God and to one another—*that's* inspired Scripture! And it assures me that God is truly GOOD! Of course, the whole story of a God-breathed Bible includes the ugly, unvarnished stuff as well as cultural assumptions about God's character just like the tribe that misunderstood the missionaries who they thought favored female circumcision. But when the time was right, they were able to correct it. Not unsimilar to what Paul said: "With all wisdom and understanding, he [God] made known to us the mystery of his will according to his good pleasure, which he purposed in Christ, to be put into effect when the *times reach their fulfillment*—to bring unity to all things in heaven and on earth under Christ" (Eph. 1:8-10, emphasis added).

"Who decided that the Bible, because it's inspired by God, has to be perfect by our standards?" Greg Boyd asks.

> Where did we get the idea that we have the right to set up the criteria to judge the Bible? Like we know what a "God breathed" book should look like ahead of time. But we don't. We don't have a clue. So, we've got to start with what we've

---

6. Greg Boyd, "The 'Problems' in Scripture," message preached at woodland Hills Church, St. Paul, MN, April 16, 2022, https://www.youtube.com/watch?v=lek7sSbcS-M, 49.00—49:22.

got. But folks start with this assumption that it's got to be perfect, and then they try to impose that on the Bible, and that causes nothing but problems.[7]

Some will say that if you don't accept every word in the Bible as literally accurate, you are making yourself a judge who can cherry-pick what you like or don't like. That can and has happened. To a degree, every translation of Scripture, every interpretation is tainted by our own subjective perspective. Don't think that you or I are exempt from that potential. However, the *objective* measure is Jesus. If some idea—any idea, no matter the source—does not conform to Jesus, it needs correction. This is even true regarding what the patriarchs and prophets of old had to say.

In the past God spoke to our ancestors through the prophets at many times and in various ways, but in these last days he has spoken to us by his Son, whom he appointed heir of all things, and through whom also he made the universe. The Son is the radiance of God's glory and *the exact representation of his being*, sustaining all things by his powerful word. After he had provided purification for sins, he sat down at the right hand of the Majesty in heaven. So he became as much superior to the angels as the name he has inherited is superior to theirs (Heb. 1:1-4, emphasis added).

Jesus, Not Ourselves, Is Our Measure of All Truth!

However, if Jesus is our measure of all truth, even to the point of correcting some Old Testament misunderstandings about God, his character, and his purposes, isn't it reasonable to expect that God would have "breathed" into the ancient writers and prophets some hints that he *wasn't* as violent and retributive as they first imagined?

I do not have any details concerning how that missionary couple began to slowly introduce God's love in a way that prepared

---

7. Greg Boyd, "The 'Problems' in Scripture," message preached at Woodland Hills Church, St. Paul, MN, April 16, 2022, https://www.youtube.com/watch?v=lek7sSbcS-M, 41:54—42:20.

the people to abandon the cruel practice of female circumcision. But I'm sure the process took place. Just as there are clues throughout Scripture that show a different view of God than that of a superhero who bashes enemies, and by example teaches us to do the same, and will bash us if we upset him. If we don't realize that's not the God we worship, then we are going to be tempted to blame God for all our suffering and pain.

But those clues about God's true character of love and grace—hidden in plain sight, even in the pages of the Old Testament—are what we're going to review in the next chapter.

Discussion Questions

1. What are some examples of how easily we desire and look for a superhero?
2. Why did God initially focus on establishing his reputation as the great I AM?
3. How do you reconcile Joseph saying to his brothers, "You intended to harm me, but God intended it for good" with the claim (according to James 1:13) that God is never the author of evil?
4. How do you understand 2 Timothy 3:16 ("All Scripture is God-breathed . . ..")? Why?
5. In what ways do you agree or disagree that any idea—no matter the source—which does not conform to Jesus needs correction?

Chapter 5
What If God
Is Not Who We Thought?

The thing that really cooked people's noodles
wasn't the question, "Is Jesus like God?"
It was, "What if God is like Jesus?"
What if God is not who we thought? . . .
What if the most reliable way to know God is to look
at how God chose to reveal God's self in Jesus?

—*Nadia Bolz-Weber, author, pastor, theologian*[1]

So, IS GOD LIKE JESUS? Shortly before he died, C.S. Lewis discussed in a letter to his friend John Beversluis, how we should regard God.

> [In] the atrocities and treacheries of Joshua, I see the grave danger . . . of believing in a God whom we cannot but regard as evil, and then—in mere terrified flattery—calling Him "good" and worshiping Him is a still greater danger. The ultimate question is whether the doctrine of the goodness of God or that of the inerrancy of Scripture is to prevail when they conflict. I think the doctrine of the goodness of God

1. Nadia Bolz-Weber, "Resurrection Is Messy," *The Corners* blog, April 9,2023. https://thecorners.substack.com/p/resurrection-is-messy?utm_source=substack&utm_medium=email.

is the more certain of the two. Indeed, only that doctrine renders this worship of Him obligatory or even permissible.[2]

Such a statement raises the obvious question of who determines what is "good"? Lewis continues:

> Some will reply "Ah, but we are fallen and don't recognize good when we see it." But God Himself does not say that we are as fallen as all that. He constantly, in Scripture, appeals to our conscience: "Why do ye not of yourselves judge what is right?"—"What fault hath my people found in me?" And so on.
>
> But of course, having said all this, we must apply it with fear and trembling. Some things which seem to us bad may be good. But [when] we . . . consult our consciences, [we must not try] to feel a thing good when it seems to us total evil. We can only pray that if there is an invisible goodness hidden in such things, God, in His own good time will enable us to see it. If we need to.[3]

The writer to the Hebrews began by saying: "In the past God spoke to our ancestors through the prophets at many times and in various ways, but in these last days he has spoken to us by his Son" (Heb. 1:1-2). Why did God find it necessary to become a little lower than the angels (Heb. 2:9) and come to earth as a human? The most obvious answer is in John 3:16-17:

> For God so loved the world that he gave his one and only Son, that whoever believes in him shall not perish but have eternal life. For God did not send his Son into the world to condemn the world, but to save the world through him.

---

2. C.S. Lewis to John Beversluis, July 3, 1963, quoted in John Beversluis, *C.S. Lewis and the Search for a Rational Religion,* Amherst, NY: Prometheus Books, 1985, 2007), 295-96.

3. Ibid. Before my edits for clarity, the third sentence in the last paragraph read: "But we must not consult our consciences by trying to feel a thing good when it seems to us totally evil."

But the Epistle to the Hebrews clearly implies there was more to Jesus' mission, as does Luke 4:18-19 where Jesus said he'd been "anointed to proclaim good news" for the poor, release for prisoners, sight for the blind, and freedom for the oppressed. After centuries of studying the sacred Law and the Prophets, could the learned Scribes and Pharisees—who thought they knew God and played a major role in structuring Jewish society according to that understanding—have actually misunderstood God's character and heart so seriously that they hurt people? What if God is far more like Jesus than how they characterized him?

Correcting Ancient Misconceptions

If the ancient prophets and writers misunderstood certain aspects of God, we shouldn't be surprised if their work nevertheless flagged some of those misconceptions. In fact, if the Scriptures truly are "God breathed," wouldn't we *expect* them to include some efforts by God to slowly correct those fallacies? In the past, the significance of those clues might have been missed, but in retrospect, wouldn't they be detectable? Wouldn't God have tried time after time to show himself to be less violent and retributive than the pagan deities? Wouldn't God have distinguished himself from being merely a tougher version of the gods worshiped by the surrounding cultures?

I believe the beginning of that process occurred in discernable ways throughout the Old Testament. In fact, at Mount Horeb (Mount Sinai) Moses admitted that there was much about God he did not understand when he said, "If you are pleased with me, *teach me your ways* so I may know you and continue to find favor with you" (Exod. 33:13, emphasis added). Later in that exchange Moses asked God to reveal his glory to him. God responded, "I will cause all my goodness to pass in front of you, and I will proclaim my name, the LORD" (v. 19). This was again the name, *Yahweh*, given to Moses when he told Moses to tell the Israelites to say, "I AM has sent me to you" (Exod. 3:14). Yes, God's greatness had

47

been proclaimed in this powerful name, but his glory was not in being the greatest. The character quality that revealed his glory was his *goodness.*

Then the Lord told Moses to chisel out two more stone tablets to replace the ones on which God had written the commandments that Moses had smashed in anger when he saw the Israelites worshiping the Golden Calf. Moses was to bring the replacement tablets when he came up on the mountain the next morning, "and I will write on them the words that were on the first tablets, which you broke" (Exod. 34:1). The next day, when they met, God again proclaimed his name, "the LORD." And he passed before Moses and proclaimed himself as . . .

"The LORD, the LORD, a God merciful and gracious, slow to anger, and abounding in steadfast love and faithfulness, keeping steadfast love for the thousandth generation, forgiving iniquity and transgression and sin, yet by no means clearing the guilty, but visiting the iniquity of the parents upon the children and the children's children to the third and the fourth generation" (Exod. 34:5-7, NRSV).

First, notice the repeated use of the name, "The LORD," *Yahweh.* There's no question that Moses was dealing with the great *I AM.*

Then God describes himself as "merciful and gracious, slow to anger, and abounding in steadfast love and faithfulness, keeping steadfast love for the thousandth generation,[4] forgiving iniquity and transgression and sin." God's glory was in that goodness. There is no contradiction between *that* characterization of God and Jesus Christ, no dissonance at all. However, that extraordinary doxology is followed by God seeming to say he will *not let the guilty go unpunished* but will visit punishment for the sins of parents upon their (innocent?) children for three and four generations. Not only is this an internal contradiction, but the principle

---

4. Some translations do not include the idea of love and forgiveness for thousands of *generations* (which is based on the Chaldee or Aramaic version of the Old Testament). Instead, they simply say "maintaining love for thousands," implying repentant individuals.

is so uncharacteristic of Jesus, that it makes one wonder whether it was an editorial addition by Moses according to what he *expected* of a great God, given his pagan roots—the idea that God will punish the innocent children for their parents' sins.

Greg Boyd uses this example to show the progressive revelation concerning God's character.[5] He says that the sentence describing punishing the children of the offenders to the third and fourth generation is repeated two other times[6] in the Pentateuch, the first five books of the Bible, usually ascribed to Moses as the author. And there is a way in which such a cycle often happens, not because God causes it, but because great evil always impacts other people, and they carry grudges and retaliate, and it goes on and on. Many wars can be traced to injustices that occurred generations earlier. But after those initial times in Scripture when that generational curse was declared, the doxology or as Boyd calls it, the "foundational confession of faith" about God's goodness is repeated over twenty times throughout Scripture *without that curse attached*. For instance, Joel 2:13 says, "Return to the LORD your God, for he is gracious and compassionate, slow to anger and abounding in love, and he relents from sending calamity."

Later in scripture, that vengeful curse is actually repudiated: "The *child will not share the guilt of the parent*, nor will the parent share the guilt of the child. The righteousness of the righteous will be credited to them, and the wickedness of the wicked will be charged against them" (Ezek. 18:20, emphasis added).

In the New Testament, when the disciples saw a man blind from birth, they asked, "Who sinned, this man or his parents?" Jesus dismissed the whole concept: "Neither this man nor his par-

---

5. Greg Boyd, "The Gift of God's Justice," Woodland Hills Church, St. Paul, MN, Nov. 26, 2023, Begin 23:40. https://www.youtube.com/watch?v=PpURsuuPXLs.

6. See Num. 14:18; Deut. 5:9. It also appears without the declarations of God's goodness in Exod. 20:5 and Isa. 65:6-7. David appears to recall it and curse his enemy Saul with the concept (but for only one generation) in Ps. 109:14. But the use of this vengeful curse clearly declines and finally disappears as representative of God's character. Then it is explicitly repudiated in Ezek. 18:20.

ents sinned" (John 9:2-3). Sin often is the source of suffering, but not in this instance, and certainly not as a punishment from God.

So, we see God progressively revealing his character as the people can understand and receive it, explicitly correcting earlier misconceptions that may have been influenced by pagan expectations that justice is achieved by revenge. In contrast, God's justice is all about restoration.

Settling the Promised Land Without War

Even before God revealed his character to Moses on Mount Sinai (also called Mount Horeb), God had instructed the people in Exodus 23 as to how they could have a peaceful society without violence. They must not spread false reports, or follow the crowd in doing wrong, or pervert justice, or show favoritism. He even said they should return an *enemy's* ox or donkey if it was found wandering off. God told the people they should help those who hated them, and not deny justice to the poor. They shouldn't accept bribes or oppress a foreigner. Don't these instructions sound like Jesus telling us to love our enemies?

But how were the Israelites to love their "enemies" while embarking on the conquest of Canaan? Following the above instructions, we encounter this extraordinary promise concerning how the people *could* settle the Promised Land, apparently without resorting to violent warfare if they would only trust God:

I will send my terror ahead of you and throw into confusion every nation you encounter. I will make all your enemies turn their backs and run. I will send the hornet ahead of you to drive the Hivites, Canaanites and Hittites out of your way. But I will not drive them out in a single year, because the land would become desolate and the wild animals too numerous for you. Little by little I will drive them out before you, until you have increased enough to take possession of the land (Exod. 23:27-30).

Later, in Exodus 33:2, God again reminded Moses of that earlier promise: "I will send an angel before you and drive out the" other tribes residing in the land.

Similarly, God promised in Leviticus 18:25 "I am punishing the people who live there. I will cause the land to vomit them out" (NLT). The context is a warning to the Israelites to avoid following any of the evil practices of the people living in the land,[7] but in so doing, God indicates that the Israelites would not need to fight. The land itself would cause the original inhabitants to migrate elsewhere.

Deuteronomy 7:20 also speaks of the role of "hornets" in clearing the land. However, this time *Moses* preceded the instruction with: "You must destroy all the peoples the LORD your God gives over to you. Do not look on them with pity and do not serve their gods, for that will be a snare to you" (v. 16), describing the "hornet" more as a means of cleaning up any survivors of the massacre.

Nevertheless, even when the people had engaged in genocide, believing their bloody efforts were necessary to secure the land, God reminded them, "I sent the hornet ahead of you, which drove them out before you—also the two Amorite kings. *You did not do it with your own sword and bow*" (Josh. 24:12, emphasis added). Note, God did not even say I made *you* strong enough to defeat them. No, he claimed for himself alone the full responsibility for clearing the land, whether in metaphorical or literal terms.[8]

Before the "Battle of Jericho," there was this extraordinary scene:

Now when Joshua was near Jericho, he looked up and saw a man standing in front of him with a drawn sword in

---

7. Verse 22 of this chapter includes the verse often quoted to condemn homosexuals. For a deeper study of this see, Dave Jackson, *Risking Grace; Loving Our Gay Family and Friends Like Jesus*, (Evanston, IL: Castle Rock Creative), 2016.

8. For further insight to the meaning of "hornets," consider, Cheri Williams, "The 'Hornet' of the Conquest in Deuteronomy 7:20: An Alternate Meaning," Ancient Hebrew Research Center. https://www.ancient-hebrew.org/biblical-history/the-hornet-of-the-conquest.htm.

his hand. Joshua went up to him and asked, "Are you for us or for our enemies?"

"Neither," he replied, "but as commander of the army of the Lord I have now come." Then Joshua fell facedown to the ground in reverence, and asked him, "What message does my Lord have for his servant?"

The commander of the Lord's army replied, "Take off your sandals, for the place where you are standing is holy." And Joshua did so. (Josh. 5:13-15).

Even as God was preparing to help the Israelites "conquer" Canaan, God made it clear that he was in charge but not as a tribal god defined as *for* one side or the other, a further revelation of God's true character.

The conquest of the city of Jericho appears to have been a mixture of God's miraculous decimation of the city walls and the efforts of the armed men who, according to *Joshua's* instruction, slaughtered every living thing within the city except those in Rahab's house. Technically, Joshua did not blame God for telling the people to slaughter everyone; Joshua was the one who told them to do that. But such instructions were later attributed to God as the Israelites faced other cities.

Generations later, Gideon's experience represents a similar example of God defeating Israel's foe without bloody warfare. In fact, the reduction of Gideon's army from 32,000 soldiers down to 300 men armed with such "lethal" weapons of trumpets, jars, and torches made his force a military joke. (See Judg. 7.) To be sure, when the Midianites fled, the Israelites chased them out of the region and killed Oreb and Zeeb, two of the Midianite leaders.

But the point is, these may be glimpses of God showing himself as other than a warrior god whom we can emulate.

Updating the Law

An "inerrant" view of Scriptural inspiration holds that "the Holy Spirit dynamically superintended the verbal expressions of the human authors of Scripture so that the very thoughts God intended were accurately penned in the wording of the original manuscripts."[9] However, if Moses accurately penned the wording of the original manuscripts *exactly as God intended*, then it wouldn't need correcting. Right?

But what if the Mosaic Law as originally written wasn't just and fair?

In its original form, it allowed only males to inherit land (Deut. 21:15-17). However, as Israel was preparing to divide up the Promised Land, five sisters—Mahlah, Noah, Hoglah, Milcah, and Tirzah—realized their family would essentially disappear because their father, Zelophehad, had died without a male heir. So, they went to Moses, Eleazar the priest, the leaders, and *the whole assembly.*

Bravely, they made their case: "Our father died in the wilderness. He was not among Korah's followers, who banded together against the LORD, but he died for his own sin and left no sons. Why should our father's name disappear from his clan because he had no son? Give us property among our father's relatives" (Num. 27:3).

Moses prayed about it, and the Lord answered: "What Zelophehad's daughters are saying is right. You must certainly give them property as an inheritance among their father's relatives and give their father's inheritance to them" (v. 7). Moses went on to rescind the old custom and detail a new law of inheritance.

Even though the sisters had to fight for its enforcement when the land was ultimately distributed (see Deut. 36:1-12 and Josh. 17:3-4), the revised law was a dramatic advancement: *God shows no favoritism!* This step of adjusting the people's earlier presumptions that had been written down *as Scripture*, represents God's progressive revelation of his own character. If we don't realize that dynamic, we can bounce like a pinball between trying to embrace and emulate the earliest images of God and then his character as Scripture unfolds until he is ultimately revealed in Jesus Christ.

But we don't have to do that. We're not living under a Bad Cop / Good Cop system, never knowing who we're dealing with. Remember, "In Christ all the fullness of the Deity lives in bodily

9. Multnomah University's Doctrinal Statement, Article 1. https://
www.multnomah.edu/doctrinal-statement/?gclid=Cj0KCQjwnMWkBhD
LARIsAHBOftqNXxnVMxoY8xvCjh4oZcKPdt-YTlPM8ofMELA1Boqbn-
SCDSrPii7UaAttlEALw_wcB.

form" (Col. 2:8), and he "is the same yesterday and today and forever" (Heb. 13:8).

But We Want to Be Like All the Other Nations

Gideon's trumpeters and torchbearers chased off the Midianites in relatively the middle of a four-hundred year period when judges such as Othniel, Ehud, Deborah, Gideon, Jephthah, and Samson governed Israel along with elders, priests, and prophets—some good, some bad. But when Samuel, one of the most highly esteemed prophets grew old, the people began clamoring for a king. "It is not you they have rejected, but they have rejected me as their king," God assured Samuel (1 Sam. 1:7). Then God told Samuel to warn the people of all the chaos, drama, and cost of installing a monarchy, but the warning meant nothing to the people. "No!" they said. "We want a king over us. Then *we will be like all the other nations*, with a king to lead us and to go out before us and fight our battles" (vv. 19-20, emphasis added).

The people's desire for a king was entirely consistent with the mindset of the day (and today?) that values tangible military might or even encourages us personally to "Stand your ground!"—over the care of God himself. In contrast to smashing one's enemies militarily or personally as one might think Old Testament events model, God may have been trying to modify that ethic by saying, "It is mine to avenge; I will repay. In due time their foot will slip; their day of disaster is near and their doom rushes upon them" (Deut. 32:35, also see Rom. 12:19). Admittedly, the context is not just a truism like, "Pride goes before a fall" (Prov. 16:18). No, it says *God* will avenge. But God's warning about the folly of their demanding a king demonstrates that he and the people were not in agreement on what was best. Still, he allowed them to proceed anyway with having a king—and even blessed them in the process—not unlike those missionaries who tolerated female circumcision (even making it safer) in order to maintain relationship with the people, knowing they might get the wrong idea in the process.

King David, Israel's most beloved and second king, was welcomed even before his coronation by the people in all the towns. "As they danced, they sang: 'Saul has slain his thousands, and David his tens of thousands'" (1 Sam. 18:7). This was after Samuel had identified David as "a man after [God's] own heart" (1 Sam. 13:14). So, does that mean God affirmed a warrior king. Was warfare in God's heart? It would be easy to think so if the biblical record is accurate in how it attributes to God the previous military conquests by Israel.

But there's more. Yes, David sought the Lord and communed with him in ways that inspire all believers, especially through the psalms he wrote. However, concerning David's military exploits, God issued this final verdict: "You are not to build my temple, for you are a warrior and have shed much blood" (1 Chron. 28:3, TLB). Why would God have made such a statement if David was simply reflecting the character of God as outlined in the "Texts of Terror"? No, the true image of God is revealed in Jesus!

God Cares about Justice and Those Who Suffer

From the outset, God seems to have begun tempering what might have been understood as a raw might-makes-right mentality. It was the *cries* of the Hebrew slaves, after all, to which he responded by freeing them from Egypt. And then the Law Moses communicated to them as they traveled in the wilderness included extraordinary protections for the poor, the oppressed, widows, orphans, foreigners, those in debt, and limitations on slavery. We sometimes forget that when Jesus identified the second greatest commandment: "Love your neighbor as yourself" (Mark 12:31), he was quoting God's Law communicated through Moses in Leviticus 19:18. God had wasted no time upgrading his people's moral code above that of the more ancient Mesopotamian collections of laws such as the Code of Hammurabi, especially in terms of justice, mercy, and protection of the oppressed.[10] But the process itself demonstrates that it was a *process*. The earlier characterizations of God as war-like, retributive, and violent were not complete, and we should never treat them as though they were accurate in those regards.

---

10. Jonathan Sarr, "The Code of Hammurabi vs. the Law of Moses," Evangel Classical School, September 27, 2012, https://evangelcs.org/news/2012/the-code-of-hammurabi-vs-the-law-of-moses/.

In terms of justice, where the Mosaic Laws addressed how people should respond when wronged, it appears to have been God's way to limit the escalation of violence. In other words, "life for life, eye for eye, tooth for tooth, hand for hand, foot for foot, burn for burn, wound for wound, bruise for bruise" limited retaliation. (See Exod. 21:24-25, Lev. 24:20, and Deut. 19:21.) One was not justified in wiping out an entire family if someone accidentally or even deliberately killed someone in their family. That restriction was a step in the right direction and totally inconsistent with the genocide of every man, woman, child, and beast in a city.

Decades after Babylon destroyed Jerusalem and took many of the people into exile, some of the Israelites were allowed to return to Jerusalem to rebuild the city. It was an exciting but trying time because some of the people opposed the rebuilding of the city's walls. In the middle of chaos, Ezra and Nehemiah tried to inspire a spiritual revival by reminding them of God's faithfulness in bringing their ancestors out of Egypt. "But you are a forgiving God, gracious and compassionate, slow to anger and abounding in love" (Neh. 9:17). It is certainly true, but it was a twist on the old claim that God had commanded them to slay one another after their lapse into worshiping the golden calf (Exod. 32:27-29), or the God who killed 14,700 of them with a plague for complaining too much (Num. 16:42-49).

Designating "cities of refuge" in the Promised Land was a tangible example of God's concern for justice at a time when God was also being reported as ruthless toward the inhabitants of Canaan as well as disobedient Israelites. In Numbers 35:6-15 God tells the people to set aside six towns where a person who had killed someone could flee and be safe from any avenger until a fair trial determined whether or not the death was accidental. If it was, the offender could return to the city and live there in safety.

God Is More than a Tribal Deity

Another modification to the might-makes-right mentality is God's promise to Abraham: "In you all the families of the earth shall be blessed" (Gen. 12:3). Despite this, because God had miraculously rescued the Children of Israel from slavery and brought them into the "Promised Land," it was easy for them to presume he was their private, tribal deity. God began correcting this presumption in the following instances by embracing foreigners, to name a few:

- Tamar, probably a Canaanite (Gen. 38:1-25), Rahab, rescued from the inhabitants of Jericho (Josh. 2), and Ruth, a Moabite (Ruth 1:4) were all "foreigners" who became ancestors of both David and Jesus.
- Elijah the prophet was sent to the widow of Zarephath in Sidon where he resurrected her son from death (1 Kings 17:7-24), and Elisha was sent to heal Naaman, a Syrian, from leprosy (2 Kings 5:1-19). When Jesus pointed out that they were foreigners who received these unique miracles, the people in the synagogue were furious (Luke 4:25-28), still having trouble with God's care for others besides themselves.
- The Book of Jonah expressed the frankly parochial mentality of the Jews in about the eighth century B.C. Jonah did not want to share their God as a blessing to all the families of the earth, and particularly not the Ninevites who were their enemies . . . because he feared God might forgive them! Which God did—one more corrective concerning what God is like.

"Love Your Enemies"—Previews of *God's* Better Way

When the king of Aram was at war with Israel (see 2 Kings 6:8-23), he realized Elisha's prophetic insights helped Israel avoid attack. So, he set up an ambush to capture Elisha at Dothan. When Elisha's servant went outside early in the morning, he saw the city surrounded by horses, chariots, and a strong force. In panic, he said to Elisha, "Oh no, my lord. What shall we do?" Elijah responded, "Don't be afraid. Those who are with us are more than those who are against us." And Elisha prayed that the eyes of his servant would be opened.

Sure enough, the hills were full of horses and chariots of fire from heaven's armies. As the enemy advanced, Elisha prayed again that the enemy would be struck with blindness, which happened. Elisha was then able to lead them away from Dothan to the City of Samaria. Once trapped inside, Elisha again prayed, this time that the eyes of the enemy forces would be opened.

"Shall I kill them?" the king of Israel asked Elisha.

> "Do not kill them," he answered. "Would you kill those you have captured with your own sword or bow? Set food and water before them so that they may eat and drink and then go back to their master." So he prepared a great feast for them, and after they had finished eating and drinking, he sent them away, and they returned to their master. So the bands from Aram stopped raiding Israel's territory (vv. 22-23).

God Is Repulsed by the People's Sacrifices

The Mosaic Law addressed three basic categories: civil, moral, and ceremonial. The latter had to do with sacrifices, festivals, and worship, and all the Law was ascribed to God. So why did David conclude in Psalm 51:16-17 that . . .

> You [O God] do not delight in sacrifice, or I would bring it;
> > you do not take pleasure in burnt offerings.
> My sacrifice, O God, is a broken spirit;
> > a broken and contrite heart
> > you, God, will not despise.

Something had gone wrong personally in his own life with his adultery and murder, and being a great man of war did not balance out those sins. In fact, as we saw earlier, his military exploits—the tens of thousands he reputedly had slain—only added to his guilt. Sacrifices and burnt offerings failed to relieve his soul.

As for all of Israel that wanted to be like the other nations, more and more of their pagan practices and influences crept in, not all at once and not with every generation or king (some were good). But by the latter half of Israel's kingdom period, the Prophet Isaiah uttered this warning as Assyria threatened their autonomy:

> "The multitude of your sacrifices—
> > what are they to me?" says the Lord.

"I have more than enough of burnt offerings,
   of rams and the fat of fattened animals;
I have no pleasure
   in the blood of bulls and lambs and goats.
When you come to appear before me,
   who has asked this of you,
   this trampling of my courts?
Stop bringing meaningless offerings!
   Your incense is detestable to me.
New Moons, Sabbaths and convocations—
   I cannot bear your worthless assemblies.
Your New Moon feasts and your appointed festivals
      I hate with all my being.
      They have become a burden to me;
      I am weary of bearing them.
      When you spread out your hands in prayer,
      I hide my eyes from you;
      even when you offer many prayers,
      I am not listening (Isa. 1:11-15a).

The Ceremonial Law given by Moses certainly called for sacrifices, and their purpose was twofold—one immediate and one prophetic. The immediate value was to help the people realize the fact and seriousness of sin, which required true repentance, "a broken and contrite heart," as David had learned. The prophetic aspect portended Jesus' sacrifice on the Cross.[11] But this passage in Isaiah certainly indicates that the people were off track in how they understood and implemented God's instructions. And the reason is explained in verses 15b-17.

Your hands are full of blood!
Wash and make yourselves clean.

---

11. Many say Jesus' death on the Cross, foreshadowed by the Old Covenant sacrifices, was to satisfy God's demand as payment for our sin—Jesus' substitutionary atonement. The question is, who was demanding that payment? I do not believe it was an angry God. But we will discuss that in Chapter 13.

> Take your evil deeds out of my sight;
> stop doing wrong.
> Learn to do right; seek justice.
> Defend the oppressed.
> Take up the cause of the fatherless;
> plead the case of the widow.

Several other prophets similarly decried the hypocrisy of the people's sacrifices. "Let justice roll down like waters, and righteousness like an ever-flowing stream," cried Amos on God's behalf (Amos 5:21). In some cases, God's wrath was kindled because the people had mixed in rituals practiced by neighboring peoples. (See Ezek. 20:16-44; Hosea 6:6; Isa. 66:1-4.)

Turning Swords into Plowshares

For a people who had gloried in the conquest of the Promised Land by what they believed was God's blessing on them as a warrior nation, the threat of Assyria and Isaiah's warning about the impending fall of Jerusalem if they persisted in idolatry and oppression of the poor must have been bewildering and terrifying. But God offers a way out: repentance! Their salvation would not come by a more powerful king or stronger army. In fact, in chapter 2, verses 2-5, Isaiah says,

> In the last days
> the mountain of the LORD's temple will be established . . .
> and all nations will stream to it.
> Many peoples will come and say,
> "Come, let us go up to the mountain of the LORD,
> to the temple of the God of Jacob.
> He will teach us his ways,
> so that we may walk in his paths."
> The law will go out from Zion,
> the word of the LORD from Jerusalem.
> He will judge between the nations
> and will settle disputes for many peoples.
> They will beat their swords into plowshares

and their spears into pruning hooks.
Nation will not take up sword against nation,
    nor will they train for war anymore.

The Suffering Servant Prophesies

We began this chapter suggesting that the biblical patriarchs, prophets, and people had impressions of God carried over from their pagan roots and surrounding cultures, primarily that God was violent and retributive. We also suggested that God tolerated this misunderstanding while establishing a relationship of trust with the people until they were slowly able to receive correction. In this chapter I've offered a litany of examples where God taught them "a different way," contrary to behaviors reflecting a violent and retributive God. Sometimes they got it, and sometimes they didn't, but until the exile, they were always dipping back into the immorality and idolatry of the cultures around them.

This was never more obvious than their image of the Messiah they believed would rescue them from their oppressors and enemies, someone who could ride in on a warhorse to organize an army and free the Jews from Rome's cruel dominion by the time the first century arrived.

But the Prophet Isaiah offered a very different image in chapter 53.

Who has believed our message
    and to whom has the arm of the LORD been revealed?
He grew up before him like a tender shoot,
    and like a root out of dry ground.
He had no beauty or majesty to attract us to him,
    nothing in his appearance that we should desire him.
He was despised and rejected by mankind,
    a man of suffering, and familiar with pain.
Like one from whom people hide their faces
    he was despised, and we held him in low esteem.
Surely he took up our pain
    and bore our suffering,
yet we considered him punished by God,
    stricken by him, and afflicted. . . .

He was oppressed and afflicted,
>   yet he did not open his mouth;
he was led like a lamb to the slaughter,
>   and as a sheep before its shearers is silent,
>   so he did not open his mouth. . . .

Many other Old Testament prophesies described the Messiah in terms other than the expected conquering hero, but it was not until Jesus came and fulfilled them all that his followers began to believe he was indeed the Messiah for whom they had waited.

In the next chapter, we'll look at some of the ideas and images about God that Jesus still needed to correct.

Discussion Questions

1. In what ways do you think God is more like Jesus than how the Patriarchs portrayed him?
2. How do you understand what transpired between Moses and God on Mount Horeb when Moses asked God to reveal himself more fully (Exod. 33:18-23)? Was anything new revealed? What?
3. What did God mean when he promised the Israelites that he would send hornets to clear the Promised Land? What does it say about God that he told Gideon to reduce his force to a mere 300 men with nonlethal weapons?

Chapter 6
Jesus, the Revisionist

"Are you the only one visiting Jerusalem who does not know the things . . . about Jesus of Nazareth? He was a prophet, powerful in word and deed before God and all the people. . . . We had hoped that he was the one who was going to redeem Israel."

—Two disciples on the Road to Emmaus,
Luke 24:18-21

WAIT! BEFORE YOUR HAIR SPONTANEOUSLY COMBUSTS over calling Jesus a revisionist, I am NOT revising his story. In fact, I strongly embrace what orthodox Christians have believed about Jesus since the early church and affirmed in the major Christian creeds. But there was some history Jesus came to revise, and religious leaders didn't like that. The word *revisionist* has been vilified by anyone opposed to efforts to correct how history was misunderstood. For whatever reasons—often political—they don't like anyone saying, "The traditional story was mistaken. You left out this and had the wrong idea about that." As we noted in the last chapter, through the prophets—sometimes, perhaps without realizing it themselves—God had been trying to correct common misunderstandings about his character and his vision for all people.

But their efforts were not enough! God had to visit us in person, to not only tell us about, but to show us God's character more clearly.

The disciples' expectations about the Messiah, quoted in the epigraph at the beginning of this chapter, is an example of the old expectation for a warrior messiah, and the people hoped to benefit from his power by being on his side. In this case, he would free them from Rome's domination and restore their political, economic, and military sovereignty to the grandeur of David's kingdom and more. But they expected such a messiah to reflect a god who ruled people by force and threat. Jesus was indeed the Messiah, but he did not reflect that kind of a God. On several occasions, Jesus had embraced the Messianic title as the Son of David (Matt. 9:27; 15:22; 20:30; 21:9), and even the name, Messiah (Mark 14:61-62; John 1:41-50; 4:25-26), the term, "I am," as God had identified himself to Moses (John 8:58; Mark 14:61-64), and as a king (John 18:36-37). All of that was true, but the disciples and most of the people understood it through the traditional lens, which needed revising.

As a revisionist, Jesus rejected the old image of the Messiah. When the crowd of five thousand whom Jesus had just miraculously fed tried to take him by force and make him a king, he slipped away to be by himself (John 6:14-15). The kind of a king they had expected did not represent the true character of God. And though at his trial before Pilate, Jesus acknowledged that he was, indeed, a king, he distinguished himself from the common expectation: "My kingdom is not of this world. If it were, my servants would fight to prevent my arrest by the Jewish leaders. But now my kingdom is from another place" (John 18:36).

When Jesus was crucified, the hopes of his followers were dashed, as the disciples on the Road to Emmaus admitted: "We had hoped that he was the one who was going to redeem Israel." But when his resurrection was confirmed, as "he appeared to them over a period of forty days and spoke about the kingdom of God" (Acts 1:3), it revived their expectations. Again "they gathered around him and asked him, 'Lord, are you at this time going to restore the kingdom to Israel?' He said to them: 'It is not for you to know the times or dates the Father has set by his own authority. But you will receive power when the Holy Spirit comes on you; and you will be my witnesses in Jerusalem, and in all Judea and Samaria, and to the ends of the earth'" (vv. 6-8).

The Need for a New Vision Secured by a New Covenant

What? No armies, no horses, no thrones? Just some kind of a baptism from the Holy Spirit that would enable them to be his witnesses. *Witnesses?* . . . Who wants to be just a witness? And witnesses to what? Well, maybe just what Jesus had commissioned them to do in Matthew 28:18-20: "All authority in heaven and on earth has been given to me. Therefore go and make disciples of all nations, baptizing them in the name of the Father and of the Son and of the Holy Spirit, and teaching them to obey everything I have commanded you. And surely I am with you always, to the very end of the age." Or maybe like he said to Peter, "Take care of my sheep" (John 21:16).

And that is exactly what they did for the next three hundred years.[1] Before this, they may have been accused of being "the people who have been turning the world upside down" (Acts 17:6, NRSV), but as Jesus had said, his servants would not fight. They would not mount armies and breach walls, steal land and build fortresses, or massacre whole people groups in the name of some manifest destiny. Instead, they preached the Gospel and planted churches embracing all racial groups, healed the sick and cared for the dying, fed the hungry and became martyrs. Jesus' example and this expression of God's Kingdom utterly transformed the ancient image of God as warlike and vindictive!

What if—some fourteen-hundred years earlier—that multitude of freed slaves coming out of Egypt had embraced such a mission? What if instead of massacring the inhabitants of Canaan and claiming the land as their own, the Israelites had slipped in peacefully, preaching good news, healing the sick, feeding the hungry, and loving their enemies? Of course, that couldn't have happened, right? We can hardly tolerate the refugees who come across our border, and we're far more secure than the Canaanites were. But it couldn't have happened for a far more fundamental reason: *The*

---

1. Constantine converted to Christianity in 312 AD after seeing a vision of the cross and believing if he fought under its sign he would have military success in conquering Rome from Maxentius, and he did. In 380 AD, he declared Christianity the official religion of the Empire. Not surprisingly, merging Christianity with an otherwise pagan nation state altered the nature of much of the Church.

Israelites weren't ready. They weren't yet sure they were following the great I AM. And they didn't yet have a relationship with a God who was so loving they could trust him whether they were received warmly, kicked out, persecuted, or even martyred. They couldn't have spread God's love until they had received God's love embodied in Jesus coming to live among them, revising their view of what they thought he was like, showing them something worth dying for, and then baptizing them with the power of his Holy Spirit to pass on that love.

The Old Covenant, established when God rescued his chosen people from Egypt, needed a New Covenant to revise their understanding of him, an understanding not based on "the blood of goats and bulls . . . [but on] the blood of Christ . . .. For this reason Christ is the mediator of a new covenant" (Heb. 9:13-15).

God Is Not Two-Faced

Without a New Covenant, consecrated by the sacrifice of Immanuel (God with us) on the Cross, the people's understanding of God's character might have appeared two-faced. On the one hand, they had been told he was violent and vindictive—thereby encouraging them to violently smash their enemies while fearing his punishment when they displeased him. On the other hand, there were clues, testimonies in the Psalms and the Prophets, that he was gracious and abounding in loving kindness. So, what was God really like? And how do we—two millennia later—escape living under a similar theological schizophrenia?

One of the most powerful Old Testament pictures of God's care is found in Psalm 91, traditionally understood to have been written by Moses.

> If you say, "The LORD is my refuge,"
>> and you make the Most High your dwelling,
> no harm will overtake you,
>> no disaster will come near your tent.
> For he will command his angels concerning you
>> to guard you in all your ways;
> they will lift you up in their hands,

so that you will not strike your foot against a stone (vv. 9-12).

Of course, there is a condition required for all this protection: *"If* you . . . make the Most High your dwelling place, no harm will overtake you, no disaster will come near your tent" (vv. 9-10, emphasis added). Which suggests that without the relationship you might not recognize the benefits. Now that's true of any relationship. However, though this psalm reveals God's great love for us, the addition of conditions invites abuse by those in power who can use them to manipulate those in need. Jesus railed against the teachers of Moses' Law and the Pharisees because . . . "They tie up heavy, cumbersome loads and put them on other people's shoulders, but they themselves are not willing to lift a finger to move them" (Matt. 23:4). Even in our day, people are confused by what might be called the two-faced representation of God—on the one hand violent and coercive, on the other hand gracious and willing to support us through all life's troubles. Unscrupulous "spiritual guides" have taken advantage of this confusion. For example, during the COVID pandemic, one preacher peddled Psalm 91 as part of a "Coronavirus Protection Packet,"[2] implying you don't need to get vaccinated because God's angels will protect you.

The entire psalm is rich with promises of God's protection, from *physical things* like the fowler's snare, the deadly pestilence, the terror by night, and the arrow that flies by day. Those promises were followed by the guarantee: "You will only observe with your eyes and see the punishment of the wicked" (v. 8). But these literal references appear to be somewhat in contrast to the more metaphorical assurances of God's presence and comfort as our Shepherd we find in Psalm 23. Jesus identified himself with Psalm 23 by saying that he was the Good Shepherd who won't flee when trouble comes but will even lay down his life for his sheep.

On the other hand, you may have noticed a portion of Moses' psalm where Jesus took issue with applying it literally. When the

---

2. Alton R. Williams, "Coronavirus Protection Packet," Understanding Life Ministries (Memphis, TN, 2020) https://worldovercomers.org/wp-content/uploads/2020/09/WOOMCs-Coronavirus-Protection-Packet.pdf.

devil tempted Jesus in the wilderness, he challenged Jesus to throw himself down from the highest point of the temple, quoting Psalm 91:

"He will command his angels concerning you
  to guard you carefully;
they will lift you up in their hands,
  so that you will not strike your foot against a stone" (Luke 4:10-11).

Jesus countered by quoting Deuteronomy 6:16: "It is said: 'Do not put the Lord your God to the test'" (Luke 4:12). Moses apparently wrote Psalm 91, but his authority is subservient to Jesus because *Jesus* is our standard. Jesus corrects our misunderstandings or misapplications from any source, even from "God breathed" scripture. Those preachers who urged their parishioners to just trust God and apply Psalm 91 literally rather than get vaccinated were not applying Jesus' corrective to avoid tempting God's grace. As a result, numerous church members died as did some of those preachers.[3]

Things that Needed Changing

Throughout his ministry, Jesus was often at odds with the Sadducees and Pharisees and their interpretation of God and how God calls us to live. Jesus often chided them for their hypocrisy. But in his Sermon on the Mount, Jesus goes farther. He identifies his objective in Matthew 5:17 as, "Do not think that I have come to abolish the Law or the Prophets; I have not come to abolish them but to fulfill them." Then in verse 21, he begins introducing insights that actually "fulfill" the Law by addressing the underlying motives the Law of Moses failed to explain. Each point began with, "You have heard it said," and Jesus quotes the laws against murder, adultery, divorce, breaking oaths, and retaliation. Then Jesus adds powerful teachings that address the *attitudes* behind these evil deeds that destroy peace in any community. This is more than

---

3. "Deaths of anti-vaccine advocates from COVID-19," Wikipedia, https://en.wikipedia.org/wiki/Deaths_of_anti-vaccine_advocates_from_COVID-19.

good expository preaching. Jesus fulfills the Law by going beyond and actually changing the commonly understood content.

However, concerning the issue of retaliation, we noted in Chapter 5 that the Mosaic Law seemed to limit retaliation—you must not do more harm to someone who has harmed you than they did to you. In other words, only a "life for life, eye for eye, tooth for tooth, hand for hand, foot for foot, burn for burn, wound for wound, bruise for bruise." What is commonly overlooked, however, is that those were not merely *permitted* responses. According to the Law, they were *required* responses: "If there is serious injury, *you are to take* life for life, . . ." (Exod. 21:23); "Anyone who injures their neighbor *is to be* injured in the same manner" (Lev. 24:19); "*Show no pity*: life for life, eye for eye, tooth for tooth, hand for hand, foot for foot" (Deut. 19:21). The principle as Moses gave it was essentially no more godly than the pagan Hammurabi Code of ancient Mesopotamia.

So, when Jesus said, "But I tell you, do not resist an evil person. If anyone slaps you on the right cheek, turn to them the other cheek also" (Matt. 5:39), he actually contradicted what Moses had commanded. He was upgrading to God's vision. He was being a revisionist.

Believing that Jesus was God incarnate, I had long accepted that he enhanced and amplified what appeared in the Old Testament. And, of course, there was the tension with the Pharisees where he challenged their abuse and misapplications of the Law. But I had never considered the possibility that he actually revised some of the old ways God had been portrayed. However, in cancelling "eye-for-an-eye" type retaliations, Jesus contradicted Moses. Then Jesus went on to say, . . .

> You have heard that it was said, "Love your neighbor and hate your enemy." But I tell you, love your enemies and pray for those who persecute you, that you may be children of your Father in heaven. He causes his sun to rise on the evil and the good, and sends rain on the righteous and the unrighteous (Matt. 5:43-45).

It's hard to commit genocide without intensely loathing and dehumanizing your enemy, but you might go to those extremes if someone suggested that God encouraged you to "hate your enemies." Such an attitude is pretty explicit in passages like the conclusion of Psalm 137: "Daughter Babylon, doomed to destruction . . .. Happy is the one who seizes your infants and dashes them against the rocks" (vv. 8-9).[4] That kind of sentiment is understandable for grieving victims, but it is not to be our ideal or what we think characterizes God. When we think it does, we are inclined to agree with Psalm 139:21-22: "Do I not hate those who hate you, Lord, and abhor those who are in rebellion against you? I have nothing but hatred for them; I count them my enemies."

Jesus not only said we should love our enemies, more importantly, loving our enemies emulates our Father in heaven, because he "causes his sun to rise on the evil and the good, and sends rain on the righteous and the unrighteous." That is a radical insight and certainly tempers any presumption that God is eager to smash anyone who doesn't please him.[5]

Go back and review all the "Texts of Terror" itemized earlier in Chapter 2 of this book—events of death and destruction directly attributed to God or similar violence he was said to have authorized or even commanded. If you were in the crowd listening to Jesus' Sermon on the Mount, would you have immediately agreed with the claim that their Father in Heaven was peace-loving and nonviolent? Not likely! Jesus was emphasizing a very different characterization of God, and he was telling his listeners that they needed to reject parts of the old image and emulate a new revelation of a loving and forgiving God.

---

4. Such "imprecatory" language (uttering a curse or prayer invoking evil) is found in Psalms 7, 12, 35, 55, 58, 59, 69, 79, 83, 109, 137,139.

5. As mentioned before, the Old Testament *does* provide glimpses of Godly grace. One example was when David did not take Saul's life when he had a chance, even though at that time Saul was certainly David's enemy. Saul said, "You have just now told me about the good you did to me; the Lord delivered me into your hands, but you did not kill me. . . . May the Lord reward you well for the way you treated me today" (1 Sam. 24:18-19). This willingness to not take vengeance may have been one reason David was called "a man after God's own heart."

For another example, recall the woman caught in adultery as recorded in John 8:1-11.[6] They brought to Jesus a woman caught in adultery (having conveniently let the man get away) and asked him what they should do. They were obviously trying to trap Jesus, but they had a point: The Law of Moses does more than allow the death penalty for adultery as an angry spouse might demand; the Law *required* the death penalty.[7] And Jesus' final instruction to the woman ("Go now and leave your life of sin.") more than suggests she had not been falsely accused. But Jesus, the only one on site "who was without sin," violates—that is reverses—the requirement of the Law and says, "Then neither do I condemn you."

Jesus' efforts at revising wrong images of God may have begun when he first announced his ministry in Nazareth. In that town where he'd been raised, he went to the synagogue and was invited to read from the Scroll of Isaiah, chapter 61.

"The Spirit of the Lord is on me, because he has anointed me to proclaim good news to the poor.

"He has sent me to proclaim freedom for the prisoners and recovery of sight for the blind, to set the oppressed free, to proclaim the year of the Lord's favor" (Luke 4:18-19).

Jesus then rolled up the scroll and gave it back to the attendant, saying, "'Today this scripture is fulfilled in your hearing.' All spoke well of him and were amazed at the gracious words that came from his lips" (vv. 21-22). Of course, Jesus had to end his text at some point, but why did he stop at that point? The *next phrase* in Isaiah declares that the anointed one would announce "the day of vengeance of our God" (Isa. 61:2). If he was the Messiah, why wouldn't Jesus declare the same thing, the arrival of God's vengeance? Because his life and ministry thereafter proved

---

6. I am aware this event was not recorded in some of the oldest manuscripts of the Gospel of John. However, it coincides with the character of Jesus. And those most likely to question whether Jesus reversed aspects of the Mosaic Law would probably defend the authenticity of this passage.

7. See Leviticus 20:10 and Deuteronomy 22:23-24.

that was not his mission. Perhaps in rejecting that expectation by the prophet, he was also beginning to modify some common expectations about God.

"By What Authority?"

"Jesus entered the temple courts, and, while he was teaching, the chief priests and the elders of the people came to him. 'By what authority are you doing these things?' they asked. 'And who gave you this authority?'" (Matt. 21:23). It was a good question, though Jesus didn't answer it in the moment because he knew they didn't really want to know the answer. They were just trying to trap him.

However, if we are going to claim that some of the violent and coercive images of God as portrayed in the Old Testament needed revision by the message and ministry of Jesus, then we need to be certain whether Jesus was speaking truth or hyperbole when he said, "Anyone who has seen me has seen the Father" (John 14:9) or in declaring, "I and my Father are one" (John 30:30).

John was totally convinced of Jesus' literal truthfulness in this matter. He began his gospel saying, "In the beginning was the Word, and the Word was with God, and the Word was God. He was with God in the beginning. Through him all things were made; without him nothing was made that has been made" (John 1:1-3). "The Word," as John used the term, is broadly affirmed as referring to Jesus, especially in the context of the whole chapter. Therefore, John was unequivocally declaring that Jesus is God, not a little god, not kind of like God, but, as the Nicene Creed explains: "very God of very God . . . by whom all things were made."[8]

John also seemed to be aware that there were differences between what Moses had offered and what Jesus brought.

---

8. I am not advocating "Modalism," the theological belief that the members of the Trinity are not three but one person, appearing in one of three modes. I believe in the Father, Son, and Holy Spirit—three distinct persons who do not play "good cop, bad cop" but are consistent in character, equally loving, and united in purpose. To get into the weeds of Modalism deeper than I dare go, see, https://christianity.stackexchange.com/questions/86808/what-is-the-difference-between-the-trinity-theory-and-modalism.

The Word became flesh and made his dwelling among us. We have seen his glory, the glory of the one and only Son, who came from the Father, full of grace and truth. . . .

For the law was given through Moses; grace and truth came through Jesus Christ (John 1:14, 17).

The contrast was between the Law on one hand and the grace and truth of Jesus on the other. And ultimately, the truth about Jesus was the thing for which he was crucified: his claim to be God. It was on the authority of his divinity that he declared and dispensed grace in ways not as obvious in the Law.

John was not the only one affirming Jesus' claim that he had this authority. Writing to the Colossian church, Paul said, "The Son is the image of the invisible God . . .. For God was pleased to have all his fullness dwell in him. . . . For in Christ all the fullness of the Deity lives in bodily form" (Col. 1:15, 19; 2:9). The writer to the Hebrews said much the same thing. We already mentioned the contrast between how "In times past God spoke to our ancestors through the prophets at many times and in various ways, but in these last days he has spoken to us by his Son" (Heb. 1:1-2). But he continues in verse 3 to say, "The Son is the radiance of God's glory and the *exact representation of his being,* sustaining all things by his powerful word" (emphasis added).

Perhaps the most definitive evidence that Jesus had the authority to correct historical misconceptions occurred near the end of his earthly ministry. Peter had made his confession that Jesus was indeed "God's Messiah" (Matt. 13:15), after which Jesus told the gathered disciples that he was going to be killed, but that "on the third day be raised to life." Apparently, given how totally disheartened they were after his death, they weren't paying much attention.

But a few days later (approximately forty days before his crucifixion), Jesus took Peter, John, and James up onto a mountain to pray when this incredible event happened:

As he was praying, the appearance of his face changed, and his clothes became as bright as a flash of lightning.

Two men, Moses and Elijah, appeared in glorious splendor, talking with Jesus. They spoke about his departure, which he was about to bring to fulfillment at Jerusalem. Peter and his companions were very sleepy, but when they became fully awake, they saw his glory and the two men standing with him. . . .

While he was speaking, a cloud appeared and covered them, and they were afraid as they entered the cloud. A voice came from the cloud, saying, "This is my Son, whom I have chosen; *listen to him*" (Luke 9:29-32, 34-35, emphasis added).[9]

"Listen to him!" God the Father said. Listen to *Jesus*, even though the two most renown prophets of old were standing right there beside him. Why not, "Listen to these three and amalgamate any apparent differences?" which is what many of us try to do.

No, if there is any difference, "Listen to Jesus!"

But Not with the Dualism of Marcion

Once the early believers got over their expectations that Jesus was going to lead a revolt against Rome (see Acts 1:6), they began taking to heart the mind-boggling reality of what it meant to follow Jesus Christ, the suffering servant who fully represented his Father God. But later, in the middle of the second century, that was too much for Marcion, the son of the bishop of Sinope. He began preaching a dualistic heresy, claiming there must be two Gods: the violent God of the Old Testament and the benevolent God of the Gospels. He rejected the entire Old Testament and several books we now include in the New Testament. For a time, he gathered a following, but he was ultimately excommunicated by the early church leaders.[10]

Marcion's denunciation of the Old Testament overlooked the fact that God had already been correcting his image by revealing his *goodness* through the history of the Jewish people as recorded in

9. Matthew 17:1-5 and Mark 9:2-7 record the same event with no variation in detail.
10. "Marcion of Sinope," *Wikipedia*.

the Old Testament until the time was ripe for Jesus' advent. It was a long but unbroken story. And it's important to be clear about its continuity, because without it we *would* be trying to amalgamate two different deities.

Instead, the Jewish confession of faith, the *Shema*, is absolutely correct: "Hear, O Israel: The LORD our God, the LORD is one" (Deut. 6:4). Christians believe that *that same God* came to earth as Jesus, the Messiah, the Christ—fully God and fully man, who is the second member of the Trinity, along with the Father and the Holy Spirit. That is not three Gods, or two, but one God, existing together in a state virtually impossible for the human mind to comprehend because we are not transcendent. The difficulty in comprehending the Trinity should tell us something about the possibility that the patriarchs—in fact, all believers, ourselves included—might not have fully grasped the nature of God and therefore ended up interpreting him according to human experience.

It isn't easy to hold that history in tension. Within a century and a half after Marcion, once Constantine had embraced Christianity, a church and state symbiotic relationship ensued, relapsing into that old violent and retributive model of God's character—a model that served the pursuit of security and power. The Church's justification for the Crusades, the Doctrine of Discovery, the Inquisition, the genocide of indigenous peoples, slavery of Africans, and the idea of Manifest Destiny are just some of the expressions of our human tendency to be seduced by the model of a violent and retributive God.

Failure to keep focused on the sequence of God's progressive revelation of his character bred antisemitism. If we have no respect for our spiritual ancestors and the fact that many segments of Judaism have also wrestled with and reformed their ancient belief in God's violence—just as Christians must do—then it becomes easy to make Jews our enemies. Antisemitism has had many expressions throughout history, far too often led by Christians, like Martin Luther, who, as Rabbi Noam Marans points out, advocated "burning or razing synagogues, destroying Jewish homes, confiscating Jewish holy books, banning Jewish religious worship, expropriating Jewish money, and deporting Jews."[11] But in the nineteenth and twentieth centuries Marcionism, itself, enjoyed a revival. According to Philosopher Samuel Loncar, "During the Third Reich, the Marcionist view of Scripture—a totally de-Judaized canon—became the center of a movement to eliminate Jewish influence on the German church and insist that Jesus was not Jewish, but Aryan."[12]

No! Jesus was Jewish, but he did not agree with what today might be considered ultra-Orthodox Jewish or biblical-literalist Christian views of God's character. He was a revisionist who revealed for us a fuller understanding of the God whom we had only begun to meet in the Torah (the first five books of the Bible).

Jesus' Unity with the Father

Near the end of his ministry, Jesus prayed an extended prayer for all believers (apparently within earshot of some of the disciples, since it was later written down) in which he spoke of being at one with God the Father:

> "My prayer is not for them alone. I pray also for those who will believe in me through their message, that all of them *may be one, Father, just as you are in me and I am in you.* May they also be in us so that the world may believe that you have sent me. I have given them the glory that you gave me, that they *may be one as we are one—I in them and you in me—so that they may be brought to complete unity.* Then the world will know that you sent me and have loved them even as you have loved me" (John 17:20-23, emphasis added).

---

11. Noam E. Marans, "On Luther and his lies," *The Christian Century*, Oct. 25, 2017. https://www.christiancentury.org/article/critical-essay/on-luther-and-lies.

12. Samuel Loncar, "Christianity's Shadow Founder: Marcion, Anti-Judaism, and the Birth of Liberal Protestantism," *Marginalia*, Nov. 19, 2021. https://themarginaliareview.com/christianitys-shadow-founder-marcion-anti-judaism-and-the-birth-of-liberal-protestantism/.

This unity includes the *character and overall purpose* of all three members of the Trinity—Father, Son, and Holy Spirit. They were united in love and in expressing love! It does not, however, eliminate differing roles. Clearly, Jesus recognized a distinction between himself and his Father and the Holy Spirit whom he would send at Pentecost to indwell the believers.

Concerning that indwelling, Paul later affirmed the unity in the Body of Christ with each believer receiving from the Holy Spirit distinct, functional gifts: "Just as a body, though one, has many parts, but all its many parts form one body, so it is with Christ" (1 Cor. 12:12). All believers were to emulate the *character* of Christ Jesus, but their functions would differ between apostles, prophets, teachers, miracle workers, healers, helpers, guides, and those able to speak in different tongues (v. 28).

Neta and I have been married for fifty-eight years. When we are our "better selves," our character is unified. One is not vengeful while the other forgives. One is not faithful while the other cheats. One is not generous while the other is stingy. It's a complement when people say we are joined at the hip—Dave-and-Neta, Neta-and-Dave. But we have different gifts, which usually leads to different (though flexible) roles in how we function.

The same is even more true between Jesus and the Father. What we see in Jesus, who lived among humans for thirty-three years, must correct any misunderstandings we have had concerning the character of God. To apply that revision, we do not have to jettison God the Father or separate Jesus from God.

Discussion Questions

1. Why do you think Jesus didn't mount a revolution to throw off Rome as most of the Jews of his day expected the Messiah to do?

2. How does God's visitation to humankind in the person of Jesus revise previous presumptions about God's character?

3. Acts 17:6 describes the believers as "the people who have been turning the world upside down." What was Jesus revising that led to his followers being described that way?

4. Some people say the Old Testament describes God one way while Jesus portrays another side. Do you see God as a little of both, or do you see the biblical record more as progressive revelation?

Chapter 7

What God Allows Is Not Necessarily What God Approves

"For I know the plans I have for you," declares
the LORD, *"plans to prosper you and not to harm*
you, plans to give you hope and a future."
—*Jeremiah 29:11*

T HE ABOVE PROMISE—spoken not to an individual but to a nation that would first endure seventy years of captivity—has
become so popular it shows up as a meme on the internet, on personal graduation cards, or posters for one's wall. I *do* believe God
has a purpose for all humanity, which he most certainly will ac
complish . . . in the end, even as he adjusts to us, his fickle and
rebellious creatures. In that sense, he is sovereign. I also believe
he has personal purposes for each of us, which we wisely seek
and follow to the best of our ability. However, there is too much
space between life as we experience it and God's ultimate victory
over sin, death, and destruction to turn God's higher *or* specific
promises into trite Band-Aids we paste on life's every twist, turn,
or even life's tragedies.[1]

One may think that if God is all powerful, knows the end from
the beginning, and has a good purpose for you, then everything
that happens must meet his approval. So, why doesn't he perform
miracles or in other ways block anything from happening that

---

1. For a valuable review of the context for Jeremiah 29:11, view the
video, "Why you should stop quoting Jeremiah 29:11," by Brandon Robbins.
https://www.youtube.com/watch?v=cKgZWy9fm1I.

would bring suffering, destruction, and death to you or any of his beloved creatures?

Good question, but the answer is not simple. It's not as simple as saying, "If God allows it, it must be good, so suck it up, and change your definition of what's 'good.'" No, God does not gaslight us. He never asks us to deny the reality of suffering by calling it "good." Suffering and death are not good! Otherwise, Jesus wouldn't have spent his ministry alleviating them. And it's not as simple as expecting God to violate the very laws of the universe he created to the point of unrecognizability. And it's not as simple as expecting God to micromanage all the factors that might impact his purposes for you . . . including your choices. Otherwise, why would Jesus have taught us to pray for God's will to be done?

Something Not God's Will

For seven years Neta and I were members of The Worship Center in Evanston, Illinois, where Ricky Byrdsong and his family were also members. Ricky had been the head basketball coach for the Northwestern University Wildcats and dreamed of writing a book for parents that would translate some of his coaching techniques into parenting skills. When Lyle Foster, the pastor of The Worship Center, realized we were authors with experience as the editors of Marriage and Family Products for David C. Cook Publishing, Co., he got us together with Ricky.

We hit it off well and realized Ricky had some unique contributions that would, indeed, help parents in ways no other book we were familiar with had addressed. We dove in, helping him plan, write, and prepare a proposal, which in time landed a contract with Bethany House Publishers for his book, *Coaching Your Kids in the Game of Life*.

But on July 3, 1999, just three weeks after receiving the incredibly joyful news of a book contract, Ricky, a handsome, 6' 6" black man, was murdered by a young man who had gone on a shooting rampage inspired by a white supremacist hate group.

To help their three children come to terms with this horror of all horrors, Ricky's wife, Sherialyn, read Ecclesiastes 3:1-2 to them. "For everything there is a season, a time for every activity under heaven. A time to be born and a time to die" (NLT). Then she explained that their daddy's time to be born was June 24, 1956, and his time to die was July 3, 1999. She said, "These times were set before the world was ever created." And since his work here on earth was done, God welcomed him into heaven. "I believe that because God is sovereign," she said, "he's in control of every situation and circumstance. I also believe that he is good and that he works all things together for good."

We finally finished writing the last third of Ricky's book with the help of Sherialyn, several of his former coaching colleagues and basketball players, and devoted family and friends. The book has blessed thousands of families. Sherialyn founded the Ricky Byrdsong Foundation that started the Ricky Byrdsong Race Against Hate, which (except for the COVID years) has drawn around five thousand participants per year. The Byrdsong children have grown up and become stellar adults, and Sherialyn has continued ministering for the Lord. So, God has unquestionably brought good things out of this tragedy.

But I'm less comfortable entertaining the unspoken—and perhaps unacknowledged—implication that if God controls every situation and circumstance, he inevitably had a hand in bringing about Ricky's murder. To be sure, that is *not* what Sherialyn said, but that's how most people understand the claim that God controls every situation and circumstance.

But God Didn't Initiate Ricky's Murder

Neta and I did extensive research into Ricky's life and background as well as the origin, activity, and objectives of the hate group that spawned the shooter who killed him. Our investigations were more than curiosity. We were writing *No Random Act: Behind the Murder of Ricky Byrdsong*. The hate group, known as the World Church of the Creator and from which the shooter came, was as diabolical as any organization can get. Don't be fooled by its name. It is not a church, and the "creator" they worship is the white man, with every intent to exterminate all Jews and people of color through Racial Holy War (RAHOWA). Their revered prophet, founder, and author of their "holy books," Ben Klassen, was a disciple of Hitler, who explained their objective as follows:

> We gird for total war against the Jews and the rest of the goddamned mud races of the world—politically, militantly, financially, morally and religiously. In fact, we regard it as the heart of our religious creed, and as the most sacred credo of all. We regard it as a holy war to the finish—a racial holy war. Rahowa! is INEVITABLE. … No longer can the mud races and the White Race live on the same planet.
>
> —Founder Ben Klassen, 1987[2]

Klassen's protégé and the current *Pontifex Maximus* is Matt Hale, who is now serving a forty-year prison sentence for soliciting an undercover FBI informant to kill Judge Joan Lefkow.[3] At the time of his conviction, Hale claimed his organization had eighty-eight chapters across the United States as well as in several foreign countries.[4]

Ben Smith, a privileged Chicago Northshore youth, had been a member of Hale's hate group, which inspired him by its ideology to go on a two-state shooting spree in which he killed Ricky Byrdsong in Skokie, Illinois, Won-Joon Yoon, a Korean doctoral student coming out of church in Indiana, along with wounding nine Jews and other blacks and Asians in Illinois, before killing himself.

In researching the hate group, we worked with the Skokie police, the FBI, the Southern Poverty Law Center, and numerous individuals familiar with the hate group as we studied its ideology, goals, and practices. Then I made two personal visits to interview

---

2. "Creativity Movement" (Formerly known as the World Church of the Creator), Southern Poverty Law Center, https://www.splcenter.org/fighting-hate/extremist-files/group/creativity-movement-0.

3. Judge Lefkow had ruled against the World Church of the Creator in 2002 in a trademark dispute with a religious organization in Oregon that had registered the term "Church of the Creator" with the U.S. Patent and Trademark Office. Hale's organization has since used the name, "Creativity Movement."

4. "Creativity Movement" (Formerly known as the World Church of the Creator), Southern Poverty Law Center, https://www.splcenter.org/fighting-hate/extremist-files/group/creativity-movement-0.

Hale in his headquarters. He's so narcissistic, he considers any publicity "good publicity" and welcomes the press no matter how critical.

As a result, I am convinced God would *never* have employed or authorized this evil group to kill one of his most dedicated servants because "God is light; in him there is no darkness at all" (1 John 1:5), and therefore God could not be party to such evil.

Prophesying Evil Is Not the Same as Causing It

There is plenty of evidence that God knows the future and sometimes communicates that knowledge to human prophets (see Amos 3:7), especially when warning people to change sinful behaviors that would otherwise result in disaster or to warn them to avoid alliances with foreign nations that would betray them or influence them for evil.

Sometimes God also reveals to his servants the impending cost—perhaps even in terms of their life—that may result from obediently fighting evil, affirming to them that he grants them freewill in saying no, even to their calling. For instance, Isaiah 50:7 says, "Because the Sovereign LORD helps me [the Messiah], I will not be disgraced. Therefore have I set my face like flint, and I know I will not be put to shame." Thus, Jesus was well aware of his imminent crucifixion. "As the time approached for him to be taken up to heaven, Jesus resolutely set out for Jerusalem" (Luke 9:51).

Even though he prayed, asking if there was any other way to accomplish his mission (Matt. 26:39), *he set his face like flint!*

But *none* of that means God caused those consequences!

If you are familiar with Dr. Martin Luther King, Jr.'s life, you may recall that for months preceding his assassination on April 4, 1968, he was haunted by a sense of impending death. He seemed to have a premonition—or what some might call "a word of knowledge"—that his life would end prematurely. And then, in his final speech before two-thousand people at the Mason Temple in Memphis, he said, "I've been to the mountaintop.... Like anybody, I would like to live a long life—longevity has its place. But I'm not concerned about that now. I just want to do God's will."

Of course, there had been bomb scares and threats. But the next day he was murdered.

In a similar way, God's spirit may have been preparing Ricky Byrdsong. Time and again he'd told God, "I want to make a difference. Even if it costs me my life, I'm willing!"

On the Sunday before Ricky was shot, he'd surprised even himself at the level of commitment he called for from the members of his church . . . but deep inside he felt God was on the verge of something big. "We all need to get there," he'd told the church. "Don't you know that I had to come to that point in my own life? Don't you know that they didn't want me talking about God to the basketball team? Don't you know that I had to say, 'But it doesn't matter now'?

"Don't you know that they didn't want me having a Bible study in my own office with my own staff? But I said, 'It doesn't matter now.' Don't you know that they'd rather that I not quote any Scriptures to the newspaper? I was a coach at a major institution, and my words were going everywhere. They wanted me to keep that kind of talk in the church. But I had to get to the point where I said, 'It doesn't *matter* now.'

"We've all got to get to that point."

On Tuesday, he felt compelled to go to the church prayer meeting and just lay himself out before God, prostrate on the floor. *Use me. I want to make a difference.*

By the time Friday, July 2, arrived, Ricky's spirit crackled with anticipation. He wasn't sure what was ahead for him, but he wanted to be ready. After work that evening, when he arrived at his beautiful home in the Chicago suburb of Skokie, he quickly put on his jogging shoes and shorts and called to his kids. "Sabrina! Kelley! Ricky-J! Let's go for a walk before it gets dark."

Sabrina, age twelve, didn't want to go. But Ricky Jr. grabbed his bike so he could keep up with his dad's long strides and Kelly went out ahead. Ricky jogged slowly as they turned the corner and headed west. The remains of a golden sunset shone through the branches of the towering elms.

It was then that Ben Smith turned onto the same street and cruised up slowly behind them. Smith had just finished shooting at and wounding six Orthodox Jews in Chicago's Rogers Park neighborhood two miles south. But now, at fifteen yards, he couldn't miss the tall black man!

I believe God knew what was going to happen, and in his grace, he prepared Ricky. In the same way many people prepare their will, medical power of attorney, and other documents when they are older. But Ricky, who was only 42, wrote a "Mission Statement for the Byrdsong Children." I think he did it more in keeping with his heart to raise his children well than in anticipation of his death, but it was a powerful legacy that God has used for good.

God Did Not Cause Ricky's Murder

If Ricky was willing to do anything God asked of him, if he wanted to make a difference and had come to the point where nothing else mattered, if God knew the danger that awaited Ricky when he went out for that run with two of his kids, and Ricky was in a zone where he was listening to God's voice enough to know that something momentous was ahead, how can we *not* fault God for letting Ricky step into the path of those bullets?

I do not know! I simply don't know!

There may be a number of things operating in the universe that give us a small glimpse into this paradox, and we'll take a look at some of them in future chapters.

However, I do not believe God *caused* Ricky's murder. "God is light; in him there is no darkness at all" (1 John 1:5), and therefore God could not be party to such evil any more than I think God inspired Hitler to murder six million Jews, or Pol Pot to kill two million Cambodians, or Idi Amin to become the "Butcher of Uganda," or any of the other atrocities in the history of humanity, including the attack on the Twin Towers on 9/11. To think God controls and therefore, by definition, sanctions such evil individuals by saying all events are part of his "plan" for humankind, would require us to believe God commissioned a *much greater evil* than all of those combined. If God controls everything as part of his plan, then God must have approved Satan's initial rebellion that created a world full of evil in which humans constantly suffer, often with the most innocent suffering the most.

85

Who Was the Beginning of All Evil?

It's a contradiction to claim God granted freewill to all sapient creatures (Satan included) but he retains control over everything that happens down to the details of what those creatures choose to do. Both conditions can't be true simultaneously. Later in this book we'll look at this paradox more closely. But for now, consider the scenario of Satan: If God controls *everything* and always has, then the source of the most egregious and pervasive pain and suffering in the entire universe began when God sanctioned (had control over) Satan's rebellion and fall from heaven. Many Bible scholars believe the "morning star, son of the dawn" (Lucifer, from the Latin) as described in Isaiah 14:12-15 and Ezekiel 28:12-19, became the Devil after his rebellion and his jealous attempt to become greater than God. He was then thrown down, out of heaven, along with a third of the angels who chose to follow him according to Revelation 12:3-9 (where the Devil is named "Satan" but also described metaphorically as "an enormous red dragon"). Elsewhere in the Bible, Satan is named as the tempter, God's adversary, our adversary, the accuser of God's followers, a roaring lion, the evil one, the god of this age (or world), the father of lies, and the thief who comes only to steal and kill and destroy. And those "fallen angels"—Satan's minions—became the demons or evil spirits who brought pain and suffering to so many people in the Bible.

People may argue that certain *specific* painful events produced enough good in the long run that God, in his sovereignty, must have caused them, but if you follow that logic to its primal origins as described by the above rehearsal of Satan's rebellion, such a drama is the mother of all evil / father of all evil in terms of the death, destruction, and suffering to God's beloved creatures. And nowhere in the Bible is God said to take responsibility for engineering *that* catastrophe. The idea is abhorrent! But to charge God as the cause of even smaller evil spectacles can only be done by incriminating him for what happened "up stream" with Satan.

But Doesn't the Bible Say God *Caused* "Evil"?

In Chapters 3 and 4, we discussed how the ancient prophets and writers of the Old Testament may have misunderstood God's character and therefore ascribed to him the source of the violence of wars and natural disasters according to their religious imaginations or ideas absorbed from the cultures around them. However, while that perspective may have framed the reports of God's role in things like the flood in Noah's day or "God's order" for Saul to slaughter all the Amalekites—men, women, children, and babies— there are other passages that don't appear to have been so infected by cultural presumptions but still seem to suggest that God caused evil or suffering if he micromanages the events of history.

One of those passages is Isaiah 45:7: "I form the light and create darkness, I bring prosperity and create disaster; I, the Lord, do all these things." Older translations say, "I . . . create evil." However, the context is a prophesy of what Cyrus, King of Persia, was going to do to liberate the Jews from captivity. Those events indeed happened, but maybe it was more a truthful prophecy than a doctrinal characterization of God.

But there are other challenging passages.

Joseph's Sojourn in Egypt

Joseph's brothers came close to killing him, but instead sold him to a caravan going to Egypt where he was made a slave. However, Joseph's harrowing experiences finally landed him in the second most powerful position in the land. When a famine struck that part of the world, he was able to provide grain to save the lives of his desperate brothers and their families.

They were terrified when they discovered who he was, thinking he would surely take revenge. But Joseph reassured them by saying, "As for you, you meant evil against me, but God meant it for good, to bring it about that many people should be kept alive, as they are today" (Gen. 50:20, ESV). The phrase, "God meant" or "God intended," implies that God planned the whole thing from the beginning, and it isn't just that phrase. The whole scenario appears as though that is what happened. But was that an event

God "meant" or planned from the foundation of the world in the way some people imagine God controls all things? If so, we must conclude God commissioned the brother's evil.

But there is another way to envision what happened.

God could have saved Jacob's clan by a myriad of means, including teaching Joseph enough humility at an early age so he didn't infuriate his brothers. With more grace, he might have been able to share his dreams in a way they could have received so *they* would have saved enough grain on their own to see the family through a famine. Instead, God gave all the characters in the story freewill—young Joseph to be a smart aleck, and his brothers to be so vengeful they got rid of him by selling him to slavers where he did learn some humility. Whether in foreknowledge or while it happened (God is not bound by time), God adjusted how he would accomplish "good" out of the evil *others chose* to do. But there is nothing in the narrative that says he inspired evil or did it himself so he could ultimately achieve good.

Didn't God Cause a Man's Blindness?

In John 9:1-5, we read the following report about Jesus:

> [1] As he went along, he saw a man blind from birth. [2] His disciples asked him, "Rabbi, who sinned, this man or his parents, that he was born blind?"
>
> [3] "Neither this man nor his parents sinned," said Jesus, "but *this happened so that* the works of God might be displayed in him. [4] As long as it is day, we must do the works of him who sent me. Night is coming, when no one can work. [5] While I am in the world, I am the light of the world" (John 9:1-5, NIV, emphasis added).

While Jesus clarifies that this man's suffering wasn't the result of anyone's sin, he appears in this translation and several others to suggest there was a divine plan *behind* the man's blindness. (Having been blind in one eye for an extended time with the fear it could happen in the other eye, I can imagine the trauma of blindness.) But was God micro-managing the universe from the beginning of time in such a way he *caused* the poor guy to spend twenty or thirty years without sight so Jesus could perform a miracle on that one day as he walked down that specific road? If so, we'd have to ask what God's purpose has been for the millions of other people who have endured a sightless life sitting by some road or stumbling along behind a white cane.

Greg Boyd, senior pastor of Woodland Hills Church in St. Paul, Minnesota, explained to me in an email that he doesn't think Jesus tried to answer *why* the man was blind, though Jesus did take a moment to dismiss the disciples' speculations by saying: "Neither this man nor his parents sinned." But then, according to Boyd, Jesus pivoted and changed the subject to move on: "Let God be glorified."[5]

It was not uncommon for Jesus to avoid engaging in unproductive discussions arising from wrong questions. And this explanation makes sense if the final phrase of verse 3 was the beginning of a new subject, leading straight into verse 4. We need to remember that the original Greek did not include punctuation, nor were the Scriptures divided by editors into verses until the mid-sixteenth century. So, here is a word-for-word translation of verses 3 and 4:

Neither this [man] sinned nor parents of him but that he may be being manifested the works of the God in him me it is binding to be working the works of the one sending me while day it is is coming night when no one can to be working.[6]

Now note what happens if you simply punctuate that word-for-word translation in a different manner than the way the NIV did. Even before smoothing out the awkward word order, it says:

Neither this [man] sinned nor the parents of him. [*Jesus says no more about the cause of the man's blindness.*] But

---

5. Greg Boyd, email to Dave Jackson concerning John 9:1-3. March 29, 2023.

6. Scripture4All, Greek Interlinear Bible (NT), John 9:3-4, https://www.scripture4all.org/OnlineInterlinear/NTpdf/joh9.pdf.

that he may be being manifested the works of the God in him, me it is binding to be working the works of the one sending me while day it is. Is coming night when no one can to be working.

Smooth up the word order slightly, and this is what you get:

Neither this man nor his parents sinned. But that the works of God should be revealed in him, I must work the works of Him who sent me while it is day; the night comes when no one can work.

Perhaps surprisingly to many, this is the New King James Version except for two punctuation: The NKJV puts a comma after "sinned" rather than a period, and a period after the first "him" rather than a comma. Don't forget, the original did not include punctuations or verse divisions. The KJV, ASV, and ESV are similar.

Neta has a plaque on one of our bookshelves which says,

Let's eat grandma.
Let's eat, grandma.
Commas save lives.

And they sure do!

On the other hand, the insertion of the "so that" as well as the supporting punctuation appearing in several other translations, was an editorial decision that some claim is justified by the Greek. But it also coincides with a theological bias that presumes God is someone who would put a person through years of suffering just to make a point.

If that were true, why would Jesus say with such urgency, "As long as it is day, we must do the works of him who sent me. Night is coming, when no one can work" (v. 4). There are a lot of people in the world who need healing. Some are suffering from direct attacks by Satan and his minions (a source of evil Jesus notes on multiple occasions), but his job and ours is to heal them and free them.

The work was so urgent that Jesus enlisted the disciples to join him in doing it "while it is still day." At one point, he even appointed seventy-two disciples to go out two-by-two to reverse the evil Satan had done in the world! When they returned, they *specifically* noted that the demons submitted to them, and Jesus responded, "I saw Satan fall like lightning from heaven." (See Luke 10:1-18.) Jesus' work of healing and freeing people from bondage and suffering was not to fix some mess God had created! Such a presumption should be denounced as blasphemy. It was to reverse what *Satan* had done! And while there are *other* reasons why people suffer, we must continue displaying the works of God in comforting and healing people. We'll discuss those other possible causes of suffering in future chapters, but here Jesus was focused on continuing his work.[7]

In answer to the question of "Does God Create Evil?" the following is a good summary by James M. Rochford:

> No! God does not cause evil. The psalmist writes, "You are not a God who takes pleasure in wickedness; *no evil dwells with You*" (Ps. 5:4). He also writes, "There is no unrighteousness in Him" (Ps. 92:15). Paul writes, "What shall we say then? There is no injustice with God, is there? May it never be!" (Rom. 9:14). James writes, "Every good thing given and every perfect gift is from above, coming down from the Father of lights, with whom there is no variation or shifting shadow" (James 1:17).[8]

So, while it's true that God often transforms evil into good, he never causes evil. What God allows is not necessarily what

---

7. For further consideration of this subject, see the word study offered on the "Monday Morning Review" from the Emmanuel Fellowship Church Weblog on August 31, 2009. https://mondaymorningreview.wordpress.com/2009/08/31/john-91-5-word-study/.

8. "Does God Create Evil?" James M. Rochford, *Evidence Unseen*, (Columbus, OH: New Paradigm Publishing, 2013), https://www.evidenceunseen.com/bible-difficulties-2/ot-difficulties/isaiah-ezekiel/isa-457-does-god-create-evil-cf-lam-338-jer-188-amos-36/. All verses in the NASB translation of the Bible.

he approves. After all, "no one should say, 'God is tempting me.' For God cannot be tempted by evil, nor does he tempt anyone" (James 1:13).

Discussion Questions

1. How would you respond to someone who says, "If God allows it, it must be good, so suck it up, and change your definition of what's 'good'"?
2. If Satan's rebellion against God was the beginning of all evil, what does that say about the claim that God controls everything?
3. How can prophesying coming destruction (as the Bible sometimes does) differ from God causing that destruction?
4. Even the best translators operate from preconceived perspectives. How did you respond to the review of John 9:1-5 about the man born blind?

Chapter 8

"I the LORD Do Not Change!" So, What Should *We* Do?

I say to God my Rock,
    "Why have you forgotten me?
Why must I go about mourning,
    Oppressed by the enemy?"
My bones suffer mortal agony
    as my foes taunt me,
saying to me all day long,
    "Where is your God?"...

Put your hope in God,
    For I will yet praise him,
    My Savior and my God.

—*Psalm 42:9-11*

IF YOU'RE ANYTHING LIKE THE PSALMIST, you may feel pretty discouraged at this point. We've taken a hard look at many of the Old Testament passages where God seemed to portray himself stronger than other deities by defeating Israel's enemies, even to the point—it appeared—of commissioning the Israelites to commit genocide. Furthermore, when God's people disobeyed him, he appeared to punish them with a vengeance. He also gave them laws to execute lawbreakers within their own community for some crimes we would never consider capital offenses. In the end, this display of strength may have been the only way the Israelites understood—given their cultural history and environment—that "the LORD your God is God of gods and Lord of lords, the great God, mighty and awesome" (Deut. 10:17). But the price involved misunderstandings concerning God's character that took centuries and finally the death of his Son, Jesus, to correct.

Today, the unbeliever still taunts, "Where is your God?" like in Psalm 42, while in our own heads we hear the question echo as: "Is *your* God good?" How do we put our hope in such a God? How do we praise him with abandon? How can we consider him *our* Savior and *our* God?

For me and maybe you, too, these questions light a fuse that many fear threatens the foundation of our trust in the Bible: the possibility that not every concept therein is presented in full detail, and therefore when "the rest of the story" is known, the picture may change. The fuse suggests that *some* of the authors may have told *parts* of the biblical report through their own culturally flawed lenses, painting God as more violent and retributive than he really is.

Of course, Paul already told us that. After reaffirming the primacy of love, he wrote, "For now we see only a reflection as in a mirror; then we shall see face to face. Now I know in part; then I shall know fully" (1 Cor. 13:12). But we probably didn't think that applied to the authors of the Bible. If we thought about it at all, we may have concluded that for the Scriptures to be "God breathed," none of the authors understood only "in part," or let their cultural presumptions leak through. But why, then, did Jesus come? Why did God feel it was necessary to walk and talk with us "face to face" on a daily basis, presenting at many points a different image than what the teachers of the Law and the Pharisees had gleaned from the Old Testament?

I've never had much trouble with what seemed to me like minor discrepancies in the biblical texts or what some label "contradictions" in the Bible when there were reasonable explanations. Who cares whether Genesis 1 and 2 differ in their reports of Creation? Both are poetic renditions of events so vast and complex we may never fully understand them, let alone be able to summarize them in fourteen-hundred words (the approximate number of English words in those two chapters).

But if Moses had to correct a portion of the Law he allegedly had written earlier so women along with men could inherit property,[1] and if Jesus explicitly reversed the law of retaliation *requiring* an eye for eye,[2] those two examples should be enough to show us that not *every* word in Scripture needs to meet some people's "inerrant" standards for God's word to be recognized as inspired or *God breathed.*

Some who say we must subscribe to their standard of inerrancy forget that until the 17th Century, everyone who claimed to be a Christian was, as John Lennox, the renowned Christian philosopher and scientist, calls them, "fixed earthers." They believed the earth was the center of the universe and rested on pillars, all based on a literalistic understanding of numerous texts, such as Psalm 104:5, "He set the earth on its foundations; it can never be moved."[3] Copernicus and Galileo used science to show that those references were metaphorical. Today, we accept that science, even though we still speak of the sun rising and setting. Lennox, addressing a whole room of Christians to whom he was lecturing, added, "How many people in this audience believe the earth is fixed relative to the stars?" He looked around and jokingly added, "So, you don't believe the Bible . . . not any of you? Because the Bible says it doesn't move." He was making the point that it's dangerous to pin our belief in the inspiration and authority of the Bible on such rigid understandings that we refuse to be corrected when our errors become obvious.[4]

Before We Move Forward

Before we move forward to explore some more helpful ways of understanding why we suffer without blaming it all on God puppet-mastering our whole life, I want to review one more chal-

---

1. Review the discussion of the appeal for justice mounted by the five sisters—Mahlah, Noah, Hoglah, Milcah, and Tirzah—as described earlier in Chapter 5.
2. See Chapter 6.
3. See also: 1 Chron. 16:30; Josh. 10:12-14; Job. 9:6-8; Ps. 19:4-6; 75:3; 93:1; 96:10; 113:3; Eccles. 1:5; Rev. 6:12.
4. John Lennox, "The Bible and age of the earth?" at SMU. July 22, 2022. https://www.youtube.com/watch?v=S26Dq3Uu6nM.

lenge for those who try to prove that the Bible is "without error in the original writings." It's not because it wouldn't be fun to have a Bible in which every detail was precisely accurate so we could solve all the puzzles of the past, present, and future like reading Tarot cards. But we—or I'll just say, I—would spend all my time trying to do just that rather than trying to grasp God's immense love found in the deeper meaning of the Cross and revealed in the sweep of the Scriptures.

One of the most challenging sections of the Bible about which to make an inerrant claim is the earliest history, from the Creation story through the flood of Noah's day. Advocates of an inerrant view tie those periods together because they believe the flood explains many of Creation's geologic phenomena, and—to be sure— the story of Noah's flood in Genesis 6-8 is richer in detail than are the Creation stories.

Creationists, as they are sometimes known, defend every aspect of the narrative of the flood as though the whole foundation of their faith depends on the literal accuracy of each detail, details as small as the implications of which preposition (*in, under,* or *above*) applies.[5] I personally have no reason to doubt that a flood happened, and it's a matter of interesting speculation as to how Noah might have built an ark, how the animals were sustained, and how the ark survived the deluge. However, it's also interesting that some secular researchers conclude that:

> Flood stories pervade hundreds of cultures and there are striking similarities to many of the accounts. It seems that at least some of these stories could be based upon actual events. Geologists have proposed the possibility of a great flood in the Middle East at the end of the last Ice Age, which

---

5. The example referred to here is a discussion among creationists concerning whether or not the flood involved the collapse of a theoretical water vapor canopy above the earth when the biblical passage doesn't even include the determinative prepositions. It's not that such speculation is wrong, it's the presumption that such minutia is the way to arrive at spiritual *or* scientific truth. See Bodie Hodge, "What Is the State of the Water Vapor Canopy Model?" https://answersingenesis.org/environmental-science/state-of-canopy-model/.

was about 7,000 years ago. At that time, the Black Sea was a freshwater lake surrounded by farmlands.

The hypothesis is that the European glaciers melted and the Mediterranean Sea overflowed with a force that was 200 times greater than Niagara Falls. That would be an incredibly fast-moving wall of floodwater. There is physical evidence that supports this theory, including stone-age structures under the Black Sea.[6]

Did all these reports come from Noah's descendants who migrated elsewhere but told different versions of the same *worldwide* flood? Or were these reports of how different cultures around the world survived the climate changes that accompanied the end of the last Ice Age when the melting ice raised sea levels nearly 400 feet and undoubtedly brought chaotic weather and great floods to many regions? Such cataclysmic surges undoubtedly flooded enormous regions of the earth and destroyed entire civilizations.

Another detail that may relate to the Black Sea and surging waters from the Mediterranean is the biblical description of Noah's flood: "On that day all the *springs of the great deep burst forth*, and the *floodgates of the heavens were opened*" (Gen. 7:11, emphasis added). Additionally, it notes the "rain fell on the earth forty days and forty nights." To me, such a description could describe torrential rains that weakened the isthmus where Istanbul and the Bosporus Strait now sit, breaking it like a dam that had previously held back the much higher waters of the Mediterranean Sea.

Whether you believe there was just one worldwide flood or various regional floods that destroyed civilizations may depend on whether you insist that the details of the event in Genesis 6—8

---

6. Lennlee Keep, "A Flood of Myths and Stories," *Independent Lens*, (PBS, Feb. 14, 2020), https://www.pbs.org/independentlens/blog/a-flood-of-myths-and-stories/amp/. Not all scientists agree that these events coincided with the era of Noah's flood because there is evidence of multiple floods as the glaciers melted. Also, the date for "end of the last Ice Age" depends on how it is defined and is often pegged at about 11,500 years ago. https://en.wikipedia.org/wiki/Last_Glacial_Period. Creationists think the last ice age began "soon after the Flood and continued for less than a millennium." https://creation.com/the-ice-age.

are precisely accurate in every respect. For instance, I don't have any trouble with the idea that the water covered all the high mountains by more than fifteen cubits (23 feet) or that the ark might have come to rest on one of those mountains when the waters receded *if* we're talking about Noah's world, the world as he knew it . . . perhaps most of the Black Sea region. But if we're talking about the whole earth where there are six major mountain ranges and at least 108 mountains with elevations greater than 23,500 feet—including Mount Everest at 29,029 feet—then where did enough water come from to rise that high, and where did it go?

Literalists offer various explanations: Aquafers below ground burst forth and/or a canopy of water vapor or ice in the stratosphere suddenly collapsed are a couple theories for where the water came from.[7] They also offer a catastrophic plate tectonics model in which they speculate that the entire earth's topography pre-Noah was much smoother or "flatter," if you will, than what exists today—seas not nearly so deep and mountains not nearly so high, which they claim explains how the sudden addition of enormous quantities of water might "cover the earth." According to this theory, the flood waters retreated when deep ocean trenches suddenly opened up and high mountain ranges erupted.

A slower movement of the earth's tectonic plates is universally accepted as causing earthquakes, triggering volcanos, forcing up most mountain ranges, and opening the fifty or so major ocean trenches (which only hold about 0.5 percent of the sea[8]). But most geologists attribute that reshaping of the earth's surface to the relatively *slow* grind of the tectonic plates over millions of years, movement that continues today.

The speculation that the entire earth was smooth enough so a deluge of forty days and forty nights could cover the *entire* world with over twenty feet of water and then suddenly convulse *so violently* that the tectonic plates burst forth to build mountain ranges

7. Don Batten, editor, "Noah's Flood—Where did the water come from?" *Creation Ministries International*. https://christiananswers.net/q-aig/aig-c010.html. Also see, Morris and Whitcomb, *The Genesis Flood*, P&R Publishing, 1961.

8. "Oceanic Trench," Wikipedia, https://en.wikipedia.org/wiki/Oceanic_trench.

five miles high and buckle down to create trenches six miles deep is mind blowing. Even harder to comprehend is that—before Noah and company could emerge from the ark—the earth's seizures had to calm down enough so tsunamis no longer sloshed back and forth to knock the ark off its perch on one of the first mountains to emerge,[9] and that the quakes and aftershocks subsided enough so the people and animals could walk around, build an altar, perhaps a shelter, and resume life on land. But the most incredible part of this scenario to me is that it *all* happened—from flood to a new world—within 371 days, the length of time the survivors remained in the ark.

It should be noted that there is geological and paleontological evidence of, not one, but five major extinctions of life on earth in the magnitude claimed by a literal reading of the Noah story. The last one ended the Cretaceous period and resulted in the loss of 76 percent of all species. But it was apparently caused by an asteroid over eight miles wide that plunged into what is today Yucatán, Mexico, digging a hole 110 miles wide and twelve miles deep (detectable today by radar from space, as well as other methods[10]). This global cataclysm kicked up so much debris and dust into the atmosphere that the sun's light and warmth was obscured, cooling the earth to the point most coldblooded animals—including the dinosaurs—died off. But that did not happen some 4,500 years ago, which might coincide with the date some creationists ascribed to the Noah flood. Instead, it happened 65 million years ago. The recovery that followed favored warm-blooded animals that could tolerate greater temperature fluctuations.[11]

---

9. Modern tsunamis rarely reach more than 200 feet high, but one triggered by an earthquake and landslide into Lituya Bay in Southeast Alaska in 1958 crashed into the opposite side at 1,720 feet high. https://geology.com/records/biggest-tsunami.shtml.

10. "Discovering the Impact Site." https://www.lpi.usra.edu/science/kring/Chicxulub/discovery/#:~:text=The%20Chicxulub%20crater%20is%20not,sediments%20that%20bury%20the%20crater.

11. Hannah Ritchie, "There have been five mass extinctions in Earth's history," *Out World Data*, Nov. 30, 2022. https://ourworldindata.org/mass-extinctions. The other mass extinctions include the end of the Ordovician period (444 million years ago), the Late Devonian period (360 million years ago), the end of the Permian period (250 million years ago), and the end of the Triassic period (200 million years ago).

Other Challenging Explanations

Literalists face other challenges with a worldwide flood. Take, for example the "two of every kind of bird" (Gen. 6:20). Currently, there over 10,000 species of birds plus many extinct species. Creationists don't claim Noah housed twenty thousand birds on the ark. Instead, they point out that he only had to collect creatures of every "kind."

Dr. Jean Lightner suggests the biblical term "kind" corresponds to the biological term "family," of which there are about 200 bird families, meaning for each kind/family Noah would have collected one representative specie pair. These, she suggests, might have divided by hybridization into double that number of species every 750 years. In 4,500 years[12] (six cycles), we could have all the "species" we see today, she says, plus some to account for extinctions.[13] Most hybridization results in infertile offspring, but speciation has occurred among "Darwin's finches" on the Galapagos islands in only two generations, far more rapidly than previously thought.[14] However, Lightner's theory requires (for birds and all living creatures) a degree of DNA mutation many biblical literalists think comes too close to the evolutionary models that—given enough time—account for the development of all other life forms now living on the earth or evident in the geologic record, including humans.

Why Did God "Regret" Creating Humans?

The most troubling question related to a worldwide flood may be: Why did God feel it was necessary to exterminate all humans on the earth except Noah and his family? Some readers point to Genesis 6:1-8 for the answer.

---

12. Strict creationists calculate Noah's flood as occurring about 4,500 years ago, far short of the 7,000 year-ago end of the last Ice Age and the Black Sea flood previously cited in Lennlee Keep's article.

13. David W. Boyd, Jr., "Bird Speciation from the Flood to the Present," *Answers in Genesis*, May 13, 2016. https://answersingenesis.org/birds/bird-speciation-flood-present/.

14. Andrew Masterson, "New species evolve in just two generations," Cosmos Magazine, Nov. 26, 2017. https://cosmosmagazine.com/science/biology/new-species-evolve-in-just-two-generations/.

When human beings began to increase in number on the earth and daughters were born to them, the sons of God saw that the daughters of humans were beautiful, and they married any of them they chose. Then the LORD said, "My Spirit will not contend with humans forever, for they are mortal [corrupt], their days will be a hundred and twenty years."

The Nephilim were on the earth in those days—and also afterward—when the sons of God went to the daughters of humans and had children by them. They were the heroes of old, men of renown.

The LORD saw how great the wickedness of the human race had become on the earth, and that every inclination of the thoughts of the human heart was only evil all the time. The LORD regretted that he had made human beings on the earth, and his heart was deeply troubled. So the LORD said, "I will wipe from the face of the earth the human race I have created—and with them the animals, the birds and the creatures that move along the ground—for I regret that I have made them." But Noah found favor in the eyes of the LORD.

Was this the reason God wiped out the whole human race except Noah (who was a righteous man according to v. 9) and his family? Some creationists and others speculate that the "sons of God" who married the "daughters of men" must have been fallen demons (incubi) who spawned a super race, the "Nephilim" that had to be eliminated. But the flood didn't eliminate them ("The Nephilim were on the earth in those days—*and also afterward*" Gen. 6:4, emphasis added), and they show up centuries later when the Israelite spies searched out Canaan (Num. 13:33).[15] And, of course, Goliath was considered a giant (1 Sam. 17:4).

Archeologists have not found evidence of any "race of giants," though the remains of individual, large humans show up

---

15. Bodie Hodge, "Nephilim: Who Were They?" *Answers in Genesis*, July 9,2008, https://answersingenesis.org/bible-characters/who-were-the-nephilim/. Also see: "Who / what were the Nephilim?" *God Questions*, https://www.gotquestions.org/Nephilim.html.

occasionally, as they do today. Currently, the only evidence that humans have mingled with other "beings" is the DNA evidence that homo sapiens living mostly in Europe and East Asia mixed with Neanderthals.[16]

If we are going to affirm every detail of the Noah story, we cannot help but continue asking what was so hopeless about God's creation—other than Noah and his family—that God decided to destroy *all* humans, innocent babies along with the most evil adults? He declared, "Every inclination of the thoughts of the human heart was only evil all the time" (Gen. 6:5). But even after the flood when God said: "Never again will I curse the ground because of humans," he added, *"even though every inclination of the human heart is evil from childhood.* And never again will I destroy all living creatures, as I have done" (Gen. 8:21, emphasis added). Apparently, nothing had changed in terms of the human condition. And yet God's perspective expressed new hope that many Christians attribute to a new plan.[17] And I believe God is always willing and able to come up with new plans based on his overarching purposes and unending love: "For God so loved the world that he gave his one and only son" to save the world (John 3:16).

If you believe that some or all of the Creationist explanations are viable, you're certainly not alone. But I personally find the contradictions between those explanations and so many fields of science embarrassingly unconvincing. Furthermore, if your view of inspiration hinges on the premise that every word of Scripture as originally written is technically and scientifically accurate, then there is a great incentive to supply those explanations, make them agree with each other, and defend them against any scientific discovery explaining things differently. While some secular scientists have made it their crusade to disprove Creationists, most are not

16. Michael Price, "Africans carry surprising amount of Neanderthal DNA," *Science*, Jan. 30, 2020, https://www.science.org/content/article/africans-carry-surprising-amount-neanderthal-dna#:~:text=For%2010%20years%2C%20geneticists%20have,interbred%20only%20outside%20of%20Africa.

17. A "new plan" did not need to be new in terms of time because God is not bound by time. Ephesians 1: 4 tells us, "For he chose us in him before the creation of the world."

driven by that objective and update their theories as new discoveries dictate. More importantly, there's no comprehensive document they're committed to defending and with which they have to make every discovery agree. Even the long-standing theory of the Big Bang is undergoing reconsideration as a result of discoveries by the James Webb Space Telescope and other findings.

To consider the Scriptures inerrant *in practical terms*, one must have inerrant authorship, inerrant canonization (for which there's always been significant disagreement concerning both the Old and New Testament), and finally, inerrant translation and interpretation.

The Cost of Depreciation

When I collected what I dubbed the "Texts of Terror" in Chapter 2, I could not reconcile that legacy of violence with either the teachings or the actions of Jesus. And the more I contemplated Jesus' claims and the witness of the New Testament writers that Jesus is our most complete expression of God—that we are to esteem him as *Immanuel*, God actually with us—I could no longer dismiss the dissonance, couldn't sweep it back under the rug, couldn't put it out of my mind. I had to face it!

But as we discovered, this correction process began *before* Jesus came as there are numerous instances in the Old Testament where God revealed his loving compassion and openness to all peoples of the world, eagerness to forgive, and his intent to teach the Israelites a less violent way of life than that of their pagan neighbors. And to me, this very fact strongly affirms the "God breathed" quality of the Bible *when taken as a whole*. It is inspired, not because someone thinks they can prove (according to their human standards) that there are no "errors" in any part of the story, but because God was brave enough to tell us the *whole story*, including parts where some details needed revision, not with a footnote after every misleading detail but through the sweep of the history, the bad and the good.

The Old Testament provides us with a progressive revelation of who God is, one prophet building on the image revealed by those who went before, adding to and sometimes correcting previous perspectives. But what I'm affirming is that the whole foundation of Christianity is the *incarnation of God in Jesus*, without depreciating Christ's divinity. He was not just the latest contributor in a parade of prophets.

A rigid understanding of inspiration can cause many to remain stuck in a primitive view of God, characterizing him as more violent and retributive *and hopeless* than I think Jesus proved to be. Recall the sentiment of Jonathan Edwards' eighteenth century sermon, "Sinners in the Hands of an Angry God" mentioned in Chapter 2: God "holds you over the pit of hell, much as one holds a spider . . . over the fire, abhors you . . . looks upon you as worthy of nothing else but to be cast into the fire." That kind of thinking is, in my opinion, the direct result of characterizing God as the one who nearly destroyed the whole human race in the flood and still thought *every inclination of the human heart* of those who remained was utterly evil.

The contradiction is not within God's character. "I the LORD do not change. So you, the descendants of Jacob, are not destroyed" (Mal. 3:6), or as Hebrews 13:8 says, "Jesus Christ is the same yesterday and today and forever." So, who changed? I think it's obvious that our human perception of God changed, in fact, needed to change. At one point, God was said to have drowned almost the entire human race. But only a short time later, God promised to never do something like that again.

Characterizing God or his sentiments toward us in the way portrayed by Noah's story leaves a deep residue of anxiety in our souls. Does God really love us, or does he regret ever having created us? Paul reminds us, "all [of us] have sinned" and "the wages of sin is death" (Rom. 3:23; 6:23), both of which, if we're honest, we can't deny. But is it *God* who demands payment of those "wages" of death characterized by the suffering described in Genesis 6-8? Or is the "gift of God eternal life in Christ Jesus our Lord" (Rom. 6:23)? We must dig deeper to see the fuller, inspired story of redemption.

Discussion Questions

1. When Paul wrote, "For now we see only a reflection . . ..
    Now I know in part; then I shall know fully" (1 Cor. 13:12),
    do you think he was including the Old Testament authors?
    Why or why not?
2. Creationists and other literalists spend great energy trying
    to prove the accuracy of every detail in the Bible. What
    aspects of your relationship with Jesus become threatened
    if they are wrong?
3. When taken as a whole, what reassures you about the
    overall "God breathed" quality of the Bible?

Chapter 9
Job's Overwhelming Suffering . . . Why?

"For my thoughts are not your thoughts,
neither are your ways my ways," declares the LORD.
"As the heavens are higher than the earth,
so are my ways higher than your ways
and my thoughts than your thoughts."

—*Isaiah 55:8-9*

SOME MIGHT SAY THE ABOVE VERSES were intended to discourage us from asking the hard, presumptuous questions. After all, who do we think we are to question God about anything? And yet, just two verses earlier, Isaiah wrote, "Seek the Lord while he may be found; call on him while he is near" (Isa. 55:6). It's true that God's thoughts are not our thoughts, and his ways are higher than our ways, but that's not to discourage our inquiries. If we are seriously asking these questions about God's goodness, we *are* seeking God, even if we feel we are on the brink of losing our faith. In this regard, Jesus' encouragement is relevant: "Keep on seeking, and you will find" (Matt. 7:7, NLT).

A great many passages in the Bible are relevant to finding peace around the question of why we suffer. In fact, the Book of Job is devoted almost entirely to that search.

Why Am I Suffering?

The Book of Job is classified in the Christian Bible as part of the Wisdom Literature, including Psalms, Proverbs, Ecclesiastes,

Song of Songs, and Job. Much of the book is an epic poem, wrestling with the perennial question of why we suffer. The literary style and language suggest it may have been written (or revised) around the sixth century B.C. However, the narrative itself does not mention many things that would be common to that era, such as: the Mosaic Law, Israel, Judah, the exile, familiar genealogies, or names of other biblical characters. Also, Job offered sacrifices, which according to the Law, was only to be performed by priests. Moses lived to 120 years of age, and no one after him is recorded as having lived longer. But if we add up the segments of Job's life, it appears he lived over two hundred years, more like the ages reported before Abraham, whose father, Terah, reached 200 years. No one after Terah reportedly lived longer than that.

All things considered, the setting for the narrative appears to be very ancient, causing some scholars to believe it is the oldest book in the Bible, written before the time of Moses.

To summarize, the Book of Job is organized in three parts: Chapters 1 and 2 are the prologue explaining who Job was and *how* his "blessed life" suddenly collapsed into overwhelming suffering. Chapters 3—37 involve conversations between Job and four of his friends in which they speculate on *why* Job was suffering. Chapters 38—42 provide God's response and dialog with Job, in which I believe God attempts to help Job understand the universe in a way that, even though it might not explain *all* the reasons for his suffering, nevertheless relieves Job of the crushing guilt and confusion caused by the common clichés of his day (and ours).

Fact or Parable?

Does the book record a historical saga or is it a parable, similar to Jesus' parables . . . only longer? If it is a parable, that does not diminish its value as inspired scripture or what it can teach us. We would only need to be cautious about literalizing every detail. For instance, in Jesus' parable of the Rich Man and Lazarus, the rich man, who was in Hades, was able to see and converse with Abraham in paradise, but that does not justify declaring that such conversations are factually possible in the afterlife, and it's certainly not the point of Jesus' message.

So, whether you believe the Book of Job attempts to report the events of a specific person's life or see it as a parable told because of its relevance to every person's experience, I offer the same cautions we've explored in previous chapters. If there is a disparity between how God is portrayed in this ancient account and the perfect revelation of God's love and character in Jesus as he lived, loved, and taught among us, then we must defer to the more perfect revelation in Jesus. In the prologue to the Book of Job (chapters 1 and 2), we have a specific example of when and how this principle might apply. There we are told that . . .

1. Job lived in the land of Uz, among "the people of the East" (Job 1:3). Some suggest this may reference the southern part of Arabia.

2. He was "blameless and upright; he feared God and shunned evil." This need not characterize Job as "sinless" in contrast to the claims of Romans 3:23 that all of us have sinned. It's more in the sense of how Cornelius was described in Acts 10 as an upright or righteous man who—though not yet a believer in Jesus—was nonetheless a devout man, who feared God, gave alms to the needy, and always prayed (vv. 2, 22). Furthermore, in this story of Job, God, himself, repeated the pronouncement that Job was blameless and upright (Job 1:8).

3. Job was very rich, owning seven thousand sheep, three thousand camels, five hundred yoke of oxen and five hundred donkeys. He also had a large number of servants and was considered "the greatest man among all the people of the East."

4. At the opening of the story, Job had ten children, whom he loved so much that he offered sacrifices on their behalf to atone for any sins they may have committed while they partied.

Finally, as the scene is set, we are told that an assembly is in progress in the courts of heaven moderated by God and attended by the angels, when Satan brazenly walks in. At this point, I become uncomfortable with any claims that this as a literal report of an historical event rather than seeing it as a parable from which we are to learn. The reason for my discomfort is this: If we are to accept the collective information regarding Satan's rebellion against God as described in Isaiah 14:12-15; Ezekiel 28:12-19; and Revelation 12:3-9, then Satan had already been thrown down out of heaven at some point *prior* to his assault on humanity in the Garden of Eden. And if, as Jesus described him, Satan "comes only to steal and kill and destroy" (John 10:10), what's he doing marching back into God's presence? But that may involve paradoxes (or even a *time warp*?) which none of us can explain.

However, what happens next is an exchange that characterizes God in a manner that seems utterly contradictory to the nature of Jesus Christ as we know him.

Did God Gamble on Job?

In this scene, God challenges Satan, "Have you considered my servant Job? There is no one on earth like him; he is blameless and upright, a man who fears God and shuns evil" (Job 1:8). In the parlance of a game of poker, Satan *sees God and raises him one*:

> "Does Job fear God for nothing?" Satan replied. "Have you not put a hedge around him and his household and everything he has? You have blessed the work of his hands, so that his flocks and herds are spread throughout the land. But now stretch out your hand and strike everything he has, and he will surely curse you to your face."
>
> The LORD said to Satan, "Very well, then, everything he has is in your power, but on the man himself do not lay a finger."
>
> Then Satan went out from the presence of the LORD (Job 1:9-11).

If that's not a wager, I don't know what is. Satan then destroyed all Job's property and killed all of Job's children. But, "In all this, Job did not sin by charging God with wrongdoing" (v. 22).

Satan came back before God to play a second hand and offered *double or nothing*:

> "A man will give all he has for his own life. But now stretch out your hand and strike his flesh and bones, and he will surely curse you to your face."
>
> The LORD said to Satan, "Very well, then, . . .but you must spare his life."
>
> So Satan went out from the presence of the LORD and afflicted Job with painful sores from the soles of his feet to the crown of his head (2:4-7).

Job's suffering was excruciating beyond description, and the idea that God as he revealed himself in Jesus Christ intentionally approved that kind of suffering on any human being just to win his argument with Satan seems beyond belief!

So, what might be going on?

If this is a parable, then that prologue was just a literary set up to tell us the much bigger story to follow, to teach us something about suffering and thereby comfort us. And the remainder of the book might have been based on the "unexplained" tragedies of one historical man, in the way modern movies are sometimes "based on a true incident" even though aspects of the story are fictional—in this case the prologue.

Whether the whole Book of Job is a parable or the part after the prologue was based on the horrible tragedies that actually happened to an ancient blameless and upright man and how he and his friends tried to make sense of it, the story is as common as the suffering humans experience every day. In the end, that's the condition into which God speaks hope through his dialog with Job in chapters 38—42. God speaking hope—not condemnation or platitudes—is exactly what Jesus would do, did do, and does do. Furthermore, God's actions *after* the prologue do not characterize God as dramatically different from Jesus, so we don't have a basis to challenge its historicity on that count.

As for the prologue, it doesn't sound like Jesus, so it may have been the speculations of an ancient author according to the common characterizations of God by the people of that day—a characterization not yet enlightened by the progressive revelation that unfolded in the remainder of the Old Testament, and certainly not by the person of Jesus Christ.

Clichés of the Day

One of the things about a cliché is that it becomes overused because it appears to be true or seems to serve a purpose, but clichés aren't necessarily true. One of the first clichés you might notice is Job's response after all his wealth was destroyed and his children killed. He said, "The LORD gave and the LORD has taken away; Blessed be the name of the LORD" (Job 1:21). The first and last part of it is true: The good things in Job's life did come from God. The Apostle James agrees: "Every good and perfect gift is from above, coming down from the Father of heavenly lights, who does not change like shifting shadows" (Jas. 1:17). And David affirms the last part of the cliché: "I will bless the LORD at all times" (Ps. 34:1), which is a good thing to always do, no matter what is happening to us.

But who did the taking away? Who destroyed everything Job had? According to the prologue, Satan did as the destroyer. In fact, Jesus explained that Satan is the one who "comes only to steal and kill and destroy. [But] I have come that they may have life, and have it to the full" (John 10:10).

Of course, I trashed the prologue, right?[1] But my questions don't mean Job didn't suffer those horrible events (whether parable or history), I just doubt the prologue *or* that Job was right in suggesting God was behind it all. Now, you may say, that begs the question of whether God is sovereign over all things. And it does, if we think like the prologue's author and many throughout history who consider God a puppet master, orchestrating every event. But what if the universe is far more complicated than any authoritarian, micromanaging model we can envision? And

---

1. Not altogether. The primary justification for questioning aspects of the prologue stem from its portrayal of God's character as being so different from the character of Jesus Christ, who is nowhere shown to cause anyone's suffering for such a capricious and self-centered reason as proving himself right.

(spoiler alert), that's what I believe God was trying to explain to Job in the concluding chapters of the book . . . on a level an ancient nonscientific person could understand.

Nevertheless, the cliché—that it was God who had "taken away"—served the purpose of giving *some* explanation to Job for the source of his pain. When any of us are going crazy under pressure and pain, we might embrace a god who is in control even if he is not a good or even a just God. Identifying *a* source for our pain brings some relief whether the answer is right or wrong. And it did help Job avoid cursing God, but it didn't bring him comfort any more than tossing that same cliché at hurting people today brings them lasting comfort.

What Job's Friends Did Right

By the end of the prologue, three of Job's friends—Eliphaz the Temanite, Bildad the Shuhite, and Zophar the Naamathite—had heard about his suffering and came to comfort him. When they saw how bad his condition was, they expressed their grief for him by tearing their clothes and throwing dust on their heads, as was the custom. "Then they sat on the ground with him for seven days and seven nights. No one said a word to him, because they saw how great his suffering was" (Job 2:13).

This morning, a friend texted me and a few other brothers (we usually share a weekly breakfast) that he'd woken up to find his wife sitting in her recliner, dead! I was stunned, and the shock wouldn't dissolve. Many family members and friends would undoubtedly reach out to offer help, provide food, whatever, but I had no idea what to do or say. Finally, I headed over to his place. He lives on a few acres out in the country, and by the time I got there, his wife's body had been taken away. The readout from her pacemaker might provide detail concerning the exact cause of death. But at that point my friend was alone, riding on his tractor, mowing the grass. He shut it off as I got out of the car and walked over. We both hugged with some tears. He offered, "I'm usually most at peace just sittin' on this thing, and the job needed doin, so . . ."

"Yeah. I understand."

We talked, but he didn't need to explain anything, and I didn't need to tell him anything, certainly not some banality like, "Well, at least she's in a better place." Which is true, and reassuring when there is doubt, but can feel hollow. So, I tried to remember the initial wisdom of Job's friends: *Just be there!*

"*Sitting shiva,*" the week-long mourning period for close relatives practiced in Judaism, has its roots in biblical times, perhaps even the story of Job. Family and friends visit the bereaved to express their condolences and provide comfort. It's a way to begin and encourage the grief process. Silence isn't required, and I didn't sit for seven days with my friend. In fact, I stayed less than an hour that first day. But I'll be checking in on him, and hopefully I'll avoid what Job's friends ended up doing, which was hurtful.

What Job's Friends Did Wrong

When Job began to talk, it was to lament his life from the day of his birth. All his past glory and privilege did not dull the pain of how things had turned out, and he began asking why.

His friends took the bait, thinking, no doubt, that some kind of an answer would help. Eliphaz began by recalling how Job has encouraged other people. "But now trouble comes to you, and you are discouraged; it strikes you, and you are dismayed. Should not your piety be your confidence and your blameless ways your hope?" (Job 4:5-6).

But then he cannot resist offering the traditional logic. "Consider now: Who, being innocent, has ever perished? Where were the upright ever destroyed? As I have observed, those who plow evil and those who sow trouble reap it" (vv. 7-8).

It's true that in many things we reap what we sow (Gal. 6:7-9). If you drive drunk, you risk creating an accident that may take a life. And if you sow according to the good fruits of the Spirit, you may reap a spiritual harvest. But unlike the Buddhist concept of karma, where our life is a scale and our good and bad deeds earn merits or demerits, we can't manipulate life. It was God who *gave* Job blessings. Job didn't earn them, and we can't retrofit the concept to explain Job's suffering as the consequence of misdeeds. But that idea was exactly what Eliphaz introduced because it was the common assumption concerning how any retributive deity acts.

"If I were you," said Eliphaz, "I would appeal to God; I would lay my cause before him. . . . Blessed is the one whom God corrects; so do not despise the discipline of the Almighty" (Job 5:8, 17). It's good advice, but issued with a presumption of guilt.

Job agrees with Eliphaz's logic in Job 6 because he also is a captive of the prevailing theology. But it doesn't explain his situation, and so he pleads his innocence. "Teach me, and I will be quiet; show me where I have been wrong. . . . But what do your arguments prove? . . . Is there any wickedness on my lips? Can my mouth not discern malice?" (6:24-25, 30). And then Job addresses his complaint to God, perhaps raising his hands to heaven in supplication. "If I have sinned, what have I done to you, you who see everything we do? Why have you made me your target? Have I become a burden to you?" (7:20).

Bildad seems offended on God's behalf. "Does God pervert justice? Does the Almighty pervert what is right? . . . But if you will seek God earnestly and plead with the Almighty, if you are pure and upright, even now he will rouse himself on your behalf and restore you to your prosperous state" (8:3, 5-6).

This hammering, which goes on and on, drives Job into deep despair.

> Although I am blameless, I have no concern for myself; I despise my own life. . . . Since I am already found guilty, why should I struggle in vain? . . . If only there were someone to mediate between us, someone to bring us together, someone to remove God's rod from me, so that his terror would frighten me no more. Then I would speak up without fear of him, but as it now stands with me, I cannot (9:21, 29, 33-35).

It's important to pause and consider in what immense need Job found himself. Paul tells us, "There is one God and one Mediator who can reconcile God and humanity—the man Christ Jesus. He gave his life to purchase freedom for everyone" (1 Tim. 2:5-6, NLT). The mediator for whom Job longed was, in fact, Christ Jesus, not to "stop" God as the source of Job's suffering as Job's friends imagined! God was not torturing Job, but Job did need rescuing! The prologue names Satan as Job's nemesis, and the rest of the Bible certainly identifies Satan as our adversary. But there are other sources of suffering, and Job needed help. The role of a mediator—whom we know is Jesus—was to empower Job (and us) to come boldly before God, to seek his help in our time of need, whatever may be the cause. As it says in the Book of Hebrews:

> Therefore, since we have a great high priest who has ascended into heaven, Jesus the Son of God, let us hold firmly to the faith we profess. . . . Let us then approach God's throne of grace with confidence, so that we may receive mercy and find grace to help us in our time of need (Heb. 4:14, 16).

Job Tries to Stand Up for Himself

Job's rebuttal to his friends in Job 12 is based on the idea that God controls everything in nature and all human activities. Therefore, God must be causing his suffering. "[Who] does not know that the hand of the LORD has done this?" (Job 12:9).

> What he tears down cannot be rebuilt; those he imprisons cannot be released. If he holds back the waters, there is drought; if he lets them loose, they devastate the land. To him belong strength and insight; both deceived and deceiver are his (vv. 14-16).

Job continues on and on, listing many examples of God's sovereignty in a manner that presumes God micromanages everything. And then in chapter 13, Job concludes that his only hope is to speak directly "to the Almighty and argue my case with God" (v. 3). "Though he slay me, yet will I hope in him; I will surely defend my ways to his face" (v. 15).

The debates with his friends continue, with them accusing him, and Job trying to defend himself, until in chapter 19, Job makes this profound statement of faith:

I know that my redeemer lives, and that in the end he will stand on the earth. And after my skin has been destroyed, yet in my flesh I will see God; I myself will see him with my own eyes—I, and not another. How my heart yearns within me! (vv. 25-27).

But he still doesn't have an answer to the question of why he is suffering.

Job's friends run out of patience with him, and Eliphaz says, "Is it for your piety that [God] rebukes you and brings charges against you? Is not your wickedness great? Are not your sins endless?" (22:4-5). Since Job can't or won't recognize his own guilt, Eliphaz starts speculating.

> You demanded security from your relatives for no reason; you stripped people of their clothing, leaving them naked.
>
> You gave no water to the weary and you withheld food from the hungry, though you were a powerful man, owning land—an honored man, living on it.
>
> And you sent widows away empty-handed and broke the strength of the fatherless.
>
> That is why snares are all around you, why sudden peril terrifies you, why it is so dark you cannot see, and why a flood of water covers you (vv. 6-11).

There are more interchanges, but Job responds in his own defense: "I will never admit you are in the right; till I die, I will not deny my integrity. I will maintain my innocence and never let go of it; my conscience will not reproach me as long as I live" (Job 27:5-6). Later, he became more specific in his rebuttal to Eliphaz's accusations:

> Whoever heard me spoke well of me, and those who saw me commended me, because I rescued the poor who cried for help, and the fatherless who had none to assist them.
>
> The one who was dying blessed me; I made the widow's heart sing.

> I put on righteousness as my clothing; justice was my robe and my turban.
>
> I was eyes to the blind and feet to the lame.
>
> I was a father to the needy; I took up the case of the stranger.
>
> I broke the fangs of the wicked and snatched the victims from their teeth (29:11-17).

> I made a covenant with my eyes not to look lustfully at a young woman. . . .
>
> If I have walked with falsehood or my foot has hurried after deceit—let God weigh me in honest scales and he will know that I am blameless—if my steps have turned from the path, if my heart has been led by my eyes, or if my hands have been defiled, then may others eat what I have sown, and may my crops be uprooted.
>
> If my heart has been enticed by a woman, or if I have lurked at my neighbor's door, then may my wife grind another man's grain, and may other men sleep with her.
>
> For that would have been wicked, a sin to be judged (31:1, 5-11).

Yes, Job was "blameless and upright" as God had said, but he still suffered. It seemed unfair, and he didn't know why.

Both Plaintiffs and Defendant Agree on Two Premises in Job's Case

Before the testimony ends, we meet a fourth witness, Elihu. He is the son of Barakel the Buzite. So far, Elihu has remained silent, apparently because he was younger than Job or his other three friends, and Elihu felt he should leave the resolution of the matter to his elders. But it had gone too far, and Elihu was "very angry with Job for justifying himself rather than God." He was also angry because his three elders couldn't refute Job (32:2-3).

In fact, we might wonder if Job's claim that God was treating him unjustly was close to blasphemy. In the prologue, Job did not curse God after Job lost his children and all his wealth. And when after Job was physically afflicted, and his wife urged him to "curse God and die!" (2:9), Job did not do so. Later, when God speaks, God does not accuse Job of cursing him. Therefore, telling God how you feel, even if you feel you've been treated unjustly, is not necessarily blasphemy. God can take it.

But there are two premises about life and the universe that Job and all *four* of the witnesses against him agreed upon:

1. All of these characters presume God actively controls *everything* that happens in the universe—good or bad, small or large. Therefore, Job's suffering *must be* the result of God's attack on him. Job's friends thought that, and so did Job.

2. They all think God blesses or afflicts people based on their behavior. Righteous behavior triggers God's blessings. Unrighteous behavior triggers God's wrath. Furthermore, based on this principle, you can accurately judge a person's character—whether they are good or bad—according to their wealth, health, and other obvious blessings. Job's friends thought that, and so did Job, and that's why he thought what had happened to him was so unfair.

These are fateful premises for surviving suffering or judging the character of other people. The sources of suffering are not that simple!

Discussion Questions

1. How do you understand the prologue to Job's story—the scenes where Satan struck a deal with God to torment Job and prove that his faith would break? Do you think Jesus would ever entertain such a wager regarding one of us?

2. Job's declaration in Job 1:21—"The LORD gave and the LORD has taken away; Blessed be the name of the LORD"—is often quoted in the middle of deep grief. Why might a be-

reaved person embrace such an explanation? Why might someone reject it?

3. What were the helpful things Job's friends did to comfort him? What was the most hurtful thing they did?

4. In Job 27:5-6, why did Job deny any culpability for wrong-doing? Under the circumstances, what do you think of that stance?

Chapter 10
Job's Magical Mystery Tour of the Universe

*"If the universe is so bad, or even half so bad, how
on earth did human beings ever come to attribute
it to the activity of a wise and good Creator?"*

—C.S. Lewis, *The Problem of Pain*[1]

WHEN GOD FINALLY RESPONDED DIRECTLY TO JOB, it is easy to hear
it as a "smack-down," a belittling rebuke that Job has no
right to question God. There may be some truth to that, but there
is another way to understand God's larger purpose in reminding
Job of what he *doesn't* know.

Then the Lord spoke to Job out of the storm. He said:
"Who is this that obscures my plans with words without
knowledge? Brace yourself like a man; I will question you,
and you shall answer me.
"Where were you when I laid the earth's foundation?
Tell me, if you understand. Who marked off its dimensions?
Surely you know!" (Job 38:1-5).

Try to get your mind around the possibility that God, who is
infinitely greater than any of us can imagine or think, has come
to the rescue of a sick and suffering man whose friends are tell-

---

1. C.S. Lewis, *The Problem of Pain*, (New York: Macmillan Paperbacks Edition, 1962), 15.

ing him it all must be his fault—blaming the victim. No human is standing with Job. Furthermore, because of the cultural presumptions in which Job lives, he agrees with the accusatory logic of his friends . . . except, he can't think of any great or protracted sin that would account for the kind of punishment God was supposedly heaping on him. And because he still doesn't believe God is unjust, all he can conclude is that there's been a mistake. If he could just explain himself directly to God, God would understand, and the whole mess could be cleared up.

But the premise on which Job and his friends think the universe works is wrong!

So, in his loving kindness, God shows Job a glimpse of how things really work. And much of what follows is a divine tour in which scene after scene, museum room after museum room, begins with God saying, "Tell me if you understand how the earth was formed, who marked off its dimensions, how it's held in place." "Tell me if you know anything about the Big Bang and the earth's molten core creating a relatively stable foundation and how I laid its magnetic cornerstones while the morning stars of other galaxies sang together, and all the angels shouted for joy" (see Job 38:6-7). Admittedly, I took some literary license there by connecting the language of the Book of Job with some of our more recent understandings about creation since the universe is the first subject God addresses.

What I'm suggesting is that a lot of the language we might read as put-downs in every scene, could be a process of orientation, helping Job to register what he *doesn't* understand so God can point out something larger and far more complex. No, God didn't speak in twenty-first century scientific language about quasars and black holes and dark matter scattered among two trillion galaxies spread across a universe 93 billion light years in diameter. That kind of talk wouldn't have meant anything to Job, but God did stretch Job's understanding to the next level. It's not unlike the Socratic method, which can sound argumentative in the questions it asks but is ultimately designed to stimulate the student's critical thinking and draw out deeper truths.

When God asked Job, "What is the way to the abode of light? And where does darkness reside? Can you take them to their places? Do you know the paths to their dwellings?" (vv.19-20), he may have been alluding to some pretty high-level physics, after which God did add some sarcasm: "You have lived so many years!" (v. 21). Why did God say that? I have no idea; maybe Job was rolling his eyes, wanting to get on with his own private question: "Why am I suffering?"

In any case, God was not distracted from his lesson plan. He soon asked:

"Can you bind the chains of the Pleiades? Can you loosen Orion's belt?

"Can you bring forth the constellations in their seasons or lead out the Bear with its cubs?

"Do you know the laws of the heavens? Can you set up God's dominion over the earth?" (vv. 31-33).

And God's ultimate objective was far more personal than to give Job a survey of creation, astronomy, meteorology, zoology, animal husbandry, botany, anthropology, and the principles of flight. All these subjects would have been "familiar" to Job and his contemporaries, even though they may have had no answers to the questions God posed regarding the various phenomena in each field. God was doing something else.

God may have been wanting Job to think bigger thoughts. In 1952, J.B. Phillips wrote a book, titled: *Your God Is Too Small*. Phillips was a cannon of the Anglican church who became beloved all over the world for his highly acclaimed translation, *The New Testament in Modern English*. For many people of my generation, it was the first translation of Scriptures we could read smoothly without being constantly jarred by unfamiliar syntax and obsolete terms. Phillips' title well encompassed his theme: *Your God Is Too Small*. He began by saying,

No one is ever really at ease in facing what we call "life" and "death" without a religious faith. The trouble with many people today is that they have not found a God big enough for modern needs. . . .

It often appears to those outside the Churches that this is precisely the attitude of Christian people. If they are not strenuously defending an outgrown conception of God, then they are cherishing a hothouse God who could only exist between the pages of the Bible or inside the four walls of a Church.[2]

I think this may have been the experience of Job and his friends. They were operating on an antiquated and inaccurate caricature of God, and it was devastating Job and would ultimately hammer his friends as well if they encountered serious suffering.

Job's cry was essentially the same as that of David, "My God, my God, why have you forsaken me?" (Ps. 22:1), which was quoted by Jesus on the Cross, "'*Eli, Eli, lema sabachthani?*' which means 'My God, my God, why have you forsaken me?'" (Matt. 27:46). But despite the way David felt at the time, God had not forsaken him. And beyond the pain Jesus was experiencing on the Cross, Jesus knew and had said, "I and the Father are one" (John 10:30). Later, Paul explained what was going on: "God was reconciling the world to himself in Christ" (2 Cor. 5:19). That is to say, they were working together in a unity we can hardly comprehend.

Some theologians disagree. They believe God the Father actually did forsake Jesus because Jesus had taken upon himself the sin of the whole world, and they think God was unable or unwilling to associate with that sin. In his book, *The Holiness of God*, R.C. Sproul says that once Jesus was . . .

. . . laden with our sin, then He became the most grotesque and vile thing on this planet. With the concentrated load of sin He carried, He became utterly repugnant to the Father. God poured out His wrath on this obscene thing. God made Christ accursed for the sin He bore.[3]

---

2. J.B. Phillips, *Your God Is Too Small*, (New York: Touchstone, 1952, 2004), 7-8.

3. R.C. Sproul, *The Holiness of God*, (Wheaton, IL: Tyndale House Publishers, 1985), 158.

But such a theory ascribes a very literal concept to the word, "forsaken," defined by a parochial understanding of space and time. (Like, how far away did God have to stay?) It also overlooks the whole ministry and demeanor of Jesus—God having chosen to be with us, "while we were yet sinners!" Sin is destructive, no question about that, but God is not afraid of getting his hands dirty in saving us. The words Jesus quoted from Psalm 22:1—"My God, my God, why have you forsaken me?"—are actually answered in that same Psalm. "For he [God] has not despised or scorned the suffering of the afflicted one; he has not hidden his face from him but has listened to his cry for help" (v.24).[4]

God did not forsake Job, either, but answered *his* cry for help.

The magical mystery tour of the universe that God gave Job did not in itself heal Job's wounds, resurrect his children, or restore his comfortable life (though some of that came later). Rather, it convinced Job that God had not abandoned him and had heard his cry. Just trying to imagine what Job had gone through brings tears to my eyes to hear Job's response after God took the time to personally enlighten him: "My ears had heard of you, but now my eyes have seen you. Therefore, I despise myself and repent in dust and ashes" (Job 42:5). That doesn't mean Job came up with a list of sins that he finally confessed to justify his suffering. No, God had not forsaken him in the sense that Job had to do something to earn his attention. Job had heard about God before, but now God had lovingly met with him personally to show him wonders too marvelous for words. And Job fell down in humble awe.

God Condemns Those Popular Theories

Do you recall how in the last chapter we identified two false premises depicted in the story of Job's suffering? The first presumed that God actively micromanages everything, and the second claimed God blesses or afflicts people based on their behavior. We noted that both Job and his friends subscribed to these

---

4. This psalm of David foretells of Christ's crucifixion with verses like, "They divide my clothes among them and cast lots for my garment" (v. 18). Thus, in the same way Jesus used verse 1 to describe how forsaken he felt, verse 24 provides assurance that God had not actually forsaken him.

bad theological concepts about how the moral universe operates. And the conflict in the story resulted from the accusations of Job's friends that his profound suffering proved he was guilty of flagrant sin. In his own defense, Job protested that he was innocent.

After God reviewed with Job some of the complexities of creation to the point where Job was humbly reassured, God turned to Eliphaz, the elder and therefore the representative of Job's friends and said . . .

"I am angry with you and your two friends, because you have not spoken the truth about me, as my servant Job has. So now take seven bulls and seven rams and go to my servant Job and sacrifice a burnt offering for yourselves. My servant Job will pray for you, and I will accept his prayer and not deal with you according to your folly. You have not spoken the truth about me, as my servant Job has" (Job 42:7-8).

So, what falsehoods did Job's friends utter in contrast to the truth that Job spoke? The narrative primarily contrasts the friends' accusations of Job's sinfulness over against his protestations of innocence. But God didn't say he was angry because these friends maligned Job. No, twice God said he was angry because "You have not spoken the truth *about me*, as my servant Job has" (emphasis added). So, what was different about what Job said and what his friends said? We noted earlier that each of these men subscribed to the falsehoods about God controlling everything and blessing or cursing people based on their behavior. So, why wasn't God equally upset with Job?

If we look a little closer, we may see a distinction. It is true that God blesses people, and it is always appropriate to thank God for any and all of his good gifts. But Jesus also said, "[God] causes his sun to rise on the evil and the good, and sends rain on the righteous and the unrighteous" (Matt. 5:45). Perhaps the offense the friends committed was to presume to judge Job. That usurped God's role and ascribed to God an evil the story that the Book of Job and other biblical passages say comes from Satan, i.e., suffering and destruction.

Admittedly, that distinction hangs on a technicality because Job also thought his suffering came from God (Job 6:4; 7:20). But Job did not judge himself guilty and persistently considered the whole mess a mistake. At the very least, I believe the takeaway for us is to never judge that a person is unrighteous because of their suffering or is righteous based on their apparent blessings. To do so triggers God's wrath. This doesn't mean we can't recognize good from evil or an upright person from an evil person, but we must never base those observations on a person's apparent blessings or sufferings.

The story of Job does not resolve the question of why we suffer; in fact, it doesn't even put to rest the two false premises embraced by the characters in the story. The prophet Jeremiah was just one of many who continued to wonder: "Why does the way of the wicked prosper? Why do all the faithless live at ease?" (Jer. 12:1), and the disciples asked Jesus, "Who sinned, this man or his parents, that he was born blind?" (John 9:1). However, if we return to God's response to Job when God took him on that "magical mystery tour of the universe," we may find that our God is too small, as Job did. And in that revelation, we may discover (in the coming chapters) other sources for suffering that don't depend on the simplistic answers originally offered by Job's friends . . . and are still offered all too often today.

Discussion Questions

1. What were the cultural presumptions Job and his friends had about suffering? And how did they complicate Job's ability to cope?
2. Why do you think God's answer to Job was so extensive?
3. What do you think about J.B. Phillips' comment, "The trouble with many people today is that they have not found a God big enough for modern needs"? Why might that still be true, three-quarters of a century later?

4. Twice God told Job's friends he was angry with them because they had not spoken the truth about him (God) as Job had. So, what was different about what Job said from what his friends said?

Chapter 11
Is Your God Too Small?

O Lord my God, when I in awesome wonder
Consider all the works Thy hands have made,
I see the stars, I hear the rolling thunder,
Thy power throughout the universe displayed!

"How Great Thou Art"
—Carl Boberg, 1886

PERHAPS LIKE JOB, WE COULD USE A "MAGICAL MYSTERY TOUR" of the universe that would put certain aspects of suffering into perspective. Such insights may not reduce our pain directly, but they can lift the blame and confusion, thereby allowing us to more fully experience God's care and closeness in our times of greatest grief.

And yet, how could studying the universe tell us things we need to know that aren't already clear in God's inspired Word, the Bible? Why look to nature? It's not a matter of pitting one source against the other. It's how one compliments the other. For instance, while the Bible tells us *that* God created everything that exists, we can study things in nature that fill in many of the blanks concerning *how* that creation happened, understandings that ancient people knew nothing about. Even the Scriptures themselves point us to the cosmos to discover new truths.

The heavens declare the glory of God; the skies proclaim the work of his hands. Day after day they pour forth speech; night after night they reveal knowledge. They have no speech, they use no words; no sound is heard from them. Yet their voice goes out into all the earth, their words to the ends of the world (Ps. 19:1-4).

"They have no speech," and yet they communicate truth, telling us—for one thing—how great God is in terms that were never articulated in the biblical texts.

Greater than We Can Imagine

Okay, I'm going to geek out here a little, but it won't be more than you can manage with some basic arithmetic. So, hang with me. Modern science tells us that the diameter of the observable universe is about 93 billion light years.

Some billionaires may have a sense of how large a billion is. But I sure don't have a feel for a number that large . . . not unless I can visualize it. So here goes: How large of a space would be required to hold 1 billion marbles, spread in a single layer? Let's start with one square foot. If each marble was a half-inch in diameter, then 576 marbles would fit into each square foot. A 4,700 sq. ft. basketball court could hold 2,707,200 marbles. (Try to visualize a gym floor covered in marbles.) A 57,600 sq. ft. football field could hold 38,177,600 marbles. However, it would require over twenty-six football fields to hold 1 billion marbles. Get that? So, since the universe is 93 billion light years across, it would take 2,418 football fields to hold as many marbles as the universe is across . . . in light years.

But that's not all (as late-night TV commercials say). A light year is the distance light can travel in one year at the speed of 186,000 miles per second. In other words, since a trillion is a thousand times one billion, when we do the math, that makes the universe about 5.8 trillion miles across. And, despite our national debt, that is a number far too large for me to imagine.

The fact that our God created such an immense universe says something about his "I AM" nature—his capacity—that is more overwhelming than the universe itself. And that is reassuring because God has revealed his glory through his mercy, grace, slowness to anger, steadfast love and faithfulness, and readiness to forgive. As David said . . .

When I consider your heavens, the work of your fingers, the moon and the stars, which you have set in place, what is mankind that you are mindful of them, human beings that you care for them? (Ps. 8:3-6).

David was so confident in God's goodness that he challenged us by saying, "Taste and see that the LORD is good; blessed is the one who takes refuge in him" (Ps. 34:8). Of course, there are deep things of the Spirit that are not understood by unbelievers, but as Paul says, "Since the creation of the world God's invisible qualities—his eternal power [the I AM] and divine nature [the glory of his goodness]—have been clearly seen, being understood from what has been made" (Rom. 1:20). God can be experienced by anyone who sincerely seeks him. We don't have to pretend, put on a holy face, or deny our doubts. All we need to do is give God a real try.

God's Purpose from the Beginning of Time

The Creator who designed the development of the universe much as modern science claims it occurred over the last 13.8 billion years, oversaw with clear purpose the emergence of homo sapiens on this planet, into which God breathed "life" (*nephesh* in Hebrew) in his image. That protracted miracle is awesome beyond all comprehension. It's true that the Scriptural description of that process was truncated into a poetic summary in the first two chapters of Genesis along with a few other briefer references elsewhere. But to suggest that those summaries incorporate the scientific details of all that actually happened simply because it's told as a "six-day" event is to reduce God to a genie in a bottle, a very small god, indeed.

The greatest of all God's creative exploits was in envisioning what would result if he set the cosmos in motion in something like the Big Bang. This venture was not like winding up a clock and letting it go on its own (as deism assumes) but by masterminding the whole creation with divine purpose—knowing what *could* happen and what *could not* happen because of impossible contradictions. But even as creation unfolded, God would have foreseen the convulsive cataclysms to be endured. In God's omnipotence, he presumably could have "pulled the plug." Had he made that decision for our star, some distant observer might have simply quipped, "Just another supernova," without ever having known God's vision for human beings.

I believe in real miracles—events God causes that defy the laws of nature as we understand them or perhaps as God created them. So I have no problem believing that during the development of the universe, God may have intervened in the natural course of some events, such as what happened when God breathed a "soul" into homo sapiens.[1] But allowing for those tweaks or nudges along the way does not conflict with acknowledging the primary sweep of what Paul called "the creation of the world . . . [that has] been clearly seen, being understood from what has been made" (Rom. 1:20). Those scientific insights remain quite reasonable. That doesn't mean theories of creation don't change. (At the moment, aspects of the Big Bang theory are being reconsidered.) However, God encourages us to see, think, study, and not to gullibly ignore the obvious.

These understandings affirm that God had a *purpose* for creation from the very beginning.

What Was Required?

Genesis 1:26 says, "Then God said, 'Let us make mankind in our own image, in our likeness . . .'" Again, this poetic revelation should not be taken as a scientific statement encouraging us to anthropomorphically envision God as having two eyes, two ears, a nose and a mouth and two arms and legs simply because that's our nomenclature. As David said, "What [are] human beings that you care for them?" Presumably, God could have breathed his spirit

---

1. There are those who claim Genesis 2:7 merely means God brought the human to life (having *just* then made him out of the "dust of the ground") through an act of "suscitation," discounting the possibility that the evolving, living creature (also from the "dust of the ground") had reached a point where God could implant a soul. They base their conclusion on the meanings of various Hebrew words translated "breath," saying the one used here doesn't necessarily mean God imparting his "spirit." However, within the poetic framework of the passage, no other creatures required God's breath or were animated in this manner. But as a result of *this* "inspiring" event, the human became an utterly unique creature.

into some other creature, and perhaps he has, "a long time ago in a galaxy far, far away."[2] Being made in the image and likeness of God has far more to do with our character—our capacity to love, create, relate—than our mere physical appearance.

However, given the creatures that we are, there were some conditions that we required in order to develop as physical beings. In the 1990s, the Hubble Deep Field telescope showed approximately 200 billion galaxies in the observable universe. However, new research raises that estimate by a factor of ten or perhaps 2 trillion galaxies,[3] and our Milky Way alone contains more than 100 billion stars.

There is a good chance that most stars have planets circling them. To date, over 5,000 exoplanets have been found.[4] Some exist in what is called the "Goldilocks Zone," not too hot or cold to allow for liquid water—a prerequisite for life as we know it.

But our earth enjoys numerous other conditions that have been necessary for us and other life forms to survive. In addition to abundant water, we have a breathable atmosphere that's thick enough to burn up most meteors. (Think of all the pock marks on the unprotected moon.) Earth has a molten iron core that produces a magnetic field protecting our planet from most deadly cosmic radiation. Our solar system floats in the middle of a peculiarly empty region of space, called a "Local Bubble," which also helps protect us from deadly galactic cosmic rays.

However, the universe—and even our earth—can be a very deadly place, producing much suffering simply by its very nature.

Let's pause a moment to review *why* we're looking at nature to discover something about God. The first answer is because the Bible invites us to do so: "When I consider your heavens . . .", David said. And Paul pointed out that creation itself reveals the in-

---

2. Before you freak out over this speculation, don't forget that the Bible itself recognizes other sentient beings equal to or greater than humans: angels, cherubim, seraphim, demons, even Satan.

3. Alastair Gunn, "How many galaxies are there in the universe?" BBC Sky At Night Magazine, Nov. 29, 2023, https://www.skyatnightmagazine.com/space-science/how-many-galaxies-in-universe.

4. "How many exoplanets are there?" https://exoplanets.nasa.gov/faq/6/how-many-exoplanets-are-there/.

visible qualities of God's character. But more importantly, this was how God brought Job peace concerning his painful suffering. God reviewed for Job aspects of nature that Job had undoubtedly heard of but had never considered as a correction to his mistaken presumptions about God's character. Hopefully, that's what we are doing as well—looking at things in creation we have heard of but never thought about in terms of God's character—that God does not initiate natural catastrophes to punish us, nor does he micromanage *everything* to interrupt the dangerous requisites of nature.

Dangers, Dangers Everywhere

When I was a boy about six or seven years old, my dad took me to a lumber mill where the entire mill was powered by a single gigantic steam engine. This was before the widespread use of hydraulics and large electric motors. Gear shafts and belt drives emanated from that steam engine throughout the mill to power the winches that pulled the logs from the holding pond and positioned them on a carriage, rotated the logs and then powered the carriages back and forth, while the huge saws cut off rough boards. The same steam engine powered the planers that smoothed and trimmed the boards.

I can still remember that steam engine. It was situated in a power room in the center of the mill. Everything was painted different bright colors according to its function. The flywheel extended high into the room and descended an equal distance below the main floor. The room was hot from the steam but not a drop of oil or a smear of dirt appeared anywhere. Everything ran smoothly and without the noise a comparable diesel engine would have made.

This was before the days of OSHA, but everyone knew that all the machinery throughout that mill was dangerous. I could sense it from the low rumble of the engine and how tightly my dad held my hand. It was big power that could kill in an instant, and accidents were common in the logging industry!

I remember it as awesome!

Our universe is far more awesome. Imbedded in the developing beauty of such a grand universe are many events we call "natural disasters." In fact, the entire universe is far more dangerous than we realize—galaxies colliding, black holes swallowing immeasurable mass. Dark matter we don't understand. Even our sun explodes at a rate equivalent to 10 billion hydrogen bombs each second. But without that kind of power, we couldn't exist. That's on the macro level. Similarly, on a micro level, even the death and decay of leaves on the forest floor provides nutrients for new life—you can't have one without the other. In fact, maybe we can't have the majesty of God's creation in many respects without the potential of "suffering" from dangerous natural events.

How dangerous? In the earth's history there have been five mass "extinctions," each of which knocked out the vast majority of life at that time, allowing the life forms that survived to repopulate the world with a very different flora and fauna than reigned in the previous era. The last such extinction occurred some 65 million years ago when a giant asteroid blazed through the atmosphere to impact Yucatán, Mexico (the location is still identifiable), causing a global cataclysm and rapid cooling that triggered the last ice age.[5] Scientists estimate that more than 99 percent of all organisms that have ever lived on Earth are now extinct.[6]

But that doesn't mean God engineered those convulsions to punish those creatures or humans since then. Jesus spoke to this conundrum in Matthew 5. After telling us to love our enemies and pray for those who persecute us, he said, so . . .

. . . that you may be children of your Father in heaven. He causes his sun to rise on the evil and the good, and sends rain on the righteous and the unrighteous (Matt. 5:45).

In Luke 13:4, he also pointed out that the eighteen people "who died when the tower of Siloam fell on them" were not being punished. "Do you think they were more guilty than all the others living in Jerusalem?"

5. Hannah Ritchie, "There have been five mass extinctions in Earth's history," *Our World Data*, Nov. 30, 2022. https://ourworldindata.org/mass-extinctions.

6. Michael Greshko, "What are mass extinctions, and what causes them?" September 26, 2019, https://www.nationalgeographic.com/science/article/mass-extinction.

That tower may have fallen because of an engineering error or a small earthquake. But natural disasters, things like a flood from too much rain or a drought from too little or a landslide—the kinds of things insurance companies label "Acts of God"—bring massive suffering, almost as much as cancer and disease. The World Health Organization estimates that seven million people have died as a result of the recent COVID-19 pandemic.[7] And one thing that surprised me (though certainly not most epidemiologists) was the speed with which the virus evolved—morphing every few weeks into a variant that circumvented much previous immunity, whether natural or from vaccines.

However, if science is correct, the same mechanism that enables a deadly virus to evolve so quickly is the same process that allowed us to become homo sapiens, ready to receive God's breath and become living souls. In other words, there are some things that we can't have both ways. You can't have an earth suitable for sustaining our life without the cataclysms that created the earth in the first place and continue to reform it. You can't have the majesty of blue whales without them eating sixteen metric tons of krill per day. You can't have forests without the microbes that ingest fallen leaves to produce nutrients that feed more trees. But sometimes those or similar microbes evolve into diseases that kill forests. And sometimes genetic changes at the cellular level result in tragic consequences for us humans such as birth defects or susceptibility to other maladies, such as heart disease.

God did not set up the universe in this way to punish us, to bring pain and suffering, but those agonizing possibilities inevitably accompany the potential for all the beauty and majesty of God's creation.

It's the same way with freewill. We cannot be the humans God made us to be without the freedom to choose between good and evil. God's natural laws govern the cosmos. God gave all living organisms varying degrees of instinct to navigate those laws, but

---

7. WHO Coronavirus (COVID-19) Dashboard, December 6, 2023, https://covid19.who.int/?mapFilter=deaths.

God gave sapient beings freewill that can override instinct and respond to or resist God's will.

As humans we have a great deal to do with the level of suffering we experience from the natural world. So many diseases and injuries are now preventable or treatable that used to cause suffering and death. We can feed vast numbers of people who would otherwise starve to death. Most of us (reading this book) live longer and in far more comfort than anyone—even kings and rulers—a few centuries ago.

Although humans can reduce much suffering, we are also responsible for creating much suffering, both directly and through abuse and neglect of God's creation.

Nevertheless, as we struggle with suffering from any source, hopefully this modern "magical mystery tour" of some working aspects of God's universe will bring comfort and reduce confusion concerning whether God is behind the consequent suffering. Then we can say with Job, "My ears had heard of you, but now my eyes have seen you" (Job 42:5), we can grieve in peace and receive God's comfort without wondering whether he was the source of our sorrow.

Discussion Questions

1. If the Bible is God's inspired revelation, what is the role of "the heavens [that] declare the glory of God"?
2. Without ascribing scientific details to the passage, what do you think Genesis 1:26-31 tells us about God's purpose for humans?
3. Can you imagine a universe that supports human life that does not have dangerous features? How would it differ from our earth? What might such a planet lack?
4. What role do humans have in caring for the earth?

Chapter 12

The Enigma of
Spacetime and Prophecy

God is working his purpose out,
as year succeeds to year;
God is working his purpose out,
and the time is drawing near;
nearer and nearer draws the time,
the time that shall surely be:
when the earth shall be filled with the glory of God
as the waters cover the sea.

— *Arthur Campbell Ainger, 1894*

W HEN I USED TO SING THE ABOVE HYMN, I imagined that *"God is working his purpose out"* in much the same way I attempt to accomplish my little plans—step by step—facing frustration or failure if any step faltered. Too often, I resorted to trying to force the matter, unintentionally manipulating people or breaking something in my attempts. But recently, I've come to understand God operates differently.

In the time before time—before the very creation of the universe—God had a purpose for humanity and for each of us. But the *way* God pursues his purposes isn't necessarily like how we humans execute our plans by micromanaging everything over which we have enough power to make each step happen. Our plans are *finite*; but God's purposes are *infinite*. Proverbs 19:21 even makes this distinction between human *plans* and God's *purposes*: "Many are the plans in a person's heart, but it is the Lord's purpose that prevails."[1] Even in the context of an active cosmic war, our omniscient God is not surprised by Satan's attacks, the seemingly random dangers in nature, or the consequences of human freewill. God doesn't need to control everything to achieve his purposes.

But the way we are locked into *our* understanding of the passage of time is pivotal to our experience of suffering. We grieve or suffer trauma over what has happened, struggle with what is happening, or wait for what we fear or hope will happen. For this reason, it's helpful to stretch our minds concerning time and thereby free our image of God from our finite, step-by-step, power-based perspectives.

As humans, we cannot escape the present except in our imagination. But we can watch things *as they happened* back in time—minutes or years ago. On the next sunny day, glance up at the sun. There is absolutely *no way* for you to see what's happening right now, but only what happened just over eight minutes ago. Find the North Star tonight, and you will see Polaris not as it is now but as it was 323 years ago. That's pretty close to going back in time, but we cannot alter the past. I'm not sure even God actually changes the past. Though there is that report in Isaiah 38:8 when God apparently "reversed" time. (We'll look at that incident later.)

Our sense of time is largely related to how much of its passage we've experienced. For a five-year-old child, a broken leg that takes two months to heal may seem to last forever because it represents a significant percentage of the child's life and far more of their consciously "experienced time." But at age fifty, the same event—though just as painful—can be taken in stride because an adult can envision the end of pain and handicap and knows that waiting represents only a small fraction of their "experienced time." Without adequate emotional support, a child's broken leg can be far more traumatic than for an adult.

Once, when one of our children experienced a traumatic event, I had little understanding of how deeply distressing it was for some-

---

1. Some Bible translations use the word *plans* to refer to God's thoughts, ways, or intentions. But there is a difference between the myopic and short-sighted ways we humans plan and how God pursues his purposes.

one so young. I did everything I knew to do at the time, but then I moved on as though I was relating to an adult who could handle it. I did not realize the long-term, unseen harm of the trauma.

Gratefully, God is not so ignorant of our situation. Perspective matters. Perhaps this is part of what Peter was referring to when he wrote, "But do not forget this one thing, dear friends; With the Lord a day is like a thousand years, and a thousand years are like a day (2 Pet. 3:8, see also Ps. 90:4).

In some situations, realizing how our experience is impacted by our perspective can ease suffering. While the old adage, "time heals all wounds," may be overstated, patience regarding its passage can ease various types of suffering. Who has not noticed that some problems resolve if we just wait? Or, they at least seem smaller? We might even say, "If I'd only known when this would be over, I could have managed it better."

In so many situations of suffering, our human experience of time involves waiting, sometimes for something we never witness happening in this life.

"The Times They Are A-Changin'"

That's more than the title of an old Bob Dylan song. I'm going to take another geek dive here to look at "time" from a perspective that's beyond our *usual* experience. Science has demonstrated that time is not an absolute constant. It *can* change, and it's literally possible to measure how time can slow down or speed up.

Any physical item—the book in your hand—occupies three dimensions in space: height, depth, and width. Those dimensions are real even if that book were the only item in the universe, but they are only relevant to us in their relationship to other objects, starting with us. But the book also resides in a fourth dimension: *time*. It is there in that space *at* a specific time, *for* a specific time. The fusion of the three dimensions of space with the fourth dimension of time is referred to as *spacetime*. But the rate at which time passes can change depending on two factors. (1) If the book is moved closer to a stronger gravitational field, *general relativity* causes that book's time to proceed more slowly than for you, if you keep your distance from that stronger gravity. Now for that difference to be measurable, the gravitational field would have to be immensely stronger, while you stayed where you were. The reverse also occurs if you move the book far away from, say, the gravitation of the earth, where you remain. (2) Additionally, the faster an object moves, the slower its time passes relative to a stationary observer. This is known as *special relativity*. You may have heard it said that if a spacecraft with a crew onboard were able to travel near the speed of light to another star and back, only a few years may have passed for the crew while we on earth would have aged greatly.

If that sounds like smoke and mirrors, it's not. It's a demonstrable phenomenon, and your cell phone factors in these "time dilation" dynamics every time you use GPS. That's because the satellites used for global positioning are far enough away from the strong gravitation of the earth that time in those satellites advances measurably faster. So, to figure out where you actually are at any one moment, a minute adjustment is made before signaling that little dot on your GPS screen to move.

The Alpha and the Omega

But what can this possibly have to do with understanding our suffering? Most of us wouldn't understand relativity even if Albert Einstein explained it to us. We can't get beyond Newtonian theories. However, there is value in acknowledging that not everything in the universe is as it first appears; space and time are two such features.

When God says, "I am the Alpha and the Omega, . . . who is, and who was, and who is to come, the Almighty" (Rev. 1:8), we have a hard time comprehending God's eternal nature, or as Daniel called him, "the Ancient of Days" (Dan. 7:9). Our conception of time is the *past*, the *present*, and the *future*—always moving in that direction at a constant pace—so we tend to imagine that God must be *outside of time* if he knows the end from the beginning. But the verse doesn't say he's outside of time. In fact, to know the end from the beginning only denotes that God knows how it will ultimately turn out—that his purposes will be fulfilled.

THE ENIGMA OF SPACETIME AND PROPHECY

The danger in imposing the analogy of God being outside of time is that because God is omniscient and knows all there is to know, then that must include everything that has happened, is happening, and will happen *inside time*, including all details. Some theologians have concluded that the reason God knows everything about the future is because he already *willed* it to come to pass. Therefore, nothing can change. From the human point of view, that feels like fatalism—whatever will be, will be—and there's nothing anyone can do about it. Theologians of this persuasion refer to their theory as "predestination," i.e., whatever God *predestines* will come to pass, and nothing else. God, rather than the *Fates*,[2] becomes a cosmic puppet master, which is exactly the way the ancients' understood their pagan gods. They believed "the gods" *caused* the arrival of all events to bless their adherents and curse their enemies.

While it's true that God *does* know all that is possible to know (and we'll discuss what that includes later in this chapter), one implication of the predestination theory is that it presumes God has already determined who will or who won't be saved, especially when applied to these verses:

> For those God foreknew he also predestined to be conformed to the image of his Son, that he might be the firstborn among many brothers and sisters. And those he predestined, he also called; those he called, he also justified; those he justified, he also glorified (Rom. 8:29-30).

However, if that means *only* those whom God has "predestined" will be saved, then that's a grim future for those not "called." And it doesn't leave much hope for anyone—even believers—caught in severe suffering either, because it's built on the philosophy of God causing everything. Esteemed theologian N.T. Wright counters such an interpretation of Romans 8:29-30 by pointing out that Paul

---

2. Greek and Roman mythology identified three "fates" that governed human destiny. They were goddess sisters: Clotho (the spinner or birth), Lachesis (the allotter of misery and suffering), and Atropos (the inevitable or death).

"is not talking about a theory of how people get saved or not." Rather, this passage is a "compressed telling of the story of Israel as the chosen people whose identity and destiny is then brought into sharp focus in Jesus."[3]

Moreover, there are so many "whosoever will" type invitations in Scripture, one must conclude that humans have or will have a *real choice*:

For God so loved the world that he gave his one and only Son, that whoever believes in him shall not perish but have eternal life (John 3:16).

And everyone who calls on the name of the Lord will be saved (Acts. 2:21).

As Scripture says, "Anyone who believes in him will never be put to shame. . . . Everyone who calls on the name of the Lord will be saved" (Rom. 10:11, 13).

If anyone acknowledges that Jesus is the Son of God, God lives in them and they in God (1 John 4:15).

This is just the tip of the great debate between Calvinism and Arminianism. In its most extreme manifestations, Calvinism can produce statements like the quote with which I began Chapter 2, where John Piper maintained that God must have *caused* the 9/11 terrorists to attack the United States because God controls everything, even things as small as "the fall of sparrows."[4] In contrast, Arminianism emphasizes the importance of freewill. There are other differences between Calvinism and Arminianism, and nuances within the adherents

---

3. N.T. Wright interviewed by Samuel Selvin, "N.T. Wright on Pre-destination and Election," Dec. 25, 2014, https://www.youtube.com/watch?v=qKwIijhZW-M. Wright also references Eph. 1:3-4 and Rom. 9—11, other passages often used to support predestination.

4. The Bible nowhere says God *causes* sparrows to fall, only that "not a single sparrow can fall to the ground without your Father knowing it" (Matt.10:29, NLT).

of either perspective, all of which is beyond the scope of this book (or my ability) to fairly review.[5]

A God Bigger than Time

I believe there are purposes God is working out, goals toward which God moves. But he is big enough to be able to accomplish them without having to micromanage all things in heaven and on earth or violate human freewill. The universe operates so consistently according to God's basic laws that we depend on them, calling them "natural laws," and yet we continually discover features that don't fit the "rules." For instance, new discoveries by the James Webb Telescope show spacetime anomalies not fully explained by the theories of *special relativity* and *general relativity* mentioned earlier.[6] But we have learned enough about nature that we trust God created an orderly universe that follows God's rules, even when we don't understand all of them.

When it comes to humans, Scripture is also replete with examples of God offering genuine choices to humans. God invites, explains, appeals, warns, scolds, even disciplines. But he does not coerce or lobotomize us. God's every interaction with us recognizes his gift to us of freewill: the forbidden fruit in the Garden of Eden; "I have set before you life and death . . . Now choose life," he told the Israelites (Deut. 30:19); "Choose for yourselves this day whom you will serve" (Josh 24:15). Even Jesus' prayer in Gethsemane models how our genuine choice can willingly honor God's sovereignty: "Father, if you are willing, take this cup from me; yet not my will, but yours be done" (Luke 22:42). References

---

5. John Piper, himself, offers a review of the "Watershed Differences Between Calvinists and Arminians." https://www.desiringgod.org/interviews/watershed-differences-between-calvinists-and-arminians.

6. Because I took strong issue with young-earth Creationists in Chapter 8, it's only fair to note that some Creationists have found within "time dilation" anomalies which they think is an explanation for how a recent creation of the universe (some 10,000 years ago) could appear to be 13.8 billion years old. See https://christiananswers.net/q-aig/aig-c005.html#11. Interesting, but I'm not convinced, and my main complaint is that Creationists' goal seems to be explaining science to fit their view of Scripture when so many fields of science conclude the universe is truly ancient, which I in no way find incompatible with God as creator.

to our freewill show up everywhere in Scripture—in every appeal that we repent, in every promise of God's redemption, in every call to service, every time God beseeches us to act justly.

However, if predestination is as comprehensive as John Piper thinks it is, what possible rationale is there for punitive justice (which people of Piper's persuasion usually support)? Why do we think that personal or judicial penalties will deter anyone from doing wrong? Logically, if they are predestined to do it and do not have freewill, there's nothing that can be done to prevent them from doing it—not even them.

Finally, there is also support for God having granted freewill in what might be called "reverse evidence." If God chose to control everything in the universe, if that is his *modus operandi*, then he must have predestined Satan to rebel against him (in contrast to *granting* Satan a freewill that Satan abused). However, James 1:13-14 tells us, "God cannot be tempted by evil, nor does he tempt anyone; but each person is tempted when they are dragged away by their own evil desires" (another evidence of freewill). Even John Piper admits that "extreme Calvinists" like himself have no rational explanation for why Satan sinned.[7] But despite that conundrum, if predestination were valid, why did Satan think he could defeat God? Why did Satan attempt to kill the baby Jesus? Satan may not be all powerful, and he may not know everything, but he certainly knows as much as any extreme Calvinist. If their theory is correct, he should have known there was absolutely no chance of winning a cosmic war against God.

So, what did Satan think he was going to gain if everything were predestined?

I don't think Satan believes in that kind of predestination. I think Satan made his move based on the understanding that God honors freewill. He apparently convinced a third of the angels to side with him based on that possibility, and he thinks he's got a chance to claim all of humanity, based on our choices to sin.

---

7. John Piper, "Where Did Satan's First Desire for Evil Come From?" *Desiring God,* Dec. 14, 2015. https://www.desiringgod.org/interviews/where-did-satans-first-desire-for-evil-come-from.

And yet in all of this, God *is* accomplishing his purposes. So, how does he do that without micromanaging all the actions of his creatures?

Calvinists and Arminians have wrestled since the sixteenth century with the apparent conundrum that if God knows the future, then we must live in compliance with that knowledge, thereby losing genuine freewill. But perhaps much of this struggle stems from our tendency to anthropomorphize God, to think his experience of time mirrors our understanding. However, what if, in a way we cannot logically understand, God *knows* the future without *causing* aspects of his knowledge to play out in a manner that manipulates humans or predestines some to receive grace while withholding the same grace from others? What if God's knowledge in no way determines anything related to salvation—it's just what he knows? That "disconnect" may seem logically impossible. But as we saw earlier, our experience of time is not the final word on its nature.

An Open View of the Future

But there is another way to understand how our eternal God may work throughout time to accomplish his purposes for us and the universe while also granting freewill to us, the sentient bearers of his image. This idea goes back to the fourth century.[8] What if God can envision and take an infinite number of paths to the future that achieve his purpose?

Think of it this way: While we humans think like amateur chess players who can envision two or three *steps* ahead (our plans), there are grand masters who can see as many as twenty moves ahead and can constantly adjust the *paths* to achieve a checkmate (the purpose). God, who is infinitely more intelligent than any grand master, can anticipate an infinite number of possibilities and therefore doesn't need to manipulate us.

This would allow for an open view of the future, sometimes called "Open Theism." Theologian Greg Boyd explains it this way:

---

8. Greg Boyd, "A Very Brief History of Open Theism," ReKnew, Oct. 29, 2019, https://reknew.org/2019/10/a-very-brief-history-of-open-theism/.

The future isn't out there as a settled reality for God to know—at least not exhaustively. But we agree [with traditional theologians] that God is omniscient, God knows all things, God knows reality exactly as reality with perfect accuracy. But where this view is distinct is that it holds that part of the "furniture of reality," if you will, is *our* possibilities.

Because God created this world with free agents (humans and angelic beings), to some degree the future is not a matter of what *will* or *will not* come to pass, but rather a matter of what *may* and *may not* come to pass. That's what's real. And since God is omniscient, God knows the possibilities as possibilities and so the future to that degree is open.[9]

Some may worry that if the future is not fixed and immutable, how can God promise to bring good out of evil? How can Paul say, "We know that in all things God works for the good of those who love him, who have been called according to his purpose"? (Rom. 8:28). But again, we need to think of a bigger God. Boyd says,

> If God has unlimited intelligence . . . then God could anticipate each and every one of a trillion, trillion possibilities to the trillionth power, each and every one as though it was the only possibility because God doesn't have to spread his intelligence thin . . .. If you just have confidence in God's intelligence, you don't need to worry about the fact that some of the future is open to him.[10]

Back in Chapter 4 of this book, I used the example from Genesis 50 where Joseph reassured his brothers: "You intended to harm me, but God intended it for good to accomplish what is now being done, the saving of many lives [from famine]" (v. 20). I said that God didn't inspire the brothers' attempt to destroy Joseph, but *when* they made their move, God countered by transforming the results into good—to save them from famine. A famine was

---

9. Greg Boyd, "Perhaps Even God Doesn't Know the Future?" *Closer to Truth,* Dec. 27, 2016. https://www.youtube.com/watch?v=wKRClBlPv24.
10. Ibid.

coming. God knew that, but there were other ways to save Jacob and his household had the human players made different/better choices. God was always pursuing his *purposes* unrestricted by human-size *plans*.

It is by *faith* that we believe God will accomplish his purposes, not by a theory of *certainty* that God is controlling or causing everything.

Prophecy and Time

In the above example of God using Joseph to save his brothers and father's household, I mentioned that God knew a famine was coming and could have saved the clan from its effect in various ways. That's because there is no conflict between God knowing how all *natural events* in the universe will transpire, on the one hand, and his granting humans freewill, on the other hand (e.g., the possibility for Joseph's brothers to behave kindly or cruelly). God doesn't need to maintain an open view regarding the movement of the stars (as though they might *choose* to change course) or the fact that an asteroid will crash into the moon or that the COVID-19 virus will mutate.

Many things appear random. However, possibly apart from quantum mechanics or chaos theory, most events have a cause, whether it can be identified or not.[11] You may have heard the Chinese proverb: "The flapping of the wings of a butterfly can be felt on the other side of the world as a tornado," which may or may not be true. However, the more we learn about the universe, the more even *we* can predict (prophesy) future physical events.

In the middle of the last century, C.S. Lewis pointed out the difficulty many people had with the idea of prayer. A man told him, "I can believe in God all right, but what I cannot swallow is the idea of him attending to several hundred million human beings who are all addressing him at the same moment."[12] Today, many may still find prayer incomprehensible, forgetting that millions of people are employing human-made two-way communica-

---

11. Full disclosure, I don't understand quantum mechanics or chaos theory enough to say more than that they wrestle with issues of predictability.
12. C.S. Lewis, *Mere Christianity*, (Westwood, NJ, Barbour and Company, 1952), Chapter 3, "Time and Beyond Time," 142.

tions with global positioning systems twenty-four-seven. I don't mean to compare our technological achievements to God. I'm just pointing out that in centuries past those achievements may have seemed just as impossible as prayer.

Not only can we predict the course of an asteroid, but NASA's Double Asteroid Redirection Test intercepted one with a rocket, altering its trajectory, and demonstrating that it's conceivable to prevent a threatening object from hitting the earth.[13]

Can God intervene in natural events? Yes, and the Bible reports many instances in which God did just that—from parting the Red Sea for the fleeing Israelites to the amazed disciples saying of Jesus, "What kind of man is this? Even the winds and the waves obey him!" The healings, people raised from the dead, feeding the multitudes—all those miracles briefly suspended natural laws. But the fact is, genuine miracles make "headlines" precisely because they are so uncommon, and therefore they represent evidence that God is *not* constantly pulling puppet strings for everything in nature. (We'll talk about the implications for us concerning how rare major miracles are in Chapter 16.)

Precisely because the natural world obeys God's laws (except when God intervenes with a miracle), God knows everything and understands all those laws and so can predict everything that will happen according to those laws.

Humans with freewill are another matter.

However, when Neta and I teach writing seminars, we encourage new fiction authors to fully develop their character's *character*—background, family status, likes and dislikes, goals, weaknesses, and strengths. Then we offer this example: Imagine your best friend's cat died. Because you know your friend thoroughly, you will *know* how she or he will respond. Will he shed a tear, sigh, and then say, "Good riddance, I was tired of that old hairball"? Or cry for a week and refuse to consider a replacement? Or get the dog she's always dreamed of? If you know your characters thoroughly, and then put them in a situa-

---

13. "NASA's DART Mission Hits Asteroid in First-Ever Planetary Defense Test." https://www.nasa.gov/news-release/nasas-dart-mission-hits-asteroid-in-first-ever-planetary-defense-test/.

tion, your story will practically write itself because you'll know what they will do next.

How much more can God accurately predict what we will do without *controlling* us? God, who understands every person better than any psychiatrist and knows every person's background, current pressures, fears, and goals would have no problem predicting what an individual will do in *most* situations. God requires no suspension of their freewill to prophesy what they will do. Will a specific king make war? Will a short little tax collector climb up into a tree when Jesus walks by? Will he be so depressed over his life situation that he will eagerly respond to Jesus' request to go to his house and talk about a change?

The implications of God's comprehensive knowledge of us cannot be overstated. Neta's novel series, *The Yada Yada Prayer Group*, is based on the meaning of the Hebrew word, *yada*, which as a root word appears 944 times in the Old Testament. It means "to know and be known intimately"—with many varied applications. Psalm 139 uses the term in so many ways, it could be called the Yada Psalm. And yet, none of them presume God has suspended our freewill. None of them suggest that God knows us with such a high level of accuracy that we are therefore locked into behaving accordingly, either to do right or to do wrong.

The theory that God functions with an "open view of the future" does not mean God doesn't know anything about what is going to happen. Physical things he knows precisely. Human responses he knows with a high probability, but he can adjust according to the possibilities.

Are there biblical examples where God adjusts, changes his mind?

Fire from Heaven

Consider the destruction of the cities of Sodom and Gomorrah in Genesis 19:24-25 by "burning sulfur . . . out of the heavens." It sounds like an asteroid, breaking up and incinerating the plain and all those living in those cities.[14] It also occurred at such a pre-

---

14. Asteroid impacts are relatively common in earth's history. One of the most destructive in modern history was the Tunguska Event in Russia

cise time that the angels had to hurry Lot and his wife and two daughters out of the city before it struck. The backstory in Genesis 18:16-ff includes the Lord telling Abraham that Sodom would be destroyed because of its wickedness, explicitly described in Ezekiel 16:49-50 as, "Now this was the sin of your sister Sodom: She and her daughters were arrogant, overfed and unconcerned; they did not help the poor and needy. They were haughty and did detestable things before me."[15] However, Abraham pleaded with God not to destroy the righteous with the wicked if there were fifty righteous people. God agreed, and Abraham, possibly knowing how bad the city was, negotiated lower and lower numbers—forty-five, forty, thirty, twenty, ten. God kept conceding, indicating his willingness to adjust. But when two angels were sent to warn the people, beginning with Abraham's nephew Lot, the residents threatened to rape the foreigners. The angels ultimately got Lot and his family out of the city in the nick of time before the cities and all who remained were incinerated.

If it was a meteor that destroyed Sodom, God would have known its precise impact point and time. The conflagration was indeed a punishment, but precisely for the reasons noted in Ezekiel: attitudes which made them unwilling to welcome the prophetic angels or heed their warning to flee. If fifty had not been so haughty and arrogant, attempting to rape the angels, wouldn't they have been saved? Or forty, even ten? Any and all were given a choice. But only Lot and his family listened to the warning and responded.

God undoubtedly knew that it was *unlikely* for others to join Lot and his family in fleeing Sodom and Gomorrah, and even Lot's wife turned back as the family fled. But the fact that God

---

on June 30, 1908 that felled 80 million trees, clearing an area larger than London. https://en.wikipedia.org/wiki/Tunguska_event.

15. The "detestable things" does not identify homosexuality as the issue the way many presume, but the intended gang rape and inevitable murder of the two foreigners. [See my book, *Risking Grace*, (Evanston, IL, Castle Rock Creative, 2016), Chapter 10.] For a similar incident, read Judges 19-20. Rape of either women or men is—as was recently demonstrated during the Hamas attack on the Israelis kibbutz—the most degrading assault possible, worse, many would say, than death itself.

negotiated with Abraham suggests the outcome was not a wholly settled matter.

The fact that God knows the human heart and the choices people—or whole nations—are *inclined* to make, does not mean he cancels freewill. Returning to our chess analogy, a master player will anticipate many of his opponent's moves. But that doesn't revoke an "open view of the future." There's always a choice until it is made. It does, however, provide the basis for prophecies related to what people are *likely* to do or not do . . . and the probable consequences.

There's Always a Choice Until It's Made

Centuries after the destruction of Sodom and Gomorrah, the wickedness of an even greater city merited sudden destruction. God sent the curmudgeon prophet, Jonah, to warn the people to repent. After trying to escape his assignment by heading in the opposite direction and nearly drowning in the sea, Jonah finally relented and traveled to Nineveh, the capital of the Assyrian Empire, the long-time enemy of Israel. They had attacked and began deporting Israelites in 732 BC. But as Jonah traversed the sprawling city, his only reported message was: "Forty more days and Nineveh will be overthrown." Rather than stone Jonah to death or try to rape him . . .

> The Ninevites believed God. A fast was proclaimed, and all of them, from the greatest to the least, put on sackcloth. . . . [The king and his nobles decreed], "Let everyone call urgently on God. Let them give up their evil ways and their violence. Who knows? God may yet relent and with compassion turn from his fierce anger so that we will not perish" (Jon. 3:5, 8-9).

The destruction Jonah announced could have come from various sources. He does not mention what *might* have happened—a meteor, an earthquake, an invading army, or even something as small as a virus.[16] However, because of the Ninevites' contrite heart at this time, God changed his mind: "He relented and did not bring on them the destruction he had threatened" (v. 10)—another example of God dynamically pursuing his greater purpose of redeeming his beloved creatures. In anger, Jonah pouted that he knew God would forgive Israel's enemies (4:2).

Promises of Good

The prophetic examples we've noted so far involved warnings, calls to repentance, and showing that God can adjust according to human choice, but God has also made promises for good that do not depend on human faithfulness. God never goes back on those unconditional promises. Even when the Jews were still "stubbornhearted," God chose to arrange for their deliverance. Isaiah prophesied that Cyrus the Great would come to power and deliver the Jews from their Babylonian captivity. If Cyrus had not done as God prophesied, God could have found some other means.

> I am God, and there is no other; I am God, and there is none like me. I make known the end from the beginning, from ancient times, what is still to come. I say, "My purpose will stand, and I will do all that I please" (Isa. 46:9-10).

At the beginning of this chapter, I mentioned the incident in Isaiah 38 where on the exterior stairway to the palace roof that was used as a sundial, the shadow cast by the sun retreated back *up* ten steps, indicating an apparent reversal of time. I have no idea what physically happened to make that shadow appear to move, but far more relevant to me is that God dynamically changed the prophecy he first gave Isaiah for king Hezekiah and issued a second one. We must conclude that the first prophecy was within God's "will." But so was the second one—two possibilities, *both* paths to fulfill God's purpose!

---

16. The date for Jonah is uncertain, but Nineveh did fall to the Babylonians in 612 BC, probably considerably after Jonah's visit.

This is what the LORD says: "Put your house in order, because you are going to die; you will not recover."

Hezekiah turned his face to the wall and prayed to the Lord, "Remember, Lord, how I have walked before you faithfully and with wholehearted devotion and have done what is good in your eyes." And Hezekiah wept bitterly.

Then the word of the LORD came to Isaiah: "Go and tell Hezekiah, 'This is what the LORD, the God of your father David, says: I have heard your prayer and seen your tears; I will add fifteen years to your life. And I will deliver you and this city from the hand of the king of Assyria. I will defend this city.

"This is the LORD's sign to you that the LORD will do what he has promised: I will make the shadow cast by the sun go back the ten steps it has gone down on the stairway of Ahaz." So the sunlight went back the ten steps it had gone down (Isa. 38:1-8).

God is not locked into some frozen steps of time, but it appears that whenever God changed his mind it was for humanity's benefit, granting forgiveness even when it didn't seem deserved, showing mercy, extending lovingkindness to honor an old king who had faithfully served him.

We can't always explain why suffering strikes or why we or someone else escapes. We've looked at several causes that don't indict God's goodness, but when we are in the middle of overwhelming pain and grief, we may still have doubts. God is not offended by those doubts, and if the Psalms teach us anything, he does not punish us for doubting. Even when God transforms evil into good, our doubts may still swirl.

If we don't feel like we can wait for God's answers, can we give ourselves the emotional space to wait in our pain. And maybe in time we will discover that . . .

> *Those who wait for the LORD*
> *shall renew their strength,*
> *they shall mount up with wings like eagles,*

they shall run and not be weary,
they shall walk and not faint.

—*Isaiah 40:31*, NRSV

Discussion Questions

1. How do God's purposes differ from how humans make plans?
2. How might recognizing the elasticity of spacetime bring some comfort to our experience of suffering?
3. When you consider the various ways Scripture appeals to our free response to God, or presumes that we humans have freewill, how do you respond to the claim that God predestines everything?
4. How do you respond to the theory that God functions with an "open view of the future" in which he can allow freewill because he can adjust infinitely and still pursue his purposes?

Chapter 13

Why I Laid Down My Gun in the Middle of a Cosmic War

"All who draw the sword will die by the sword."
—*Matthew 26:52*

The weapons we fight with are not the weapons of the world. On the contrary, they have divine power to demolish strongholds.
—*2 Corinthians 10:4*

A S I WRITE THIS CHAPTER, the Israel Defense Forces and Hamas are locked in raging battles with a "biblical" caricature. Hamas employs *Jihad* (holy war), intent on completely replacing Israel with an Islamic state.[1] Israel tries to annihilate Hamas, the ruling body of Gaza.[2]

The collateral damage *both sides* tolerate sounds like they've been emboldened to "destroy all that belongs to [the enemy]. Do not spare them; put to death men and women, children and infants" (1 Sam. 15:3), and "make no treaty with them, and show them no mercy" (Deut. 7:1-2), or any of the other "Texts of Terror" we looked at in Chapter 2.

The utter destruction is sickening!

---

1. "Hamas Charter," August 18, 1988, revised May 1, 2017. See Article 6, 7, and 30. https://www.palestine-studies.org/sites/default/files/attachments/jps-articles/2538093.pdf.
2. Israeli Prime Minister Benjamin Netanyahu, interview with Steve Inskeep on NPR *Morning Edition*, November 17, 2023.

Meanwhile, war grinds on in Ukraine, month after month, and we all worry that either conflict (or other "hot spots") could escalate into a nuclear encounter engulfing the whole world.

Few human activities cause more suffering than war. For that reason, I don't think Satan cares who wins because he's not fighting for one side or the other; he's only interested in pitting us against one another—*that* will bring the most suffering humans can inflict on one another. Whether personal or corporate, direct or commissioned, death and destruction are Satan's goals, which puts us in the middle of a *cosmic war* in which the whole creation groans.

In the last few chapters, we have looked at aspects of the universe that are far greater than we naturally imagined—whether the size of the universe, its age, or God's incomprehensible ability to navigate through spacetime, making adjustments to achieve his infinite purposes without forcing finite plans on humans in a way that cancels their freewill. It's mind-blowing! We can start to see why Job said, "My ears had heard of you but now my eyes have seen you" (Job 42:5). In the next verse, Job said, "Therefore I despise myself and repent in dust and ashes." I don't think this refers to confessing sin, as we usually think of repentance. In verse 3, he had admitted, "Surely I spoke of things I did not understand, things too wonderful for me to know." He was simply acknowledging that he had no idea what was going on "out there." And we are in the same boat, despite all our scientific discoveries.

Is Something Else Going On?

Back in Chapter 11 we took a brief "magical mystery tour" of the universe, noting that it is much larger and older than most of us can comprehend. We peeked at the mysteries of spacetime, realizing that not everything is as it first appears. We can thank science for stretching our minds concerning "How Great Is Our God," to quote a praise and worship anthem. But another possibility some scientists are considering is whether alternate parallel universes might exist in the cosmos. Most religions have affirmed this idea from their beginning—and been scoffed at by secularists who think it's just the way ignorant people explain the unexplainable.

And that's certainly true in many cases. But there may be more to it as scientists have explored the mysteries of unseen dark matter in the universe, which may outweigh ordinary matter by a factor of six to one.

Dark matter and dark energy were initially thought to be no more than a kind of scaffolding for the observable universe, but an article in the *Scientific American* seriously asks . . .

Could there be a hidden world that is an exact copy of ours, containing hidden versions of electrons and protons, which combine to form hidden atoms and molecules, which combine to form hidden planets, hidden stars and even hidden people?[3]

When cosmologists speak of dark energy and dark matter, they're not implying a moral quality, and I doubt many were envisioning the spirit world, but there definitely is more going on than meets the eye. The Bible refers to creatures that coexist with our space and time and influence us for better or worse. There are angels and archangels and cherubim that serve God and help us. But there is also Satan and his minions that wreak havoc.

Social psychologists have wondered about the dynamics of mob mentality that led otherwise intelligent, upstanding people to go along with the barbaric violence against millions of Jews in Nazi Germany, the raw slaughter of the Tutsi minority by the Hutu majority during the Rwandan genocide in 1994, or the gleeful lynching of black people by white mobs in the United States.[4]

Something more sinister seems to be at work, and this is why the Apostle Paul says, "The weapons we fight with [must not be] the weapons of the world. On the contrary, [our weapons] have divine

---

3. Jonathan Feng & Mark Trodden, "Could Dark Matter Make Invisible Parallel Universes?" *Scientific American*, August 1, 2014. https://www.scientificamerican.com/article/could-dark-matter-make-invisible-parallel-universes/.

4. Greg Boyd, "The Spirit of Us," Feb. 18, 2024, Woodland Hills Church, about how crowds who are formed around evil agendas serve as seedbeds for Satan's influence. https://www.youtube.com/watch?v=nn07oFeovhs&t=1291s. (Begin at about minute 21.00.)

power to demolish strongholds" (2 Cor. 10:4). And those strongholds involve far more than military ventures. There are many ways Satan can deceive and entice us to destroy one another. "For our struggle is not against flesh and blood, but against the rulers, against the authorities, against the powers of this dark world and against the spiritual forces of evil in the heavenly realms" (Eph, 6:12).

Could We Be in the Middle of a Cosmic War?

As we watch the daily newsfeed, there unquestionably seems to be an evil dynamic at work that goes beyond mere circumstances or explainable self-interest. Some think of it more like a mob hysteria to which humans are susceptible rather than the result of calculated tactics by an actual evil being dedicated to the bondage and destruction of humanity. We hesitate to identify it as an actual *cosmic war*, something greater than *Star Wars*, something that's active now, and has been with us for all of history.

I grew up hearing messages about Satan as our foe, usually trying to tempt us to sin or keep us out of heaven. But rarely did theologians speak of more than the personal implications. While I was not taught that humanity was getting better and better (there's that old problem of sin), when it came to what was happening in the world or between countries, I thought that if the "good guys" won, democracy could survive and possibly expand, the Gospel could go forth, people would get "saved" and behave better. So, fight—if need be—for your country. *Fight*? Yeah, you know, do your duty!

And then Something Happened . . .

In 1968, not long after Neta and I were married, we lived in Elgin, Illinois, over thirty miles west of Chicago, but our church was in the city, on Chicago's near West Side in what was then called the ghetto. Each Sunday we made the trek to Faith Community Church. I brought my Bible and taught Sunday school to the young teens.

On Thursday, April 4, 1968, Dr. Martin Luther King, Jr., was assassinated, and Chicago—like so many other cities around the country—went up in flames of rage and despair. Dr. King had been telling black people they could achieve freedom through peace and nonviolence. But he'd been murdered, and they were angry!

All the National Guard units in the region were activated and deployed to many of the distinct neighborhoods that make up Chicago. I was a member of an Illinois National Guard unit thirty miles outside of the city, and to my shock we were assigned to the blocks immediately around my inner-city church! *How did that happen?* But instead of carrying my Bible with the good news of Jesus, I arrived riding in the back of a duce-and-a-half Army truck, brandishing a rifle tipped with a jagged bayonet as we bounced over the spider web of firehoses that laced the streets. "Keep those weapons high," the sergeant barked. "Make *those people* see you mean business." But what business did *I* mean?

I knew who lived in that next building, and Willie Mae's apartment was just around the corner. I could imagine her beaming face in the choir as she sang, *"We've come this far by faith, leaning on the Lord."* Who was *I* leaning on?

Mayor Daley ordered: "Shoot to kill arsonists," but I saw the cops shoot at a carload of people who had simply made a U-turn when they realized they couldn't get through a road-blocked intersection.

We patrolled those streets for a week. One night my squad was ordered to clear an alley of a suspected sniper up on the third floor. The wrought-iron zig-zag frame of a fire escape was barely visible as it clung to the side of the apartment building while we crept through the dark. We heard a clang from above and froze, weapons at the ready, squinting to see our target. And then a window sash flew up, and a woman yelled, "Roger, get your raggedy ass back in here right now, boy. It's way past your bedtime."

What was I *doing?*

These people weren't my enemy. In fact, despite the rioting and the fires that had gutted pawn shops, liquor stores, over-priced appliance merchants, and other exploitive businesses along Roosevelt Road, I feared my brothers and sisters from church were in far more danger from the occupying army patrolling their streets. When you join an army, you swear to obey the orders. The year before, forty-three people had been killed in Detroit when the Michigan National Guard was deployed to quell that riot. So what army was I in? The Lord's army or some other army?

Approximately 10,500 police and more than 6,700 Illinois National Guard troops were dispatched to quell the rioting in Chicago. Finally, the billows of acrid smoke subsided, and our unit packed up and left without killing anyone. However, published accounts said eleven citizens died and forty-eight were wounded by police gunfire during the action. Interestingly, reporter Clay Risen pointed out that, "The South Side escaped the major chaos mainly because the two large street gangs, the Blackstone Rangers and the East Side Disciples, cooperated to control their neighborhoods . . . due in part to King's direct involvement with these groups in 1966."[5]

I think in my being assigned to the area around my church, God saw an opportunity to teach me something. I got a small glimpse into what was actually happening behind the scenes, if you will, of the transcendent cosmic war where Satan eagerly employs swords and guns or any other "weapons of the world" to bring suffering to all God's creation. No matter what my intentions, was it possible to use those worldly weapons of violence to accomplish God's objectives?

Many honorable people, including sincere Christians, say, yes, it is possible if you operate within "the law." But whose law? Roman law? The law of the Crusaders? The doctrine of discovery? Modern principles governing warfare? What happens if "survival" necessitates something more? Some of us don't realize that subconsciously we're subtly influenced by those early biblical examples claiming *God* ordered warfare or violent punishment. We've not unequivocally renounced those biblical examples as no standard for a follower of Jesus. It's just too easy to block out that comparison. Think of the justifications offered by the IDF and Hamas, or maybe the decision to drop atomic bombs on Hiroshima and Nagasaki or conduct the secret carpet bombing of Cambodia that killed 150,000 civilians.

---

5. Clay Risen, "April 5: 'There Are no Ghettos in Chicago,'" *A Nation on Fire: America in the Wake of the King Assassination* (Hoboken, NJ: John Wiley & Sons, 2009).

Examples Influencing Me

All my uncles fought in World War II. One was an Air Force Colonel—a decorated fighter pilot in World War II and the Korean War, and even a transport pilot into the Vietnam War. My dad was exempt because he had such a high management position in Lockheed Aircraft Company building war planes. I recall my paternal grandmother's funeral. My cousin was allowed to attend just before being deployed to Vietnam, and I was given leave in the middle of my advanced infantry training.

Six of us men—all six-foot tall or better—made an impressive "Jackson squad," even at Grandma's funeral, and I felt proud to wear the uniform. In fact, during basic training, I'd been honored as "The Outstanding Trainee of the Cycle"[6] out of the whole battalion—nearly a thousand men. Physically, mentally, and the training in tactics and on various weapons were all challenges I relished. I do recall, however, taking uncomfortable note of the fact that the targets on the ranges all had human shapes.

Of course, there was always the possibility of being activated and sent to Vietnam, though I hoped not, because by then I didn't think *that* war was legitimate or "just" in how it was being conducted. But hey, that was a *political* opinion, and soldiers didn't have a say in where they were ordered to serve. I counted on going home to be part of an Army National Guard unit, possibly getting called up to fight forest fires or help fill sandbags during a flood where those rifle-range targets would never turn into real people.

But they did become real people, people around my church whom I knew, a whole community whose rage I, as a white guy, had started to understand, at least enough to not think of them as "those people" or the enemy whom I needed to threaten by "meaning business."

What position was I filling in that larger cosmic war between God's commitment to life and Satan's commitment to death? As far as I know, there was no one from my church who took part in anything illegal during the civil disorder following Dr. King's

---

6. This simply reflected my commitment and effort during training and *was in no way* comparable to the commendations soldiers receive for valor or sacrifice in combat.

murder. Many people would say the force of the National Guard—lethal though it was—did not threaten law-abiding residents. But the context did not protect them either, as I saw that night with the little boy on the fire escape. "Collateral damage" might have killed him as easily as it has killed untold millions of innocent people throughout history.

In August, because of the planned protest for the 1968 Democratic National Convention in Chicago, 6,000 National Guard troops were again deployed to avert the violence promised by some radical groups. My unit was among them, and we saw plenty of action as crowds of thousands marched in Grant Park. It was our responsibility to prevent them from crossing the bridges from the park to Michigan Avenue where high-end stores might have been vandalized. Under the burning fog of teargas, we mostly held the bridges while squads of Chicago police swept through the crowds, bloodying heads with their batons. That night we were repositioned along Michigan Avenue right in front of the Conrad Hilton Hotel, which served as the headquarters for most convention attenders. Interestingly, when the police pulled back and left the National Guard to face the crowds, the violence subsided while hippies put flowers in the muzzles of our weapons and taunted us with anti-war chants. I took lots of pictures of those events, but it didn't change my growing conviction that I was in the wrong army.

After we went home, I dedicated myself to reading nothing other than the New Testament for the next month as I tried to hear what God wanted me to do. At the end of that search, with the blessing of Neta and my pastor from Faith Community Church on the West Side, I decided I needed to get out of the military, even if it meant fleeing to Canada as so many "draft dodgers" had done.

The Uniform Code of Military Justice

Having made my decision, I sought the help of advisors and was referred to *The Uniform Code of Military Justice*, the tome that contains the substantive and procedural laws enacted by Congress that govern the military justice system. During times when an active military draft operates, it had been possible for individuals to declare themselves Conscientious Objectors to military service and receive an exemption from the draft. That was the only kind of a CO I'd ever heard about. However, within the UCMJ, I discovered a little-known provision for someone *already in the military* to declare that they were or had become a CO and be granted a discharge . . . without, I suddenly realized, having to flee to Canada.

Was that me? Was I a CO?

I had not come from a peace-church background—Mennonite, Brethren, Quaker, etc.—but they had something to teach me, and it was right along the lines that I had come to realize after having been put into a "quasi-combat" situation where I was threatening people with death. Of course, there were all the obvious questions: Wasn't WWII justified? How about the Just War theory? What would I do if someone were threatening me with death? Would I be willing to use lethal violence to protect my wife and family?

In a way, those were specious questions. The only thing I could say with certainty was that I'd come to believe that I did not want to kill anyone and therefore shouldn't prepare or arm myself to kill anyone and needed to recant my oath to obey orders that might require me to kill someone.[7]

I studied the details of the law in the UCMJ and then scheduled a meeting (which I recorded) with my commanding officer in which I told him of my decision. He was very respectful. He even acknowledged the moral dilemma of being assigned to duty around my church. And he asked all those "obvious questions." I answered as clearly as I could, and then I promised him: "I want to assure you that I am not going to cause you any unnecessary trouble, and that's because I am determined to get out. So, I don't want to do anything that would jeopardize that goal." He appreciated that, and from that day on, I was not required to carry or maintain any weapons.

---

7. According to the International Humanitarian Law, Rule 154: "Every combatant has a duty to disobey a manifestly unlawful order." However, in the "fog of war" it's often nearly impossible to know what is or isn't an "illegal order."

The process took forever. There were the obvious officers up the chain of command who needed to review the validity of my case. But there were others who were just curious and had no authority other than their rank to question me. Still, I cooperated as graciously as I could.

Finally, I got out—the first person ever to be honorably discharged from the Illinois National Guard as a Conscientious Objector.

Am I a Backslider?

That old revivalist term is a strange one, isn't it. And I've often wondered about myself. I recognize that personally I have a combative spirit, and I haven't shied away from dangerous situations. Three times in my life, I've been threatened with a gun. Once, was on Chicago's West Side by a gang member. The second time occurred on the South Side when a guy demanded illegal access to a building I was managing. The third time was an apparent road-rage incident while driving through Indiana. I had flashed my emergency lights when a guy in a pickup was tailgating me. As soon as he could get around me, he pulled alongside and pointed a gun at me as he passed. In all three incidents, I realize that if I'd been carrying, and pulled a weapon in my defense, I'd probably be dead. Even the idea of personal self-defense is an uncertain option at best.

There was another incident when a crazed drug addict pulled a large knife and pointed it at my throat. In an instant, I believe God spoke to me and said, "Grab the person's arms, do a take-down, and no one will be hurt." Which I did. So, maybe there are other options than deadly force. In that instance, I followed up and visited the person in prison. They became a believer, and when released, lived a productive life for the Lord. Neta and I have stayed in their home, and they have stayed in ours. We continue to be good friends.

But I've wavered. In reality, I know nothing about being in the middle of real combat. So, who am I to pontificate about what others have suffered under the devastation of all-out war? After the 9/11 terrorist attacks on the United States, I started to wonder again whether there might be situations—such as ISIS or the Nazis—that justified going to war. Our best intelligence and General Colin Powell, whom I respected, claimed to be certain that Iraq still harbored Weapons of Mass Destruction—chemical, biological, and even nuclear.[8] Certainly, that was one exception that we couldn't allow to go unchecked. So, after the September 11, 2001, attacks, the United States hammered Iraq in the Second Gulf War until we pulled a whimpering Saddam Hussein out of a spider hole, but no new stockpiles of WMD were discovered. And now the legacy of that war reverberates in the Middle East as violence goes around and comes around, again and again.

In spite of my doubts, Jesus' maxim is immutable: "All who draw the sword will die by the sword" (Matt. 26:52).

But what about Paul's recognition in Romans concerning the legitimacy of the state?

Let everyone be subject to the governing authorities, for there is no authority except that which God has established. The authorities that exist have been established by God. Consequently, whoever rebels against the authority is rebelling against what God has instituted, and those who do so will bring judgment on themselves. For rulers hold no terror for those who do right, but for those who do wrong. Do you want to be free from fear of the one in authority? Then do what is right and you will be commended. For the one in authority is God's servant for your good. But if you do wrong, be afraid, for rulers do not bear the sword for no reason. They are God's servants, agents of wrath to bring punishment on the wrongdoer. Therefore, it is necessary to submit to the authorities, not only because of possible punishment but also as a matter of conscience (Rom. 13:1-5).

---

8. Saddam Hussein was condemned for his use of chemical weapons during the 1980s campaign against Iraq and Kurdish civilians. And Iraq had actively researched and later employed weapons of mass destruction from 1962 to 1991. But before the Second Gulf War, it destroyed its chemical weapons stockpile and halted its biological and nuclear weapon programs as required by the United Nations Security Council. https://en.wikipedia. org/wiki/Iraq_and_weapons_of_mass_destruction.

There is a God-given role for government, and it is to maintain order and justice. That's why I followed the requirements of the UCMJ and was prepared to bear the consequences if I had to break it. Obviously, Paul recognized this for himself and other believers since he and many of them were put to death for preaching the Gospel. Like many "natural" dynamics in the cosmos, governments can produce both blessings and disasters. When a group of soldiers asked John the Baptist what they should do to show repentance and please God, he answered, simply, "Do not intimidate anyone or accuse falsely; and be content with your wages" (Luke 3:14, NKJV).[9] How could a member of the ruthless Roman army conduct their duties without threatening violence and terrifying the populace?

It's a hard decision, and I humbly accept that there are many honorable people in the military or police forces who believe in Jesus and strive to be true peacekeepers. May God bless and guide them. I respect and do not denigrate them for their convictions, but every believer must consider whether their occupation is compatible with Jesus' way of life.

In honest consideration, most of us will recognize that wielding deadly force carries a high risk of bringing more suffering than peace.

But What About Armageddon?

The word *Armageddon* appears only once in the Greek New Testament: "Then they gathered the kings together to the place that in Hebrew is called Armageddon" (Rev. 16:16). The word literally means, a mountain. But it is understood by many to be the place where God's wrath is poured out in the form of huge hailstones weighing about a hundred pounds each that fall on the people. Nevertheless, Armageddon has become a catch-all referring to God's apocalyptic destruction of the world and all who have not been "saved" through repentance and belief in Jesus.

---

9. Some Bible translations emphasize the extortion element, but there is good reason to translate the Greek word, *diaseio*, as a violent threat.

As part of an extended series, Greg Boyd directly addresses the characterization of Jesus in the Book of Revelation and shows that the metaphorical images for him do not attribute physical violence to Jesus. For instance, the only weapon Jesus wields is the symbolic "sword" coming out of his mouth—the Word of truth![10] Others disagree with this interpretation, which of course does not coincide with those end-times, apocalyptic scenarios made popular by books like *The Late, Great Planet Earth* or the more recent *Left Behind* novels and movies. To be sure, those renditions reflect the same violent and retributive view of God presented by the early writers of the Old Testament. But it does not coincide with the Jesus of the Gospels.

Furthermore, if you really think Jesus is going to wage a great military battle at the end of the age, which earthly army should you join? Which one will be on the "right" side? Most of us think *our* military has been in the right during history. But really? We end up in the military of our home country . . . or, deceived by the heresy of "Christian nationalism," some are even now arming themselves to "liberate our country." Pick a time, pick a place, and you will still find Satan spreading suffering on all sides.

Mike Cosper, the director of CT Media, recently published an extended article in *Christianity Today* magazine[11] detailing the antisemitic ideology and persecution of Jewish people for millennia, leading to the massacre by Hamas of the men, women and children, including rape and mutilation, in the Kfar Aza kibbutz, October 7, 2023. He rightly pointed out that for centuries, Christians were some of the primary proponents of antisemitic hate, blaming Jews for the murder of Jesus, the Plague, and even generating conspiracy theories involving the sacrifice of children. One objective of Nazism, as well as Hamas and other radical Islamist organizations, has been the annihilation of all Jews. In this regard, Cosper's condemnation of Hamas is certainly justified.

---

10. Greg Boyd, "Slaughtering Lies," Woodland Hills Church, St. Paul, MN, Nov. 19, 2023, begin at 28:35, https://whchurch.org/sermon/slaughtering-lies/.

11. Mike Cosper, "The Aftermath of Kfar Aza," *Christianity Today*, March 2024, 32-43.

But his focus seems to be on justifying Israel's devastating military response. In a comment that restricts Jesus' ethic of nonretaliation to nothing more than a personal mandate, Cosper contrasts "the attitude of an individual who must turn the other cheek when wronged by another" from "the responsibility of a tribe to defend its people from annihilation." He even seems to dismiss the significance of Prime Minister Netanyahu reminding his Israeli forces to "remember what Amalek did to you." This was a reference to one of ancient Israel's most ruthless enemies and God's supposed instruction to King Saul to "attack the Amalekites and totally destroy all that belongs to them. Do not spare them; put to death men and women, children and infants, cattle and sheep, camels and donkeys" (1 Sam. 15:3). And just like those ancient models of violence and retaliation, the IDF has inflicted death on more than 40,000 Gazans, the destruction of most hospitals, starvation and rampant disease among children, and the razing of half the buildings and 70 percent of the homes in Gaza.

Morally, there's little difference between the goal of Hamas and the goal pursued by Netanyahu. Both serve Satan's objective to steal, kill and destroy God's children. Both employ genocidal tactics and objectives!

This is why, "The weapons we fight with [must not be] the weapons of the world. On the contrary, [our weapons] have divine power to demolish strongholds" (2 Cor. 10:4). And those strongholds involve far more than military ventures. There are many ways Satan can deceive and entice us to hate one another and destroy one another. But "our struggle is not against flesh and blood, but against the rulers, against the authorities, against the powers of this dark world and against the spiritual forces of evil in the heavenly realms" (Eph, 6:12).

Discussion Questions

1. In what ways might unseen creatures influence our "world" for better or worse?

2. What do you think Paul meant when he wrote, "The weapons we fight with are not the weapons of the world. On the contrary, they have divine power to demolish strongholds" (2 Cor. 10:4)?

3. What are some risks of taking up the "weapons of the world" in a cosmic war?

4. Why did Jesus tell the disciples to buy a sword (Luke 22:36), then immediately told them two were enough (v. 38), but only a few hours later rebuked Peter when he drew one, telling him, "All who draw the sword will die by the sword" (Matt. 26:52)?

Chapter 14
Who Demanded that Aslan Die?

> The LORD is my light and my
> salvation—whom shall I fear?
> The LORD is the stronghold of my life—
> of whom shall I be afraid?
>
> . . . I remain confident of this: I will see the
> goodness of the LORD in the land of the living.
> Wait for the LORD; be strong and take
> heart and wait for the LORD.
>
> —Psalm 27:1, 13-14

I HOPE YOU'VE HAD THE JOY OF READING C.S. LEWIS'S classic series, *The Chronicles of Narnia*. The seven books relate the adventures of some children who are transported into a fantasy world where they encounter talking animals and mythical beasts and are caught up in an epic struggle between good and evil.

In the first novel, *The Lion, the Witch, and the Wardrobe*, young Edmond succumbed to the temptations of the evil White Witch and ended up betraying his three siblings and all of Narnia by telling her about the lion Aslan's plan to end her rule over Narnia. Within this setting, Lewis communicates an allegory of the Gospel message showing how Jesus' crucifixion and resurrection redeems us from our bondage to Satan and the death he demands of us.

The White Witch claimed that the Deep Magic of the Emperor Beyond the Sea from the Dawn of Time said that any treachery committed in Narnia would be punishable by death at the

Witch's hand. Hence, because Edmund was a traitor, he must forfeit his life to her. But a *deeper* magic written *before* the Dawn of Time[1] trumped her intent when Aslan offered himself in place of the traitor, and in fact, Aslan's death was reversed when he was resurrected.

Allegorically, Lewis asserts several presumptions about Christ's *atonement* for our sins—what Christ accomplished by his death on the cross. (1) The White Witch (Satan), *not* the Emperor Beyond the Sea (God), demanded death ("the wages of sin"). (2) While the Deep Magic (the Law of Moses) was commonly understood to represent the Emperor Beyond the Sea (God), it was not a complete representation of the Emperor's true character or his will from *before* the Dawn of Time, which was only fully revealed in Aslan (Christ). (3) Therefore, Aslan's (Christ's) sacrifice was not to appease any demand made by the Emperor (God), but it was to defeat the White Witch (Satan) and cancel any claim she had on humans.

If this allegory is true, it is very relevant to our understanding of suffering: God does not demand our death, and therefore Jesus did not die to syphon off *God's wrath toward us* but to free us from the *claim Satan makes on us* for having surrendered our will to Satan. This understanding of the atonement was favored by the early church and came to be known as the "Ransom Theory" according to the Swedish theologian Gustaf Aulen in his book, *Christus Victor*.[2] However, after the Middle Ages the "Penal Substitutionary Theory" became more prominent. *Penal*, of course, refers to the punishment thought to be required by God to appease his wrath toward us for our sins.

The issue from my perspective is not the substitutionary quality of Christ's atonement. In both views, Jesus offers himself as the substitute for the consequences of our sin. The question is, *who* is demanding our death and consignment to hell and why?

---

1. There are five New Testament passages that speak similarly of conditions God established "before the creation of the world" or "before the beginning of time": John 17:24; Eph. 1:4; 1 Pet. 1:20; 2 Tim. 1:9; Titus 1:2.

2. Because of the title of Gustaf Aulen's book, the "Ransom Theory" is often called "Christus Victor," Latin for Christ the Conqueror. See https://www.compellingtruth.org/Christus-Victor.html.

God or Satan? To whom are we in bondage? From whom do we need to be freed?

Roots of the *Penal* Theory

If you're like me, when you try to read through the Bible, you cringe at those "Texts of Terror" in the Old Testament that I urged each of us to face into more bravely back in Chapter 2. Even if we know those models shouldn't be followed today, we can't remain unaffected by that approach to evil which suggests: Destroy the evil doers! Too many preachers like Jonathan Edwards have railed at us, saying, or at least implying, that we sinners are so loathsome that God abhorred us, and therefore we *deserve* to be cast into the fires of hell. Even when we were also told God loved us, it was only *after* Jesus paid the price to placate God's great anger and intolerance of us.

In subsequent chapters, we saw how God began to reveal his glory through his goodness as the story of the Old Testament progressed, thereby correcting the leftover pagan-tainted characterizations of God. Nevertheless, even four centuries after the close of the Old Testament, Jesus' disciples were still imagining God as a violent deity, who, if he was on their side, would violently rescue them from their enemy, Rome. In Luke 7, John the Baptist asked Jesus, "Are you the expected one who is to come [meaning the Messiah who would throw off Rome's oppression], or should we expect someone else?" The Pharisees and ultimately the Roman authorities feared Jesus might make such a move, and that led to his arrest and crucifixion. But before that, when Jesus was traveling with the disciples and they were not welcomed in a Samaritan village, James and John asked, "Lord, do you want us to call fire down from heaven to destroy them [just as Elijah did]?" (Luke 9:54). Jesus rebuked them, but their expectations were obvious. On the night of Jesus' betrayal, Peter was quick to draw a sword, showing his eagerness to fight by cutting off the ear of the high priest's servant. Again, Jesus rebuked Peter's rash initiative. Even after Jesus' resurrection, the disciples still asked, "Lord, are you at this time going to restore the kingdom to Israel?" (Acts 1:6).

Also, there's no question that in the Old Testament the imagery and practice for achieving forgiveness for sin was through the bloody violence of animal sacrifices, reminding the people that they were guilty and deserving of just such destruction because it showed how angry God was over their sin. All of which shows how easy it is to presume God's way is the way of violence and retribution and punishment. No wonder theologians and street preachers default to interpreting Jesus' atonement as the necessary sacrifice to appease God's demand for violent punishment.

Furthermore, it's true that we, like Edmond in C.S. Lewis's story of Narnia, have gotten ourselves in *big* trouble. We "all have sinned and fall short," and "the wages of sin is death!" There's no question it destroys us. But who is demanding our death? Is it God? No, "the gift of God is eternal life in Christ Jesus our Lord" (cf., Rom. 3:23; 6:23).

Nevertheless, there are passages in the New Testament that seem to favor the Penal Substitutionary Theory, especially if you are inclined to embrace that idea. Jesus is called the "propitiation" (*hilasmos* in Greek) for our sin (1 John 2:2; 4:10) and the "expiation" (*hilastērion* in Greek) (Rom. 3:25). In the New Testament, these terms harken back to the Old Testament sacrifices for sin. In both English and Greek, those words are rarely used outside religious contexts where they refer to appeasing or quenching the wrath of an angry god (whether a pagan god or the Judeo-Christian God). Paul actually says in verses like Romans 5:9, "Since we have now been justified by his [Christ's] blood, how much more shall we *be saved from God's wrath* through him!" (emphasis added).

However, as Greg Boyd points out, there are several problems with the idea of God accepting Jesus' death in place of our death, such as, "If the Father gets paid off by Jesus' death, did he really forgive our sins?"[3]

---

3. Greg Boyd, "The 'Christus Victor' View of the Atonement," *ReKnew*, November 29, 2018, https://reknew.org/2018/11/the-christus-victor-view-of-the-atonement/.

But Christ's Atonement on the Cross Did Pay a *Ransom*

Both Matthew and Luke report an occasion when Jesus instructed the twelve disciples on what awaited them in ministry. Theirs was a scary venture, and they would ultimately face arrest and persecution . . . and perhaps worse (a foreshadowing of Jesus' own death). But Jesus urged them to nevertheless speak boldly. Then he said, according to Matthew:

> Do not be afraid of those who kill the body but cannot kill the soul. Rather, be afraid of the One who can destroy soul and body in hell (Matt. 10:28).

Luke reported it this way:

> But I will show you whom you should fear: Fear him who, after your body has been killed, has authority to throw you into hell. Yes, I tell you, fear him (Luke 12:5).

Most commentaries and even some Bible translators suggest Jesus was saying we should fear God as the one who would throw us into hell. But why did they presume that? Perhaps because they think that role is consistent with God's character as they still understand him, that God is angry and vindictive, determined to throw sinners into hell.

However, consider the context of Jesus' statement. He was trying to encourage the disciples, not frighten them. Knowing his own mission was to break the powers of sin and hell, he continued by assuring his disciples in the following verses that God loved them even more than he cares for a sparrow that falls to the ground. In fact, he watches over them so carefully that he knows the number of hairs in their heads. "So don't be afraid; you are worth more than many sparrows" (Matt. 10:31 and Luke 5:7), is how Jesus concludes his encouragement.

Was Jesus telling the disciples they should be afraid of God? I don't think so. In fact, he was telling them they didn't even need to fear death. The only malevolent entity anyone needs to fear is Satan.

You'll notice in the Matthew passage quoted above how the New International Version translators capitalized the pronoun "One" to indicate it refers to God. But the original Greek does not capitalize pronouns for God. The Holman Christian Standard Bible and the New King James Version says, "fear Him" (capitalized). And The New Living Translation goes even further: "Fear only God." Clearly, these are editorial insertions based on the translators' presumptions and not based on the actual text. New Testament scholar N.T. Wright points this out and explains, "The one who can kill the body is the imagined enemy, Rome. Who then is the real enemy? Surely not Israel's own God. The real enemy is the accuser, the Satan."[4]

Many scriptures speak of Christ *redeeming* us from our bondage to sin and death. Obviously, God is not the one to hold us in any kind of bondage. After all, "God so loved [us] that he gave his one and only Son, that [we] shall not perish but have eternal life" (John 3:16).

Since the children have flesh and blood, he [Jesus] too shared in their humanity so that by his death he might break the power of him who holds the power of death—that is, the devil—and free those who all their lives were held in slavery by their fear of death (Heb. 2:14-15).

For even the Son of Man did not come to be served, but to serve, and to give his life as a ransom for many (Mark 10:45).

For there is one God and one mediator between God and mankind, the man Christ Jesus, who gave himself as a

---

4. N.T. Wright, *Jesus and the Victory of God*, (Minneapolis, MN: Fortress Press, 1997), 454-455. Wright's understanding of Christ's atonement, however, is more complicated than pitting the Penal Theory against the Ransom Theory. See: https://www.modernreformation.org/resources/interviews/from-plato-to-glory.

ransom for all people. This has now been witnessed to at the proper time (1 Tim. 2:5-6).

We wait for the blessed hope—the appearing of the glory of our great God and Savior, Jesus Christ, who gave himself for us to redeem us from all wickedness and to purify for himself a people that are his very own, eager to do what is good (Titus 2:13-14).

In the fifth century, St. Augustine explained what was essentially the Ransom Theory in this way:

The Redeemer came and the deceiver was overcome. What did our Redeemer do to our Captor? In payment for us He set the trap, His Cross, with His blood for bait. He [Satan] could indeed shed that blood; but . . . by shedding the blood of One who was not his debtor, he was forced to release his debtors.[5]

The Sacrifice that Redeemed Us

In Hebrews 9 we have what some might see as a melding of the two theories. In Verse 16 the writer speaks of how Christ "has died as a *ransom to set them free* from the sins committed under the first covenant." But verse 22 says, "Without the *shedding of blood* there is no forgiveness," referencing the ceremonial sacrifices prescribed under the Law back in Leviticus 17:11. To me, there seems to be no question that the Old Testament sacrifices—bloody (and inadequate) as they were—foreshadowed Christ's effective sacrifice on the Cross. And yes, God was so angry about sin that he wanted us to realize its seriousness, not because he is personally affronted, but because he knows how it destroys our relationship with him, our relationship with one another, our care for all of God's creation, and ultimately results in our death. His wrath *over sin* rages! But not *at us* his creatures. Instead, he rages over the suffering and

---

5. Doctrine of Atonement, *The Catholic Encyclopedia.*

death sin brings to us, his beloved creatures, and yes, at Satan himself, the ultimate source and minister of that death.

So, if the wrath of God was satisfied on Calvary, it was *not* because he vented it on Jesus rather than on us. It was because the ransom Christ's blood paid to Satan by his death set us, the captives, free and broke the bonds of death and hell, rendering them forever powerless.

In his blog, *Sacred Writings*, Terry Wright suggests that the line in the contemporary anthem, "In Christ Alone," which says:

> *Till on that cross as Jesus died,*
> *The wrath of God was satisfied.*

. . . might better be revised to say:

> *Till on that cross as Jesus died,*
> *The love of God was satisfied.*[6]

It would be a useful correction, primarily because it is so easy for us to presume God's wrath is all focused on us.

I just got word that an old friend of mine with whom I shared many joyful fishing and bowhunting trips has died from brain cancer. Once again (*again* because it's happened with other friends) my heart rages: *"I hate that cancer!"* I hate all suffering! But I don't hate the victims. I don't loath being with them. I wish I could have visited my friend.

But what about the perpetrators of evil and suffering? Can I really love them while they harm me or others? That's harder and sometimes dangerous if our "love" ends up enabling their evil. However, we can learn how to be more loving even when such people are our enemies. Jesus told us to "Love your enemies and pray for those who persecute you, that you may be children of your

---

6. Terry Wright, "'In Christ Alone': What should we sing instead of 'The wrath of God was satisfied'?" *Sacred Wrightings*, April 17, 2017. https://sacredwrightings.blogspot.com/2017/04/in-christ-alone-what-should-we-sing.html. Also see: Stuart Townend, "In Christ Alone, 2001, Integrity Music.

Father in heaven" (Matt. 5:44, 45). In saying this, Jesus revealed something about God. He then clarifies it further: "Be perfect, therefore as your heavenly Father is perfect" (v. 48). In our search for why we suffer, Jesus is telling us that God *actually loves* his enemies. So, the next time you suffer—even if you wonder whether you share some responsibility because of something you've done or failed to do so—be assured that God loves you and is not venting his wrath on you.

Discussion Questions

1. What about Aslan's voluntary forfeiture of his life made his sacrifice sufficient to replace the White Witch's claim on Edmund's life and, in fact, to save all Narnia from her curse?
2. How does Lewis' representation of Christ's atonement for our sins differ from the currently more common view often called the Penal Substitutionary Theory?
3. If it is God's wrath that demands our death for sin, and God continues to insist on payment, how does Jesus' death in our place represent God's forgiveness (or was it just payment with no forgiveness)?

Chapter 15
Judgment: What Is God's Goal?

Search me, O God, and know my heart today;
Try me, O Savior, know my thoughts, I pray.
See if there be some wicked way in me;
Cleanse me from every sin and set me free.

—*J. Edwin Orr*
Based on Psalm 139:23, 24.

WHEN I WAS TEN YEARS OLD, I lived with my family in a small ranching and logging town in the mountains of Northern California, population about four hundred. The town had a grocery store, a gas station, a post office, a small general store, two bars, and one church . . . that my dad pastored. There was also an abandoned motel consisting of about four rooms that were really nothing more than shacks.

Some friends and I found a skeleton key that opened the doors and made one of the rooms into our clubhouse. We didn't think anybody would care, so we freely wrote our names on the wall as "members" and ended up trashing the place. When the owner discovered the mess and saw our names on the wall, he contacted our parents, and we got in *big* trouble—at least I did. My dad ended up giving me a whipping and telling me that if the owner required it, I would have to pay for repairing the damage.

It wasn't my first whipping, but it's the only one where I remember the reason. Had the principles of "victim offender reconciliation" been articulated back then, those of us who had trashed that motel room might have been required to sit down with the owner and hear what our vandalism had cost him and how disrespected and angry it made him feel. Even without such a meeting, I got the message! But it wasn't the whipping that communicated. It was the realization that I needed to repair, repaint, and clean up the damage we'd done.

I also realized that my dad was a secondary "victim." My folks weren't ones to make me feel responsible for the success of their ministry, but I could tell my dad was deeply disappointed and worried that in such a small town, it wouldn't be good if the pastor's son was seen as a vandal.

We may sometimes do the right thing to avoid punishment—obeying the speed limit, for example. But the threat of punishment doesn't change a person's character and therefore often doesn't "work." Even when we consider the most heinous offenses, there is no evidence that the threat of the death penalty deters murder,[1] and it can even interfere with the healing process of the victim's family members.[2] So, maybe something else is more important than punishment. Maybe it's far better to understand *why* a wrong is in fact wrong or *why* doing right is right. But that only happens when the nature and consequences of "sin" are brought into the light in a way the offender can understand and empathize—that's a *revelation*.

The Big Reveal

On the eighth day after Jesus' birth, when Joseph and Mary presented him at the temple, the old man Simeon prophesied about Jesus, declaring that he was God's promised "salvation . . . a light for *revelation* to the Gentiles . . . [by whom] the thoughts of many hearts will be *revealed*" (Luke 2:30, 31, 35, emphasis added).

During his ministry, Jesus emphasized his unity with his Father in heaven by saying, "Moreover, the Father judges no one, but has entrusted all judgment to the Son, that all may honor the Son just

---

1. "Murder Rate of Death Penalty States Compared to Non-Death Penalty States," Death Penalty Information Center, 2020, https://deathpenaltyinfo.org/facts-and-research/murder-rates/murder-rate-of-death-penalty-states-compared-to-non-death-penalty-states.
2. "Victims' Families," Death Penalty Information Center, 2024, https://deathpenaltyinfo.org/policy-issues/victims-families.

as they honor the Father" (John 2:22, 23). The nature of Jesus' judgment essentially involves *revealing the truth*.

> For the word of God is alive and active. Sharper than any doubled-edged sword, it judges the thoughts and attitudes of the heart. Nothing in all creation is hidden from God's sight. Everything is uncovered and laid bare before the eyes of him to whom we must give account (Heb. 4:12, 13).

Many refer to the last book in the New Testament as "the Apocalypse" because the name in Greek is *apokalypsis*. But the word actually means the "unveiling," "disclosure," or "revelation." Hence, the English title: the *Book of Revelation*. There's much debate over the metaphorical symbolism within the book, whether it is code for political conditions faced by early Christians, or the culmination of the cosmic war with Christ triumphing over Satan, or both. Within the text, there are many references to warfare, massacres, monsters, plagues, and finally victory—even Christ's robe is described as "dipped in blood."[3] However, as we noted back in Chapter 13, the only "weapon" with which the Lamb (Jesus) "judges and wages war" is a sword coming out of his mouth. In fact, he is named, "the Word of God." (See Rev. 19, also 2:16.) That may call to mind the verses we just looked at in Hebrews 4:12, 13, where the "word of God is alive and active. Sharper than any doubled-edged sword, it judges the thoughts and attitudes of the heart."

To be sure, the Book of Revelation is about God's judgment—the big reveal, the unequivocal truth shown to all creation regarding Jesus "who is, and who was, and who is to come, the Almighty!" (Rev. 1:8).

---

3. There is much debate as to whether the blood on Jesus' robe represented his own blood shed on the Cross, the blood of Christian martyrs, or the blood of enemies shed in battle. However, Ted Grimsrud points out that "each direct reference and each allusion to 'blood' in Revelation where we do know whose blood is in mind, is a reference or allusion to Jesus' blood or that of his followers." https://thinkingpacifism.net/2017/10/11/the-book-of-revelation-and-the-problem-of-violence-a-response-to-john-dominic-crossan/.

Who Jesus Was

I have maintained that God is not an angry and vindictive deity, offended by our slights and disobedience, who is therefore fixated on punishing us. And I've pointed to Jesus, who is Immanuel (God with us) as the evidence, because Jesus didn't behave that way. But Jesus did do a lot of revealing, exposing hypocrisy, uncovering the thoughts and intent of people's hearts. He did not hesitate to issue judgments like, "Woe to you, teachers of the law and Pharisees, you hypocrites! You are like whitewashed tombs, which look beautiful on the outside but on the inside are full of the bones of the dead and everything unclean" (Matt. 23:27). He readily judged in the sense of revealing the truth.

But there is another kind of judgment: the dispensing of punishment. Regarding this kind of judging, Jesus told us, "Do not judge, or you too will be judged. For in the same way you judge others, you will be judged, and with the measure you use, it will be measured to you" (Matt. 7:1, 2). And he practiced what he preached. He did not call down fire from heaven on the inhospitable Samaritans. At his arrest he did not summon legions of angels to fight on his behalf. At his trial he renounced an earthly kingdom with its concomitant violence. He rejected the invitation of the crowds and even his own disciples to set up an earthy kingdom. He taught his followers to not strike back, but to turn the other cheek. Some would say, "Well, it just wasn't the right time," as though he was itching to "go postal" but strategically held back for a later date.

Did Jesus ever dispense punishment? Possibly. There are those who think turning over the tables of the crooked money changers and driving their livestock out of the temple was a violent act. It messed up their business, but they were probably back the next day. When Jesus freed two demon-possessed men by sending the demons into a herd of pigs (at the demons' request), the pigs ran headlong into the lake and drowned.

There was also an incident where Jesus healed a man who had been an invalid for thirty-eight years. He lay daily by the Pool of Bethesda, hoping to get into the pool when an angel stirred the waters, believing the first person in would be healed. But others always beat him into the pool. With compassion, Jesus said, "'Get up! Pick up your mat and walk.' At once the man was cured" (John 5:8-9). It was a remarkable miracle, which infuriated the religious leaders.

> Later Jesus found him at the temple and said to him, "See, you are well again. Stop sinning or something worse may happen to you." The man went away and told the Jewish leaders that it was Jesus who had made him well (vss. 14, 15).

It was commonly believed in biblical times that *all* suffering was the result of God's punishment for sin (see the Book of Job), and at first glance, many of us may have made that assumption here. But in Chapter 7 we saw how Jesus renounced that sweeping explanation concerning the man born blind (John 9). However, in this instance we must ask why Jesus would say to the man by the pool whom he had healed, "You are well *again*," indicating that he had once been whole, followed by, "Stop sinning or something worse may happen to you." Was Jesus implying a connection between the man's sin and the consequences he'd suffered? We do not know the nature of the man's disability—was it the result of a birth defect, an injury, disease? And there is no hint as to how the man's sin might have been connected to his condition. But Jesus seems to be saying, "Don't keep on sinning or something worse [i.e., the consequences of sin, not necessarily God's punishment] may happen to you."

On another occasion—when the friends of a paralyzed man lowered him through the roof of a packed house—Jesus healed him by first saying, "Son, your sins are forgiven" (Mk. 2:5). When some of the teachers of the law challenged Jesus for presuming he could forgive sin, Jesus said, "Which is easier: to say to this paralyzed man, 'Your sins are forgiven,' or to say, 'Get up, take your mat and walk'? But I want you to know that the Son of Man has authority on earth to forgive sins"(vv. 9, 10). So, in that case as well, Jesus made some connection between sin and specific consequences. But again, in none of these three instances (the man by the pool, the blind man, or the man let down through the roof) do we see Jesus saying the person's malady was a punishment from *God*.

"The wages of sin is death," Paul asserts in Romans 6:23. That's Satan's price tag, but he also collects as much suffering as he can in this life, and the consequences for some sins can be very physical. Today, when you go to the doctor, there is a whole range of maladies for which the doctor might say: "You need to make a lifestyle change, or you're going to face worse." Might any of those lifestyle issues be considered "sin"? Maybe . . . gluttony, excessive drinking, promiscuity, rage, perhaps texting while driving? Okay, okay, the concept gets pretty dicey, especially since Christians have had such a bad habit of pointing to other people's "sins," like *smoking*.

Thankfully, Paul gives us the good news in that verse: "But the gift of God is eternal life in Christ Jesus our Lord." Perhaps Jesus was instructing the man from the Pool of Bethesda: "You've been freed from one kind of suffering, take care of the even more important cause."

Jesus' Confrontation with the Pharisees

Even if Jesus didn't dispense punishments during his ministry, he certainly warned that there are limits to what God will tolerate. On one occasion after Jesus publicly healed a demon-possessed man, the Pharisees mocked the event as an act of Satan. Jesus then said, "Anyone who speaks a word against the Son of Man [Jesus himself] will be forgiven, but anyone who speaks against the Holy Spirit will not be forgiven, either in this age or in the age to come" (Matt.12:32).

Some people call this the "unforgivable sin" and use it to frighten people. But I don't think Jesus intended to create a spiritual bludgeon. He was dramatically revealing how serious the Pharisees' mockery was because of their position and influence on others. If anything, he was calling them out for scaring people away from the truth.

The crowd had been astonished at the healing, thinking Jesus must be the Messiah. But the Pharisees said, "It is only by [Satan],[4]

---

4. Literally, "Beelzebul."

the prince of demons, that this fellow drives out demons" (v. 24). They could not deny that the man had been healed, but they weren't about to admit that Jesus might be the Messiah. They could have said, "He must be a prophet" or some other innocuous admission. But knowingly and willfully ascribing this obvious act of God to Satan turned the whole event upside down, the epitome of what we now call *gaslighting*. It was telling the people that the wonderful thing they'd seen with their own eyes was not good, but evil! It was saying, *they*, the people, were the crazy ones and they should not trust what they had experienced. The reason that Jesus said this was an offense against the Holy Spirit was because, as Jesus said on another occasion, "When he, the Spirit of truth, comes, he will guide you into all truth" (John 16:13). The Holy Spirit had not yet come in the way Jesus was then referencing, and yet, it is the role of the Holy Spirit to confirm the truth in our hearts. And for the Pharisees to attack that reality was serious, indeed.

"Judgments" in the Early Church

Judgment of the revelatory type—exposing falsehoods, renouncing hypocrisy, and revealing truth—continued to characterize the preaching of the early church leaders. But there were some incidents that *appear* like punishments for evil.

In Acts 5:1-11, we read about Ananias and Sapphira, a married couple who conspired to make themselves look good by claiming to give all the proceeds from the sale of a piece of their property to the newly formed church when, in fact, they held back a portion of it. When Ananias delivered the money, Peter exposed him for lying to God in claiming to give all the money while keeping back a portion. Peter reminded Ananias that the property was his as were the proceeds. He wasn't required to give any of it to the church. So far, the judgment was revelatory in nature. Then Peter said . . .

> "What made you think of doing such a thing? You have not lied just to human beings but to God." When Ananias heard this, he fell down and died.

... About three hours later his wife came in, not knowing what had happened. Peter asked her, "Tell me, is this the price you and Ananias got for the land?"

"Yes," she said, "that is the price."

Peter said to her, "How could you conspire to test the Spirit of the Lord? Listen! The feet of the men who buried your husband are at the door, and they will carry you out also."

At that moment she fell down at his feet and died. Then the young men came in and, finding her dead, carried her out and buried her beside her husband. Great fear seized the whole church and all who heard about these events (Acts 5:4-11).

This event does not resemble anything Jesus ever did. But whether it was the shock of having their lies revealed that caused a stroke or heart attack or something else, this sounds very much like God executed Ananias and Sapphira. And that's apparently how Peter and the whole church understood what happened.

Sometime later, when Philip went down to a city in Samaria to preach the Gospel, he did many miracles. Simon the Sorcerer, who had been a renowned wizard in the region, heard the Gospel and followed Philip's ministry closely. He believed and was baptized. When the disciples in Jerusalem heard that many in Samaria had believed in Jesus, they sent Peter and John to investigate and support what was happening. Upon arriving, they found that the Holy Spirit had not yet been given to the new Samaritan believers, so they laid hands on them and prayed for them, and they, too, received the Holy Spirit. Then ...

When Simon saw that the Spirit was given at the laying on of the apostles' hands, he offered them money and said, "Give me also this ability so that everyone on whom I lay my hands may receive the Holy Spirit."

Peter answered: "May your money perish with you, because you thought you could buy the gift of God with money! You have no part or share in this ministry, because your heart is not right before God. Repent of this wickedness and pray to the Lord in the hope that he may forgive you for having such a thought in your heart. For I see that you are full of bitterness and captive to sin."

Then Simon answered, "Pray to the Lord for me so that nothing you have said may happen to me" (Acts 8:18-24).

Did Peter curse him or was he stating the obvious: Whoever makes money their god will die that way. Simon's plea for the apostles to pray for him suggests he realized the seriousness of his behavior, but there's no further mention of this Simon in Scripture. Some extra-biblical sources say his repentance was genuine and he continued as a member of the church in Samaria. Others say he continued in his sorcery, even founding the cult of Gnosticism.

Acts 9 relates the conversion of Saul of Tarsus, later known as Paul. He was a Pharisee, dedicated to the persecution of the early Christians. While traveling from Jerusalem to Damascus to arrest believers as part of a pogrom to wipe out the Jesus followers, he was struck blind by a flash of light and "fell to the ground and heard a voice say to him, 'Saul, Saul, why do you persecute me?' 'Who are you, Lord?' Saul asked. 'I am Jesus whom you are persecuting,' he replied" (Acts 9:4, 5). Some might say being blinded was a punishment that resulted in Saul's conversion. But the "reveal" in what God *said* to Saul may have been the thing that led to his genuine repentance. Also, his sight was restored (at least partially).[5] Later, he became the renowned Apostle Paul, who is thought to have written fourteen books of the New Testament.

In Acts 12:20-23 we find the report of King Herod Agrippa's death. He had been responsible for persecuting the believers, including beheading James, the brother of John, and imprisoning Peter (though an angel miraculously released Peter). Later, in a public speech, Herod boasted of bringing peace to the cities of Tyre and Sidon. The crowd shouted . . . "'This is the voice of a god, not

---

5. There's evidence that Paul's sight may have remained compromised as he apparently used a scribe to write most of his letters but said near the end of Galatians, "See what large letters I use as I write to you with my own hand!" (6:11).

of a man.'⁶ Immediately, because Herod did not give praise to God, an angel of the Lord struck him down, and he was eaten by worms and died" (vv. 22, 23).⁷

In 1 Corinthians 11, where Paul chided the church of Corinth for desecrating the observance of the Lord's Supper, he wrote: "That is why many among you are weak and sick, and a number of you have fallen asleep [i.e., have died]" (v. 30).

These understandings of Ananias and Sapphira's fate, Simon's greed, King Herod Agrippa's death, and the health or life of some at Corinth, all reflect the traditional ideas of how God treats his enemies and those who cross him. However, they do not reflect how Jesus treated any of his enemies. Even though he had many opportunities to take vengeance, he taught, "Love your enemies . . . that you may be children of your Father in heaven. He causes his sun to rise on the evil and the good, and sends rain on the righteous and the unrighteous. . . . Be perfect, therefore as your heavenly Father is perfect" (Matt. 5:44-48).⁸ That not only says a great deal about how *we* are to behave, but it also says *the same thing* about how God behaves. So, what was going on? Were the new believers still interpreting events according to a pre-Jesus theology? Had Luke not yet noticed that Jesus' characterization of God seemed to contradict the old interpretation of events in a way that commonly saw them as instances of God's vengeance?

Nevertheless, When We Die, We All Face Judgment

There's a verse in Hebrews 9 that I recall often being used in evangelistic services to urge unbelievers to make a decision for Christ: "People are destined to die once, and after that to face judgment" (v. 27). In context, it's more of an aside as the author was making the case that Christ's death was far superior to any of the animal sacrifices under the old covenant because when Christ "died as a ransom to set [us] free from the sins" (v. 15), the sacrifice did not

6. Most Roman rulers claimed to be divine, and to gain their favor, the public usually acquiesced.

7. Interestingly, according to Acts 13:1, Manaen, one of the leaders of the church at Antioch, was the childhood companion (perhaps stepbrother) of Herod Agrippa.

8. Luke reported essential the same teaching in Luke 6:27-36.

have to be repeated again and again. "But he has appeared once for all . . . to do away with sin by the sacrifice of himself" (v. 26).

In those evangelistic services, verse 27 was often used to remind people that after death, we'll all have to face judgment where the only question will be whether *your* name will be found "written in the Lamb's book of life?"[9] If so, you're in. If not, you're out.

However, if we *all* face judgment as certainly as we will all die, what will that mean? It might mean more than getting your name checked off on the "members list." Perhaps the judgment everyone faces is more a process of unveiling, disclosure, and revelation than a sentencing to punishment.

I mentioned my father earlier, and I really did / do love him. But something happened toward the end of his life that shocked me and caused me to do some deep thinking. My mother developed dementia—perhaps Alzheimer's—severe enough that she could not speak or make decisions. At one point, my dad lamented with a sigh that sounded like defeat, "I've lost her." But you could tell by watching my mom that she remained quite aware of many things going on around her. She lived in the memory wing of the assisted living facility while my dad lived in an adjoining wing. He, too, had some memory issues (couldn't find his way home from the post office one time) and reported a couple of hallucinations to me, but he was otherwise mostly "with it." Except that he developed a romantic relationship with another woman in the facility.

All our family members were appalled and angry because my mom saw it happening, and you could see the anguish on her face as she observed my dad and the other woman sitting together, sometimes with his arm around her as they talked for hours while he no longer spent much time with my mom.

I confronted him in the strongest possible terms, and he admitted he was wrong, but his behavior continued. So, what was going on? I have since learned that incidents of emotional infidelity are not uncommon in nursing homes, but I didn't know that at the time, and because my dad seemed aware of what he was doing and could see—if he took note—that it was deeply wounding his

---

9. This supposedly referenced Revelation 13:7, 8; 20:12; 21:7, etc.

wife, it seemed the height of unfaithfulness. I was angry, the whole family was angry, and to those whose faith was tenuous, this *pastor's* misbehavior discredited the Gospel.

What did my dad face when he died?

Certainly, some unveiling needed to take place, some facing into the truth about the hurt and harm, some repentance on my dad's part before heaven could remain *heaven* to my mom, who preceded him in death.

Paul speaks about "the Day [of judgment that] will bring [all things] to light. It will be revealed with fire, and the fire will test the quality of each person's work" (1 Cor. 3:13). Paul was speaking about the efficacy of each person's ministry, but then he adds, "If it is burned up, the builder will suffer loss but yet will be saved— even though only as one escaping through the flames" (v. 15).

I know very little about the Catholic doctrine of purgatory, and I have no reason to think that this *judgment* of which Paul speaks involves some kind of suffering, even though he uses the metaphor of fire that burns up wood, hay, and stubble but proves the lasting quality of gold, silver, and costly stones. If the process involved suffering, why would those who have accomplished the good works of gold, silver, and costly stones have to undergo suffering to reveal the quality of their faithful efforts? In addition, I can think of no Scriptural basis for thinking the process will be protracted. It could happen in a flash relative to our "earth time," and, if my efforts prove to amount to no more than wood, hay, and stubble, that revelation would bring remorse, but that's not necessarily the same thing as suffering. But I think some such judgment, some such "revealing," will happen for every one of us, and that takes nothing away from the all-sufficiency of Christ's atonement on the Cross.

I have become more persuaded of this possibility as I think about my own life. There are many points over the years where if I had died, I would have taken with me sinful attitudes and behaviors which had not yet been revealed, judged, or even faced. I will mention three areas: prejudice against other races, women, and LGBTQ people. This is not the time or place to rehearse what God has been revealing to me, but my attitudes and behaviors have hurt people, and I have had to repent and change. And I'm sure there's more still to come.

If my dad's example or my example don't resonate with you, think of a devout Christian two hundred years ago who owned a score of enslaved people. Don't you think that person would need an "attitude adjustment" (you could even call it judgment if you define it as *revealing the truth*) once he or she died?

Some call the process of revealing the truth in a way that changes us "sanctification," and we all need it now *and* later. C.S. Lewis explored this possibility as a process that may continue even after death in his allegory, *The Great Divorce*, as well as in some of his essays and letters.[10] When we understand what we've done, we will undoubtedly experience remorse, but not condemnation or torture to force us to repent. "For God did not send his Son into the world to condemn the world, but to save the world through him" (John 3:17). Therefore, it needn't be scary to "own up" to our wrongs because God is not violent and vindictive. In the end, God will "wipe every tear from [our] eyes. There will be no more death or mourning or crying or pain" (Rev. 21:4). We usually think of this promise as applying to the suffering *we have experienced* ourselves, but logically it may help heal us from the harm we have *done to others* as well. Because when we hurt others, it twists and damages us, leaving us in need of not just forgiveness but the healing that comes only with acknowledgment and repentance. That's the magnificent mystery of God's love.

This whole book is based on the premise that the Old Testament patriarchs needed some "sanctification" regarding their attitudes and actions that misunderstood the character of God. Few theologians would claim that the patriarchs were humanly infallible, but because of their definition of inspiration, some think God prevented any personal deficits from corrupting the scripture they wrote. Yes, Moses disobeyed God's command to speak to the rock to provide water for the people and violently struck it twice,[11] but

---

10. Nicholas Harelson, "The Salvation Theology of C.S. Lewis," *The North American Anglican*, April 23, 2021. https://northamanglican.com/the-salvation-theology-of-c-s-lewis/.

11. Numbers 20:7-13.

his "pen" never miswrote. And yet many of Moses' actions lived out the *Texts of Terror* he thought represented God's character and direction. In part, this may be why the author of the Book to the Hebrews began this way:

> In the past God spoke to our ancestors through the prophets at many times and in various ways, but in these last days he has spoken to us by his Son, whom he appointed heir of all things, and through whom also he made the universe. The Son is the radiance of God's glory and the exact representation of his being, sustaining all things by his powerful word (1:1-3).

Could it be that by the time Moses and Elijah appeared alongside Jesus on the Mount of Transfiguration, they had already experienced the kind of "judgment" that reveals the truth and corrects? Were they therefore content when God's voice from heaven directed Peter, James, and John to *listen to Jesus* with no mention of them?[12]

This does not negate the debt we owe the patriarchs for introducing us to God, but it certainly confirms that something else was needed, the actual visitation of Immanuel (God living with us). Even still, the nature of God's perfect love is something we don't fully comprehend. Paul put it this way: "For we know in part and we prophesy in part, but when completeness comes, what is in part disappears. . . . For now we see only a reflection as in a mirror . . .. Now I know in part; then I shall know fully, even as I am fully known" (1 Cor. 13:9-10, 12). For me, even as a follower of Jesus, I know there's certainly more to understand, more that needs conforming to his image.

Grace for Those Far Off

Many Christian traditions think of salvation as happening *instantly* to those who hear and comprehend the Gospel and "believe in Jesus" before they die. Some add baptism as a requirement—even baptism by a specific mode or including specific language.

---

12. Luke 9:28-36.

Others dismiss the necessity of full comprehension (after all, who fully understands?) but insist even infants must be baptized.

Most of these traditions, however, maintain that those who have *not* been "saved" by their prescribed method are destined for hell, usually described as a place of eternal torment. But C.S. Lewis' vision that sanctification is a process that may extend beyond the grave, leaves open the possibility that some may arrive in the afterlife in varying degrees of ignorance regarding the person and work of Christ. This possibility has huge implications for the billions and billions of people who have lived and died without having heard anything about Christ.[13] And that is one of the other great objections people have for why they abandon or avoid the faith. They cannot believe God is good or just if we tell them he will send the vast, *vast* majority of people to an eternal hell when those people's ignorance of the Gospel was in no way their fault. And to be honest, many of the "lost" are not the monsters Christians often paint the "heathen" to be. In fact, many religions reflect a moral code I believe is planted in the hearts of all humans by God, himself.

Though there are differing interpretations, various Scriptures leave open this door . . . at least a crack. As John 3:16-17 says, God sent Jesus into the world to save the world. What does it mean if *we* claim he succeeded in saving only a *very* small fraction of the population? In his sacrifice on the Cross, didn't Jesus redeem all sinners from Satan's claim? 2 Peter 3:9 tells us God is patient, "not wanting anyone to perish, but everyone to come to repentance." Paul says, "God was pleased to . . . through [Jesus] reconcile to himself all things, whether things on earth or things in heaven, by making peace through his blood, shed on the cross." So, if God is reconciling *all things* to himself, doesn't that have to include at least an opportunity for *all people*?

---

13. Estimates suggest that over the last 10 thousand years, 108 billion humans have lived on earth (https://www.prb.org/articles/how-many-people-have-ever-lived-on-earth/). Currently, about one third of the 8 billion people on earth claim to be Christian, but Christianity has only been around for one fifth of the 10-thousand-year time frame, so the total percentage of Christians is very small.

Peter gives us a peek into a very interesting thing that happened after Christ's crucifixion.

> Christ also suffered once for sins, the righteous for the unrighteous, to bring you to God. He was put to death in the body but made alive in the Spirit. After being made alive, he went and made proclamation to the imprisoned spirits—to those who were disobedient long ago when God waited patiently in the days of Noah while the ark was being built (1 Pet. 3:18-20).

While this passage identifies only a specific population to which Jesus preached, where were they waiting? And given the fact that the Noahians were described as so depraved God had given up on them, why would Jesus go to give them a second chance but deny the same to the billions who, because of the conscience God planted within them, did *not* give themselves over to total evil?

In Ephesians 4, Paul was explaining that Christ had "ascended on high" to give spiritual gifts for ministry to "his people." And then as something of an aside, he wrote, "What does 'he ascended' mean except that he also descended to the lower, earthly regions?" (Eph. 4:9). Could that also have been a reference to Jesus "preaching to the dead"? It's not conclusive, but in an attempt by the early church to clarify their beliefs and refute heresy, the Apostles Creed includes this statement:

> [Jesus] suffered under Pontius Pilate,
> was crucified, died, and was buried.
> He descended into hell.[14]
> On the third day he rose again from the dead.
> He ascended into heaven,
> and is seated at the right hand of God the Father almighty.

---

14. More contemporary versions say, "He descended to the dead." The Old Testament word *sheol* is not as precise as we commonly may think of *hell* and is also sometimes translated "the grave," "the pit," or "place of the dead."

Make what you will of the above conjectures, but I'm reminded again of Jesus' instruction in Matthew 7:1: "Do not judge, or you too will be judged." It is not for me to usurp his role as judge by presuming I can declare who, specifically, is condemned. I think there is reason to believe that Jesus will give a full and fair chance for *everyone* to accept him. That must include those who haven't heard as well as those who have been so wounded by the church that while they may have heard the Gospel, they can't believe until Jesus sets things right, either in this life or the next.

What About Satan?

Satan and his minions deliberately and knowingly continue to rebel against God and endeavor to destroy God's creation and his beloved people. There are no Scriptural suggestions that Satan was deceived or seduced into the evil he perpetrates. There is no obvious "revelation" needed before he can understand the harm he has done. What we do see, however, are numerous references to Satan's ultimate exile to a place of gloom, separation, destruction, and—yes—eternal "fire," whatever that may be. There are also many warnings to humans who persist in siding with Satan and his evil plans lest they accompany him into *his* hell.

So, what about them, those humans who have been determined to pursue evil with eyes seemingly wide open? Philippians 2:9-11 says:

> God exalted [Jesus] to the highest place and gave him the name that is above every name, that at the name of Jesus every knee should bow, in heaven and on earth and under the earth, and every tongue acknowledge that Jesus Christ is Lord, to the glory of God the Father.

That "every knee will bow" sounds like ultimate universalism. Does it mean Satan and every determined follower of Satan will be *coerced* to renounce him? Not likely. Will they be allowed to bring Satan's evil schemes, attitudes, and history into heaven? That is even more unlikely, as heaven would no longer be heaven for everyone else, would it? So, I have no idea what such a "surrender ceremony" will accomplish because there are still those passages declaring Satan's ultimate destiny. Perhaps it represents what Samuel Butler (1612-1680) said in his poem, "Hudibras":

> *He that complies against his will*
> *Is of his own opinion still*
> *Which he may adhere to, yet disown,*
> *For reasons to himself best known.*

If so, that should caution us against trying to scare people into heaven. Genuine converts love and follow Jesus out of gratitude for freeing us from Satan's power and planting within us a love for others. Such a transformation *is* to be "born again."

In this life or the life to come, I'm convinced that God's primary goal for judgment is to reveal the truth in such a way as to transform our character and save us from our sinful ways. Will there be punishment for sin? I don't think we've been told enough to be dogmatic one way or the other. But I'm grateful to not live in fear. After all, "God is love. . . . There is no fear in love. But perfect love drives out fear, because fear has to do with punishment" (1 John 4:16, 18).

Discussion Questions

1. Describe a time when the punishment you received for wrongdoing eclipsed your assimilation of the nature and / or seriousness of the wrongdoing itself?
2. The fear of judgment is often seen as a deterrent for wrongdoing. What do you think is God's primary goal regarding judgment? What does God want to accomplish?
3. What do you think Jesus meant when he told the crippled man he'd healed, "Stop sinning or something worse may happen to you" (John 5:14)?

4. What attitudes or behaviors in your life resulted in painful consequences to you or others? Do you consider the consequences God's punishment?

5. When you die, what kind of "unveiling" do you anticipate?

Chapter 16
Why Doesn't God
Perform More Miracles?

When peace, like a river, attendeth my way,
When sorrows like sea billows roll;
Whatever my lot, Thou hast taught me to say,
It is well, it is well with my soul.

— *"It Is Well with My Soul," Horatio G. Spafford, 1873*

HISTORICALLY, WHEN DID THE MOST MIRACLES OCCUR in the shortest period of time? Most of us would agree it was during Christ's three-year ministry . . . and the effect transformed history! Even healing events and healing ministries *after* Christ's ascension have had historic impacts. Locations have become shrines, healers have become celebrities, movements have garnered millions of followers. But too often what began as an authentic event, devolved into a scam that fleeced and manipulated followers. And yet, many of us would like to see more miracles happen . . . especially miracles that would alleviate suffering.

That sentiment is natural and usually good.

Dictionaries define a miracle as some welcome event that defies or circumvents natural laws. And those are indeed the kind of events the Bible records as "miracles"—feeding the five thousand or raising Lazarus from the dead or calming a raging sea, etc. But God doesn't perform such miracles nearly as often as we wish he would, which may be why you're reading this book. However, there are other good gifts from God that may not defy the laws of nature, but nevertheless seem so unlikely and yet so crucial that we call them miracles, even though there are explanations regarding how they came about.

For example, when Neta and I decided to quit our day jobs and go freelance as writers, getting started was financially tough. A couple of years into the venture, I felt challenged by the example of George Müller,[1] who in the mid-nineteenth century established homes that cared for over ten thousand orphans in England without appealing to the public for financial support. Instead, Müller privately prayed for what he needed, and God supplied, often in amazing and timely ways. So, when I calculated that our coming year's financial needs—to upgrade office equipment, replace our car, pay extra taxes, take a much-needed vacation, etc.—would cost twice our anticipated income, I decided to simply pray. I didn't consider it a rule that had to be followed or an attempt to manipulate God, just a voluntary discipline to pray every day for "our daily bread." When the year was over, every single need had been met, even though our income had not doubled, and there was no suspension of natural laws. In fact, I can explain each provision. For instance, to fulfill a major contract, we needed a much higher quality printer that was going to cost $2,000. But during that year, the manufacturer of the printer we already owned released a new upgraded motherboard that more than accomplished the higher quality . . . for only $300. Each provision was like that, a gift from God as clearly as the food on our table, and we thanked God for each one.

I wouldn't necessarily claim that those good gifts from God impacted history, but there are other seeming interventions by God that so significantly affect us, they definitely change our personal history and perhaps more. Dare we call them "miracles"?

Why Am I Still Here?

I am not unique in identifying occasions in the past when I could have died . . . but didn't. Most people can name similar "close calls."

---

1. My challenge came while writing *The Bandit of Ashley Downs*, one of our Trailblazer Books for young readers that features George Müller.

Near the beginning of this book, I mentioned an eighteen-month period when my body seemed to be falling apart. My left eye went blind, I was diagnosed with thyroid cancer, and I underwent open-heart surgery. God brought me through all those challenges, but while I recovered most of the sight in that eye, I did lose some of my peripheral vision on my left side. When focusing on something straight ahead, the average person can still see about 100° to either side. But my left eye can only catch movement about 40° to the left. I try to remember to compensate by glancing to the left before turning that way, so I won't bump into people.

Throwing Myself Under a Bus

In 2010, Neta and I spent nearly a month in China teaching writing seminars for expat kids in five cities. We were unable to bring sets of our Trailblazer Books, so we sold e-book editions on CDs. But when we were in Xining, the capital of Qinghai province in north-central China, we ran short. So, I left our hotel, looking for a store that sold blank CDs. As usual, the streets were packed with cyclists, cabs, busses, and an occasional donkey cart. Everybody rushed, seemingly oblivious of any traffic laws. I thought I saw a good break in the traffic and *thought* I sensed people to my right stepping off the curb. I started to do the same, when something jerked me back . . . just as a bus whipped past me, its front wheel in the gutter, right where I would have stepped.

The bus was moving fast, fast enough to have killed or mangled me severely. I almost collapsed in shock, but no one on either side of me seemed to have noticed. It was then I realized I hadn't actually been grabbed by my collar or arm or hit in the chest to knock me back. Still, I'd felt "jerked back."

Was it a miracle? Had God intervened?

Thoroughly shaken, I tried to figure out what had happened. Maybe I'd glanced to my left and glimpsed the bus without realizing it. But I don't remember seeing anything until the bus's mirror whizzed past my face, nearly giving me a shave. Whatever the case, I strongly felt God's protection.

Playing Chicken with a Logging Truck

And then there was the time years before that, when as a college student I'd been driving on a winding two-way road in the mountains of Oregon and foolishly passed a slow car on a curve, only to barely get back into my lane in time to avoid an oncoming logging truck, blaring its air horn at me!

Flying Into a "Shoe"

Even earlier, on my sixteenth birthday, Dad took me for a father-son plane trip. Hoping to change the focus of his ministry from being a pastor to becoming a missionary pilot, he'd gotten his pilot's license and had rebuilt a Cessna 170 in the process of getting his mechanic's license. We flew it from Hollister, California, north to San Jose, then jogged east over into the Sacramento Valley, where we again headed north toward Redding, our destination at the very northern tip of the valley—nearly a 300-mile trip. As is often the case, scattered fog mottled the valley floor, and there was also a cloud cover above us, but the weather service said that north of Sacramento things were breaking up. But the further we flew, that didn't happen. The ground fog became denser, and the cloud ceiling dropped lower until the Sierra Nevada Range to our east was totally socked in, and the passes west through the Northern Coastal Range became uncertain at best. It was as though we were flying into the toe of a shoe. But the weather service assured us that if we continued north, Red Bluff and Redding were still open. The plane's instruments and Dad's rating required us to fly only under visual flight rules (VFR). We had to be able to see where we were flying. But by this time, our fuel was too low to turn around and head back south without knowing how far we'd have to go to find an open airport.

Trusting the weather service, we continued flying into that tunnel with no certainty as to how we'd get out. As we approached Red Bluff, we couldn't see ground anywhere, and it didn't look any better on toward Redding at the tip of the valley. And then suddenly, a small hole opened in the ground fog right below us, and through it we could see a piece of the Sacramento

River. Calculating where we were, my dad figured the Red Bluff airport had to be about a mile west of the river. He did a tight stomach-flopping spiral, slowed the plane to almost stall speed, and floated down through that hole in the fog, grateful to find that there was a couple hundred-foot gap between the bottom of the fog deck and the river, a space through which we could squeeze to get to the airport.

"Mining" for Trouble

When I was only about twelve years old, a neighbor kid and I decided we wanted to dig a "mine" into the side of the steep hill across the road from where we lived. It was easy digging because the hill is quite sandy. The hole wasn't much larger than what we could crawl into one at a time, and we used boards to build shoring every foot or so to keep the tunnel from caving in. We only got about four or five feet in, but that was good enough for one day's work. I don't recall whether our parents found out or we went on to some other adventure like throwing hand axes to stick them into a tree or forging our own Bowie knives, but later, when an earthquake caused a landside on that hill, our tunnel got buried. Hollister, California, sits right on the San Andreas Fault and experiences earthquakes all the time. Fortunately, our "mine" didn't collapse while we were in it!

The Impact of Miracles

Like most people, there were probably other occasions when I "cheated death" without even realizing it. And as far as I know, none of my "escapes" required the suspension of natural laws. So, someone might argue that avoiding such disasters were just plain "luck," whatever luck is.

Such instances of God's protection may not require the suspension of natural laws or draw much attention in themselves, but they have huge implication for *some* people—in my case, me, my wife, our kids and grandkids . . . and whatever we do in the world. Who can tell how far the ripple effects might extend . . . or not?

If you've ever thought about time travel and the potential paradoxes even minor tinkering with past events could create, then you have some idea of the complexities that *any* intervention in the "natural" flow of events could have on unfolding history. Whenever we regret something and say, "If only I'd . . ." we're contemplating alternative scenarios and possibly different outcomes. In her novel, *Beautiful Lies*,[2] author Lisa Unger says through her character, Ridley, "I don't believe in regret. . . . Regret is imagining that you know what would have happened if you took that job in California, or married your high school sweetheart, or just looked one more time before you stepped out into the street . . . or didn't. But you don't know; you can't possibly know."[3]

So, when we ask God for a miracle—whether it's a big Miracle with a capital "M" that would override the laws of nature or a "smaller miracle" that represents God's protection by helping us avoid doing something foolish or enabling our body to fight off a virus more effectively—I think we need to recognize that *any* intervention in what is or might happen could involve more complications than we realize. Recognizing this potential for paradoxes can help us accept that there can be times when God seems to say no to our requests.

How Jesus Navigated a Paradox

I've noted earlier that Jesus shows us the goodness of God not only in what he said and taught but also in how he lived. That was never truer than when he withheld a badly needed miracle from his close friends. But the object lesson of what he said and did reveals the necessity of avoiding contradictions they had no way of foreseeing.

In John 11 we read the report of Jesus raising Lazarus from the dead. I encourage you to read the whole chapter rather than me quoting it here. Prior to this incident, Jesus' enemies attempted to stone Jesus, not for his miracles, but for blasphemy because he claimed to be God. However, he escaped their grasp

2. Lisa Unger, *Beautiful Lies*, (New York, Crown, 2006), Kindle, 89%.
3. This doesn't mean we can't learn from past mistakes, but brooding on them serves no useful purpose.

and fled Jerusalem into the wilderness where John the Baptist had earlier preached.

Lazarus and his sisters, Mary and Martha, lived in Bethany, a small village near Jerusalem, and Jesus had enjoyed pleasant days with them when he needed a retreat from the crowds. So, when Lazarus became deathly ill, Mary and Martha sent for Jesus to come and heal him. Jesus waited two days, choosing not to respond with the miracle of healing that Lazarus needed, but Jesus knew how the ordeal would end and said, "This sickness will not end in death. No, it is for God's glory so that God's Son may be glorified through it" (John 11:4).[4] There was no question in Jesus' mind that he had the power to heal Lazarus, but instead he waited until Lazarus died. Then he said, "[Now] let's go back to Judea." The disciples protested that returning to the Jerusalem area was dangerous because he was likely to be stoned.

When Jesus finally made it clear that Lazarus had died, he added, "and for your sake I am glad I was not there, so that you may believe. But let us go to him" (vv. 14, 15). Thomas then responded, perhaps sarcastically, "Let us also go, that we may die with him."

When they arrived at Bethany, Jesus immersed himself in the profound pain Mary and Martha and their friends were experiencing, and "Jesus wept" (v. 35). His grief was not from hopelessness—he knew he was going to raise Lazarus back to life—but it resulted from embracing the suffering Lazarus, his sisters, and friends had endured. A premature death often involves frightening pain and struggle, and Jesus cared! Without a doubt, if he could have spared them that terror, I believe he would have done so! The fact that he didn't perform the miracle they wanted had nothing to do with his not caring or not having enough power to heal Lazarus. Martha, Mary, and several of the gathered mourners all affirmed that Jesus *could* have healed Lazarus (vv. 21, 32, 37).

A lack of God's care or a lack of enough power are never the reasons we don't experience the miracles we seek.

---

4. In Chapter 5, I suggested that when God revealed himself to Moses on Mount Horeb and said, "I will cause all my goodness to pass in front of you" (Exod. 33:13), that "goodness" was new to Moses, who had been more familiar with God's power.

Everything has consequences—some big, some trivial. This occasion was history-making. When you look at the timeline, it appears that Jesus didn't heal Lazarus because he foresaw the consequences such healing would have caused *in contrast* to the consequences of waiting and raising him from the dead. Earlier, when the Pharisees prepared to stone Jesus, they said, "We are not stoning you for any good work but for blasphemy, because you, a mere man, claim to be God" (John 10:33). While Jesus' miracles validated his claims, they also endeared him to the people, so the Pharisees hesitated to object directly to his "good works." Had Jesus merely healed Lazarus, they might have dismissed it as: "Jesus just happened to drop by to visit his sick friend and Lazarus got better. So what?" However, Jesus' other option was to wait until Lazarus died, had been in the grave four days, and numerous witnesses were gathered to help mourn his passing. *Then*, raise him back to life! That would be undeniable, impossible to dismiss, and far more conclusive evidence of his divinity.[5] So, that's what Jesus chose.

Indeed, it was too much. "The chief priests and the Pharisees called a meeting of the Sanhedrin" and hatched a plot to arrest and kill Jesus (v. 47, ff). Foreseeing these consequences, Jesus had chosen this harder path rather than the simpler one of healing Lazarus as his sisters had earlier requested because that was the path that led to the fulfillment of Jesus' purpose of giving his own life as a ransom to free us from Satan's power.

In this narrative, there is no hint that God caused Lazarus' sickness, and no evidence that he inspired the rulers to kill Jesus. The first condition was the result of a natural phenomenon; the second component resulted from human freewill collaborating with Satan's plan. We can be certain that, as complicated as "what happens" might appear, God was not the initiator of evil and suffering.

---

5. On two other occasions Jesus raised people from the dead: the widow of Nain's son (Luke 7:11-17) and Jairus's daughter (Luke 8:40-56). Both were revived rather soon after their deaths, and for Jairus' daughter, only the girl's parents and Peter, James, and John were direct witnesses. But Lazarus had been dead for four days, and there were numerous reputable witnesses who reported the event.

One might speculate other paths that would not have extended and intensified the suffering Lazarus and his sisters experienced even in the short term, but that kind of speculation involves "what-ifs" or "if-onlys" of the past and implications for the future we cannot possibly know. I admit that sometimes my desire for a miracle is more like: *POOF!* a universal start over without any history, flaws, and sins from the past or present. And God does promise us a place in a new heaven and new earth, but that vision includes our redemption and transformation. And in that there is hope.

Even Jesus Didn't Always Get What He Asked for

Jesus taught us to pray: "Your will be done, on earth as it is in heaven" (Matt. 6:10). We often forget that both Jesus and Paul[6] prayed three times for God to intervene on their behalf, but God chose not to do so. The fact that even in his time of great desperation before his crucifixion, Jesus prayed, "Not as I will, but let yours be done" (Matt. 26:39), and taught us to pray in the same spirit, reinforces for me that we do not live in a world where God micromanages all events. God *is* working his purposes out, but if everything were predestined, there would be no cause to pray as Jesus taught us to pray and prayed himself, because we would be mere puppets of fate, nothing more than cogs in a cosmic machine. Worse still, any presumed relationship with God would be meaningless because our communication with God would have no effect one way or the other.

But it is because we exist *with* God in an unimaginably complex universe that Jesus told us to "always pray and not give up" (Luke

---

6. In 2 Corinthians 12:7, Paul says, "In order to keep me from becoming conceited, I was given a thorn in the flesh, a messenger of Satan to torment me. Three times I pleaded with the Lord to take it away from me. But he said to me. 'My grace is sufficient for you, for my power is made perfect in weakness.'" Not unlike Jesus' destiny, Paul accepted his suffering as something essential within his spirit to help facilitate God's cosmic purpose in spreading the Gospel, and he submitted. However, in terms of my contention that God is not the source of our suffering, I admit that Paul appears to disagree at least in terms of his "thorn in the flesh," though it was still Satan who administered the torment.

18:1). It is with the generosity of a gracious parent that God eagerly blesses us. Remember what Jesus taught us:

> "Ask and it will be given to you; seek and you will find; knock and the door will be opened to you. For everyone who asks receives; the one who seeks finds; and to the one who knocks, the door will be opened.
>
> "Which of you, if your son or daughter asks for bread, will give them a stone? Or if they ask for a fish, will give a snake? If you, then, though you are evil, know how to give good gifts to your children, how much more will your Father in heaven give good gifts to those who ask him!" (Matt. 7:7-11).

The Principle of Non-Contradiction

It is easy to presume that if God were truly good and truly all-powerful, he could prevent all suffering—whether it was Lazarus' death, Jesus' own crucifixion, or your suffering. But that may not always be the case. It's like C.S. Lewis said in *The Lion, the Witch, and the Wardrobe*, there may be a "deeper magic from before the dawn of time," meaning principles woven into the very fabric of the universe that cannot be contradicted—not even by a miracle.

Consider again the simplistic example of a chess game: If your king is in "check," there is at least one path (and possibly more) whereby you can escape. That path may be very costly—the loss of your queen or other important chess pieces, for instance. However, if you do not take that path, your opponent's next move will put you into "checkmate," from which there is *no* escape, and the game is over. That is a fact, it cannot be contradicted!

Perhaps Jesus faced something like that both in not healing Lazarus when he would have liked to and in not avoiding his own crucifixion. Some steps had to transpire, steps that led to his own self-sacrifice to redeem us from Satan's claim on us. There was no other way!

There may be more of those junctures in the course of the universe than we realize, not in terms of our suffering saving the world, but in terms of "things that have to be" for our reality to exist. We can rehearse in our minds all the "what ifs" and "if onlys" we can imagine, but we really have no certainty as to where they might have led. Acknowledging that there may be *some* junctures in the course of time where multiple alternatives are not available for accomplishing God's purpose is not the same as accepting general predestination regarding all or even most events.

Neta and I recently returned from the one-hundredth anniversary commemorating the Lorain, Ohio, tornado of June 28, 1924, which decimated that small town, killing some eighty-five people and leaving about seven thousand homeless. Neta's mother was age thirteen and, along with her family, was visiting their Van Deusen relatives in Lorain when the tornado struck the Van Deusen home. Everybody went down into the basement except Neta's mother, who was apparently so engrossed in a book she didn't hear the warning. The tornado picked up the house and smashed it down, collapsing the first floor into the basement like an accordion. Neta's mother's parents and two siblings were killed, leaving her an orphan. The three-year-old Van Deusen child was also killed. Other Van Deusens were seriously injured.

I have no idea why God did not direct that tornado around the town of Lorain or what might have been the "what-if" results. And I am grateful for the over thirty-five thousand other Lorain residents who survived and all the good that came from their lives and subsequent generations. But I can also speculate on some results that might have happened if Neta's mother *had not* been saved. First of all, Neta would not exist, nor would her siblings and all the good they have done. Neither would our children and grandchildren. I have no idea what would have happened to me since Neta has been so instrumental to who I've become. But without her, I doubt I would have written the book you are now reading or any other book. As a child, I loved good stories, but I was a slow reader and poor speller and never imagined I could become a writer. Instead, I was good at math and science and went to college thinking I would become a chemistry teacher. There I met Neta, who knew she wanted to become an author. Enchanted by her, I began to wonder for the first time whether I could also write, and ultimately switched my major to journalism.

I'm sure you have similar stories where you can trace the influences that have shaped your life—some may seem good and some not so good. But events have consequences far greater than we anticipate. And without micromanaging human choices or doing evil, God may face would-be contradictions that cannot be violated and purposes that must be pursued which in no way nullify his goodness or power or human freewill.

Responding to God's Intervention

I've been sobered by what I believe were God's miracles in my life—to save me from "a speeding bus" or the still small voice that seemed to say, "This is the way; walk in it." How do I let those gifts affect change in me? Do I charge on, presuming they represent God's endorsement of all my attitudes, behavior, and character, and so I don't need any change? Or, having encountered God, am I humbled like Isaiah, and say, "Woe is me, for I am undone! Because I am a man of unclean lips, and I dwell in the midst of a people of unclean lips" (Isa. 6:5, NKJV)?

Recently, a candidate for President of the United States escaped an assassination attempt when he momentarily turned to the right just enough so the bullet intended to explode his head did no more than clip the upper edge of his right ear. It might seem like a supernatural intervention, but to what end? I'm flabbergasted that it brought no pause in the vitriol, lies, threats, and divisiveness that continue to come from his lips. And I despair that so many of his followers cheered him on, declaring that his rescue proves God's approval, even anointing.

We may think that if God speaks "loudly" like that to us, we'd know it, and respond appropriately, but what about those times God speaks in a "still small voice?"[7] Will we hear that? That still small voice may be, as it was for Elijah, an important word of encouragement *and* correction. I believe the Spirit can also nudge me in a helpful direction *if I'm listening*. But I shouldn't make doctrines

---

7. 1 Kings 19:12. This word of encouragement came to a suicidally depressed Elijah (see v. 4) who, thinking he was alone, had fled into the wilderness to escape King Ahab's threats. God's correction was essentially, "Get back in the game."

out of those nudges or judge others who disagree with them, and I try not to follow them into stupid ventures, because I can be mistaken and need God's correction.

The prosperity preachers would have you believe that things are so much simpler, that there's a formula by which you can manipulate God into giving you everything you want. But it does not exist! The fact that God desires to speak to us, his creatures, is a miracle. Isaiah 30:21 says, "Whether you turn to the right or to the left, your ears will hear a voice behind you, saying, 'This is the way; walk in it.'" In context, this was moral instruction to the "People of Zion" and not a magic formula for how to find a parking space. However, except for that incident when I almost stepped in front of a bus in China, it was only as I got older and thought back, that I realized there were other occasions when God miraculously protected me. Even the smaller gifts we receive on a daily basis are only half the blessing if we fail to notice and recognize the Giver. James tells us, "*Every* good and perfect gift is from above, coming down from the Father of heavenly lights" (James 1:17, emphasis added).

In the black church, it is common to hear someone giving a testimony or beginning a prayer by saying, "Thank you, Lord, for waking me up this morning, clothed and in my right mind. You put food on my table and clothes on my back, and you got me up and on my way. . . ." Then the person reviews other large or small gifts the Lord has provided, or the choir breaks into "As I look back over my life . . . I can truly say that I've been blessed."[8] In my opinion, that tradition is essential to surviving suffering, and who better than our African American brothers and sisters to teach us that skill? God causes the rain to fall on the righteous and the unrighteous, the just and the unjust, but we are blessed and strengthened when we thank God for *all* good things rather than attribute them to chance or luck or our own efforts.

So, why give credit to luck? Instead, thank God as the giver of all good things and praise Jesus for fulfilling his promise to be with us

8. Rev. Clay Evans, "I've Got a Testimony," written by Anthony Tidwell, Meek Gospel Music, Inc., 1995.

to the very end of the age (Matt. 28:20). Jesus may have been speaking of a more transcendent presence, a promise to guide the church through the ages to a final victory in the cosmic war or maybe a reminder that he'll be with us through "the valley of the shadow of death" (Ps. 23). But if you're anything like me, doubts and fears chill my soul over far more mundane matters in this life. Like the old hymn says, "I need Thee every hour,"[9] and I'm not too hard-bitten to admit it. It helps to listen to the wisdom of the psalmist.

> *I cried out to God for help;*
>> *I cried out to God to hear me.*
> *When I was in distress, I sought the Lord. . . .*
> *Then I thought, "To this I will appeal: . . .*
> *I will remember the deeds of the Lord;*
>> *yes, I will remember your miracles of long ago.*
> *I will consider all your works*
>> *and meditate on all your mighty deeds."*
>> —Psalm 77:1-2, 10-12

Discussion Questions

1. Presuming you pray, why? And what do you expect?
2. Describe a situation where you might have died? Why didn't you die (luck, your efforts, or a gift)?
3. Most of us indulge in "what if . . .?" and "if only . . ." speculations. Pick one such possibility from your life and imagine some of the complexities *any* intervention in the "natural" flow of events might have had on extended history.
4. In raising Lazarus from the dead, what were the consequences Jesus may have been strategically navigating? If he knew what was to happen, why did he weep?
5. What can we learn from how Jesus and Paul prayed even though they didn't get what they asked for?

---

9. Annie Sherwood Hawks and Robert Lowry, "I Need Thee Every Hour," 1872.

Chapter 17
What about Discipline?

Do not make light of the Lord's discipline,
and do not lose heart when he rebukes you,
because the Lord disciplines the one he loves,
and he chastens everyone he accepts as his child.

—Hebrews 12:5-6

SOME PEOPLE MAKE EXCUSES FOR SUFFERING by claiming (usually telling others) that it's God's discipline, and we should welcome it because it proves we are God's children. That can be true if it is, in fact, *discipline* and not destructive *suffering*. Suffering harms, destroys, and even kills, which we have seen is Satan's bailiwick.

Back in the day, I mean, *way back* in the day, Neta wrote an article titled, "Let's Talk About Spanking."[1] It was a good article, talking about when, why, and how judicious spanking might be done in a way that would not harm a child physically or emotionally. Such an article was needed because there was a growing controversy between those who quoted, "Whoever spares the rod hates their children" (Prov. 13:24), and others who recognized that physical abuse can truly damage children emotionally and sometimes physically.

Neta's article undoubtedly helped a lot of parents avoid harming their children, and as it turned out, our own children chose *not* to use corporal punishment at all with our grandchildren. But they

---

1. Neta Jackson, "Let's Talk About Spanking," *Family Life Today*, September 1981.

did receive correction and discipline, which coincides with the last half of that verse from Proverbs: "But the one who loves their children is careful to discipline them." The point is that some Old Testament language regarding discipline—which includes mention of "the rod" and even "flogging" or "stripes" (Ps. 89:32)— causes us to presume God's discipline involves dreadful forms of suffering and might even include annihilation . . . especially if we think it was God who ordered those consequences in Old Testament times.

Discipline That Heals

If we still think God was responsible for—or maybe even the direct cause of—all deadly floods, famines, plagues, and wars in ancient times, and we say those events are God's retribution for sin, we are likely to transfer that assumption to the New Testament where it speaks of God disciplining us. For instance, consider this passage from Hebrews 12:4-13.

> [4] In your struggle against sin, you have not yet resisted to the point of shedding your blood. [5] And have you completely forgotten this word of encouragement that addresses you as a father addresses his son? It says,
>
> > "My son, do not make light of the Lord's discipline,
> > and do not lose heart when he rebukes you,
> > > [6] because the Lord disciplines the one he loves,
> > > and he chastens everyone he accepts as his son."
>
> [7] Endure hardship as discipline; God is treating you as his children. For what children are not disciplined by their father? [8] If you are not disciplined—and everyone undergoes discipline—then you are not legitimate, not true sons and daughters at all. [9] Moreover, we have all had human fathers who disciplined us and we respected them for it. How much more should we submit to the Father of spirits and live! [10] They disciplined us for a little while as they thought best; but God disciplines us for our good, in order that we may share in his holiness. [11] No discipline seems pleasant at the

time, but painful. Later on, however, it produces a harvest of righteousness and peace for those who have been trained by it.

[12] Therefore, strengthen your feeble arms and weak knees. [13] "Make level paths for your feet," so that the lame may not be disabled, but rather healed.[2]

Do not be confused by words like *discipline, rebuke,* or even *chasten*. This chapter is *not* about punishment for the reader's sin. The writer is trying to encourage believers who are facing persecution not from God and not as a consequence for their own sin but from the evil acts of those who might shed their blood (v. 4). Earlier, in verse 1, he told them that there is a "great cloud of witnesses" [presumably watching from heaven] who are in essence cheering them on, and he reminds the believers to "run with perseverance the race marked out for us, fixing our eyes on Jesus" (vv. 1, 2).

The point is that "God disciplines us for our *good*" (v. 10), and the writer employs two analogies to help his readers make the most of their training: a loving father and—based on the sports imagery—a good coach (v. 13). No good father or good coach will maim, disable, or kill their child or athlete. Yes, training is hard, and we may be tempted to give up, but even if we should be injured from other sources or if our blood is shed by our persecutors, the loving Father's objective is to strengthen the "feeble arms" and heal the "weak knees." Anything that would disable or damage the body or spirit is not from God because it would defeat God's objective.

Pruning That Strengthens

Another New Testament passage often cited as "proof" of God being the cause of suffering in our lives is John 15:1-8.

[1] "I am the true vine, and my Father is the gardener. [2] He cuts off every branch in me that bears no fruit, while every branch that does bear fruit he prunes so that it will be even

---

2. The first quotation in verses 5 and 6 of this passage in Hebrews comes from Proverbs 3:11-12, and the second one in verse 13 comes from Proverbs 4:26. Both are encouragements and wisdom from a loving father to a son.

more fruitful. ³ You are already clean because of the word I have spoken to you. ⁴ Remain in me, as I also remain in you. No branch can bear fruit by itself; it must remain in the vine. Neither can you bear fruit unless you remain in me.

⁵ "I am the vine; you are the branches. If you remain in me and I in you, you will bear much fruit; apart from me you can do nothing. ⁶ If you do not remain in me, you are like a branch that is thrown away and withers; such branches are picked up, thrown into the fire and burned. ⁷ If you remain in me and my words remain in you, ask whatever you wish, and it will be done for you. ⁸ This is to my Father's glory, that you bear much fruit, showing yourselves to be my disciples."

For those of us not *vignerons* (those who cultivate vineyards), this parable can be scary. Will we be "cut off" and "thrown into the fire"? Bible teacher and author Bruce Wilkinson feels Jesus' allegory about the vine and branches has been broadly misunderstood, even by most translators. He explains:

> First, a clearer translation of the Greek word *airo*, rendered in John 15 as ["cut off" in the above NIV translation] would be "take up" or "lift up." We find accurate renderings of *airo*, for example, when the disciples "took up" twelve baskets of food after the feeding of the five thousand (Matt. 14:20), when Simon was forced to "bear" Christ's cross (Matt. 27:32), and when John the Baptist called Jesus the Lamb of God who "takes away" the sin of the world. (John 1:29).
>
> In fact, in both the Bible and in Greek literature, *airo* never means "cut off." Therefore, when some Bibles render the word as "takes away" or "cut off" in John 15, it is an unfortunate interpretation rather than a clear translation.

Wilkinson finally understood the background of Jesus' analogy when an experienced vineyard owner explained to him the agricultural process Jesus was referencing with his parable of the vine.

"New branches have a natural tendency to trail down and grow along the ground," [the vineyard owner] explained. "But they don't bear fruit down there. When branches grow along the ground, the leaves get coated in dust. When it rains, they get muddy and mildewed. The branch becomes sick and useless."

"What do you do?" I asked. "Cut it off and throw it away?"

"Oh, no!" he exclaimed. "The branch is much too valuable for that. We go through the vineyard with a bucket of water looking for those branches. We lift them up and wash them off. . . . Then we wrap them around the trellis or tie them up. Pretty soon they're thriving."[3]

This understanding is even referenced in verse 3 where Jesus emphasized the importance of cleaning when he told the disciples, "You are already clean because of the word I have spoken to you." But that's the point: Keep the branches healthy; don't cut them off. I have never worked in or been around a vineyard as most of Jesus' disciples probably had. But I've done my share of vegetable gardening, and yes, you do cut off suckers—that's pruning—but suckers are not branches. One of the consequences of the common misunderstanding of Jesus' story is that it implies that authentic branches which were once part of the vine might be cut off if they don't do enough good works. Some Christian sects do preach that we can lose our salvation, but that fear flies in the face of Jesus' promise: "I give them eternal life, and they shall never perish; no one will snatch them out of my hand" (John 10:28). Or as Paul put it:

For I am convinced that neither death nor life, neither angels nor demons, neither the present nor the future, nor any powers, neither height nor depth, nor anything else in all creation, will be able to separate us from the love of God that is in Christ Jesus our Lord (Rom. 8:38-39).

3. Bruce Wilkinson, *Secrets of the Vine: Breaking Through to Abundance* (Colorado Springs, CO, Multnomah Publishers, 2006), 33-35.

If all those forces cannot separate us from the love of God, how could our own failures cause us to "lose our salvation"? Hopefully, our faith results *in* fruit (good works), but our good works did not secure our salvation (Titus 3:5), nor do they preserve it. The easy out for those who still think God the gardener cuts off branches is to say that such people were never true branches in the first place. Theoretically, maybe they were just suckers. But that's not a judgment for us to make nor an accusation with which we should threaten anyone.

But Doesn't Suffering Produce Strength?

Yes! But it can also crush and destroy. For the Christian, growth is not achieved by increasing our *self-confidence* but by increasing our confidence in God's sustaining presence with us no matter what our circumstances. Real suffering (not just the troubles and hardships of the world) is what maims, destroys, or even kills—which are Satan's intentions. If we think God plans, initiates, and delivers destructive suffering, we are going to be in trouble and find it very hard to believe that God is with us, cares about us, and longs to deliver us. That's the very confusion with which Satan loves to infect our minds and hearts.

But when suffering does come from whatever ungodly quarter—and it will—if we are confident of God's presence and care, God can transform that suffering into strength for us. Paul even admits, "We know that suffering produces perseverance; perseverance, character; and character, hope. And hope does not put us to shame, because God's love has been poured out into our hearts" (Rom. 5:3-5). In that sense, suffering can produce growth—not *self*-confidence but hope in God's love and goodness. That's how saints throughout the ages have grown stronger through suffering and prepared for persecution.

Neta and I have had the privilege of researching and writing up the stories of hundreds of believers who have, over the centuries, suffered for Christ.[4] Before returning to heaven, Jesus told

4. Published in *On Fire for Christ* (stories about anabaptist martyrs drawn from the 16th century records found in *Martyrs' Mirror*); 40 *Trailblazer Books* for young readers about great Christian heroes; five volumes of *Hero*

his disciples, "Go into all the world and preach the gospel to all creation" (Mark 16:15). Nothing has brought more persecution to Christians than their efforts to obey this command. In fact, except for the Reformation, all major waves of persecution of Christians throughout the centuries corresponded to the church's evangelistic surges. That's why Jesus wisely warned his followers:

> "Be on your guard; you will be handed over to the local councils and be flogged in the synagogues. On my account you will be brought before governors and kings as witnesses to them and to the Gentiles. But when they arrest you, do not worry about what to say or how to say it. At that time you will be given what to say, for it will not be you speaking, but the Spirit of your Father speaking through you.
>
> "Brother will betray brother to death, and a father his child; children will rebel against their parents and have them put to death. You will be hated by everyone because of me, but the one who stands firm to the end will be saved" (Matt. 10:17-22).

Note that Jesus said, "*When* they arrest you" (emphasis added), with no question in his mind that this would be the fate of his followers. But he also identified the reason: "You will be hated by everyone because of me" (v. 22).

In the book of Acts, we read that the church grew from 120 to 3,000, then 5,000 men (plus women and children). At multiple points, we read that the number of believers multiplied or greatly increased. Some estimates suggest there may have been well over 10,000 or more believers in Jerusalem at the time of Stephen's martyrdom and the subsequent persecution from which "all the believers except the apostles fled. . . . But the believers who had fled Jerusalem went everywhere preaching the Good News about Jesus" (Acts 8:1, 4, NLT).

Tales featuring character qualities for family reading; and *Fear Not,* over 200 stories of God's faithfulness to men and women through the centuries who have weathered the worst.

Persecution followed them just as Jesus had predicted, first in the person of Saul of Tarsus and his posse tracking down and arresting Christians to bring them back to Jerusalem for imprisonment, and then by those who resisted the gospel in the towns and cities around the Mediterranean to which the Christians had fled.

After Herod executed James (Acts 12:2), the apostles and other leaders also dispersed from Jerusalem. Tradition (and in some cases Scripture) identifies these destinations and the martyrdom of those leaders:

- Andrew .... Achaia
- Antipas.......... Turkey
- Barnabas......... Cyprus
- Bartholomew....Armenia
- James the Less..... Egypt
- John............ Ephesus
- Jude Thaddeus .... Persia
- Luke ....Greece
- Mark............. Egypt
- Matthew ....Ethiopia
- Matthias........... Judea
- Paul .... Rome
- Peter.............. Rome
- Philip .... Hierapolis
- Simon..............Syria
- Thomas ....India
- Timon........... Philippi
- Timothy.........Ephesus

Only the Apostle John was said to have died a "natural" death on the island of Patmos to which he had been exiled and from which he wrote the Book of Revelation.

This is why there are frequent encouragements, especially in the New Testament epistles, to remain faithful during persecution. At that time, torture was a real possibility for every follower of Jesus. Waves of intense persecution occurred during the reign of the fifty-four Roman emperors from A.D. 30 to A.D. 311. In fact, between A.D. 249–251, Emperor Decius made an empire-wide attempt to wipe out Christianity.

In studying persecution throughout the history of the church, some believers who thought that *everything* came directly from God—whether it was good or bad—seemed to interpret that to mean they were invincible "until God called them home." And that mindset produced a certain kind of brave behavior.

For instance, David Livingstone's harrowing experiences in Africa seemed to embolden him in his fight against the slave trade. He survived being mauled by a lion, abandonment by staff members and his government, and severe bouts of malaria and hemorrhoids. One night some tribal warriors confronted him, thinking *he* was one of the slavers. Livingstone brazenly opened his shirt, exposing his white chest in the moonlight. The warriors stopped in their tracks, and then one of them cautiously moved forward, his spear extended. He brought it right up to Livingston's chest and drew it slowly across his white skin. A tiny trickle of blood oozed out, looking black rather than red in the pale moonlight. Suddenly, the warriors let out a cry, turned, and fled back into the jungle.

Whether God increased Livingstone's confidence through those crises or not, it's important to remember what Jesus said when Satan dared him to leap off the pinnacle of the temple: "It is written, 'You shall not tempt the Lord your God'" (Matt. 4:7).

Suffering Can Develop Empathy

In reviewing Professor of Philosophy Michael Brady's book, *Suffering and Virtue* (Oxford University Press, 2018), Amy Coplan and Heather Battaly summarized:

[I]n Brady's view, suffering is both causally necessary for the development of many . . . virtues in individuals, as well as . . . for groups to develop and express the virtues of justice, love, faith, and trust. . . . [W]ithout it, we would sometimes fail to respond to bad things in appropriate ways and thereby fail to be virtuous. In this manner, Brady argues that suffering can be intrinsically good as a fitting response to bad things, even though it is also intrinsically bad.[5]

At times I have said I find it hard to trust any pastor who has not suffered, either because they haven't lived *long* enough or *through*

---

5. Amy Coplan and Heather Battaly, "Enough Suffering: Thoughts on *Suffering and Virtue*," National Library of Medicine, Oct. 21, 2021. https://www.ncbi.nlm.nih.gov/pmc/articles/PMC8528655/.

enough to transmit empathetic care to others. (This is of particular concern for any pastor who wields significant power.) You can learn theology, you can learn management, and you can learn how to preach, but to care for others . . . you must have been in need yourself. Paul reminded us of "the God of all comfort, who comforts us in all our troubles, so that we can comfort those in any trouble with the comfort we ourselves receive from God" (2 Cor. 1:3-4).

This can result from the disciplinary training God initiates, which is designed to strengthen and even toughen us up, showing us that we can do far more than we thought we could do.

While I was in basic and advanced training for the infantry, we crawled under barbed wire as live machine gun rounds screamed overhead, controlled our panic in a gas chamber while we put on and cleared a gas mask, navigated extreme obstacle courses and went on twenty-mile forced marches carrying over sixty pounds of gear. It was not intended to break us, but to test us, strengthen us, and show us we could do far more than we had imagined and to teach us how to work together as a team. I embraced that training, confident that the Army had no intention of destroying me. Once, when being tested on the parallel bars, I kept going when the callouses on my hands tore off and blood streamed down my arms. As I mentioned before, when the six months were over, I received "The Trainee of the Cycle" award and returned to my National Guard unit. But that same Army sent many of my comrades to Vietnam where they experienced mayhem, dismemberment, torture, and even death. Those who returned required extended therapy to heal from PTSD. Some never recovered.

While God can redeem Satan's most destructive suffering, Brady's right: real suffering is "intrinsically bad." Therefore, it's never wise to seek it for its own sake. Unfortunately, there have been times in church history (as well as in other religions) when suffering was sought for its own sake or even self-inflicted. For instance, until the 1960s, self-flagellation was widespread in some sectors of the Catholic Church.[6]

---

6. "Why do some Catholics self-flagellate?" *News Magazine*, Nov. 24, 2009. http://news.bbc.co.uk/2/hi/uk_news/magazine/8375174.stm.

When Jesus sent his disciples out into a hostile world, he advised them: "Be wise as serpents and harmless as doves" (Matt. 10:16, NKJV). I think that's what the three Hebrew children did centuries earlier when they told King Nebuchadnezzar, "If we are thrown into the blazing furnace, the God we serve is able to deliver us from it, and he will deliver us from Your Majesty's hand. *But even if he does not*, we want you to know, Your Majesty, that we will not serve your gods or worship the image of gold you have set up" (Dan. 3:17-18, emphasis added). That was a delicate balance of confidence in who God is and why they would remain faithful to him without presuming how God would respond. Most importantly, when the king did throw them into the furnace, there appeared a fourth being with them who looked like "a son of the gods" (v. 25).

While God had the power and did in fact rescue these young men from harm in the furnace, such specific miracles are not promised—sometimes they happen, and sometimes they don't. This does not mean God is capricious. Instead, God is aware of *all* the complex and possibly far-reaching implications of any action and makes his decision accordingly. However, Shadrach, Meshach, and Abednego seemed to have put their faith in the promise in Deuteronomy 31:8: "The Lord himself goes before you and will be with you; he will never leave you nor forsake you. Do not be afraid; do not be discouraged." Some theologians think the person with them in the fire was a *Christophany*, an Old Testament manifestation of Jesus himself.

In the five waves of major persecution of Christians over the centuries, many believers have found strength to remain faithful by remembering that promise in Deuteronomy as well as Jesus' renewal of it in Matthew 28:20: "Surely, I am with you always, to the very end of the age." Our experiences of discipline are to prepare us to be faithful under any circumstances.

Discussion Questions

1. If "God disciplines us for *our good*" (Heb. 12:10), why might someone think things that destroy or seriously harm us are from God?

2. What do you think of Bruce Wilkinson's explanation of John 15:1-8 in which he says the Greek word *airo* is wrongly translated "cut off" and should be rendered "lift up" or "take up"?

3. What kind of discipline do you imagine was necessary to build up the early Christians so they could survive the persecution they faced? What might you need to prepare you for your calling?

Chapter 18
Embracing Redemptive Suffering

When Christ calls a man, he bids him come and die.

—*Dietrich Bonhoeffer, The Cost of Discipleship, 1937*[1]

DIETRICH BONHOEFFER WAS A PASTOR AND THEOLOGIAN in Germany during the rise of Nazism. The more aware he became of Hitler's intentions to exterminate the Jews and pursue world domination, the stronger he felt a call from God to resist. While most German Protestant churches cooperated with Hitler and the Nazi pogrom, Bonhoeffer was one of the founding members of what became known as the "Confessing Church," a minority of believers who risked their lives to oppose Hitler.

Years before, as part of his pastoral training, Bonhoeffer had taught a confirmation class for children in the slums of Berlin, worked with the poor and unemployed in Barcelona, and—during a period when he was a student at Union Theological Seminary in New York—worshiped with the Abyssinian Baptist Church of Harlem. Each experience heightened his understanding of the Gospel from the view of people who suffer.

One of his classmates in New York was a black student named Frank Fisher. One day Dietrich and Frank and a few other fellows from the seminary went out to a restaurant. The waiter took orders from the young white men but ignored Frank. When Bonhoeffer realized what was happening, he stood up in disgust. "If Frank

---

1. Dietrich Bonhoeffer, *The Cost of Discipleship* (New York: Touchstone, 1995), 89.

cannot get service here, none of us will eat here." And he led the group out of the restaurant.

That was a small price to pay but the beginning of Bonhoeffer's conviction that "When Christ calls a man, he bids him come and die," which became his understanding of redemptive suffering.

The Apostle Paul noted that "Very rarely will anyone die for a righteous person, though for a good person someone might possibly dare to die. But God demonstrates his own love for us in this: While we were still sinners, Christ died for us" (Rom. 5:7, 8). Later—perhaps realizing the end of his own life was near—Paul wrote, "Join with me in suffering, like a good soldier of Christ Jesus" (2 Tim. 2:3). Back in Germany and fully aware of the possible consequences, Dietrich Bonhoeffer "joined" Paul.

As part of his active resistance, Bonhoeffer smuggled Jews out of Germany. One day at the Swiss border, a Nazi guard looked at Bonhoeffer's papers and said, "So. You are an agent in the *Abwehr* [the German military intelligence service]," said the guard. He glared into the car. "Who are these others?"

"Civilian agents with the Abwehr on special assignment," said Bonhoeffer casually, leaning against the car, hands in his pockets. "It's all there in the papers."

"How long will you be staying in Switzerland?" the guard pressed.

"That, sir, is secret Abwehr business," said Bonhoeffer pointedly, getting back in the car. "May we go through now?"

With a shrug, the guard handed the papers back through the open car window and lifted the barrier so the car could go through. A few miles down the road, the fearful people in the car began to relax. Bonhoeffer grinned. "Well," he joked to his relieved passengers, who were all German Jews, "smuggling Jews into Switzerland is secret business, right?"

Bonhoeffer was arrested by the Gestapo in 1943 and hung on April 9, 1945—one month before Germany surrendered to the Allies.[2]

---

2. Adapted from Dave and Neta Jackson, *Hero Tales II*, (Champaign, IL: Castle Rock Creative, 1997, 2021), 9-18.

A Different Kind of Suffering

Redemptive suffering is different from any suffering we've discussed so far. While God does not cause it (he does not *cause* destructive suffering), he is aware of its threatening potential and gives us a degree of agency in terms of embracing the risk or not. We may be victims when it comes to other kinds of suffering—the tornado that strikes your house, the drunk driver who hits your kid, the war that wipes out your town, the cancer that ravages your pancreas. But voluntarily taking a risk that puts us in harm's way while we help someone else is the first characteristic of redemptive suffering. And that is what distinguishes it from the self-inflicted suffering cautioned against in the previous chapter. Redemptive suffering cannot be for the purpose of building up one's personal strength or glory but only to help others.

When we embrace redemptive suffering, we may not understand all the consequences—what they will be, when they will strike, and how severe they will get—but we have some choice in whether we take the risk. Redemptive suffering is seen most profoundly in Jesus' struggle as he prayed in the Garden of Gethsemane, contemplating the suffering before him. It involved a *call* and Jesus' *agreement* to follow: "Not my will, but yours be done" (Luke 22:42). He really did have a choice.

The second characteristic of this kind of suffering is that it has the potential of accomplishing good: spreading the Gospel, pushing back injustice, and relieving someone else's suffering. It's a *call* to enter the battle against Satan and his schemes!

We Join with but Do Not Replace Christ

In Chapter 14 we looked at Christ's suffering and death as he surrendered his life as a ransom to redeem us from Satan's demand for our death. That's truly redemptive suffering on a cosmic scale, something we can't accomplish for anyone else, even if we die.

Perhaps because of the hostility toward Christians at the time, New Testament calls to suffer often focus on being willing to preach the Gospel no matter what the risk. In the last chapter we noted that all the early leaders of the church in Jerusalem except

John were probably martyred. So, when Paul says, "I want to know Christ—yes, to know the power of his resurrection and participation in his sufferings, becoming like him in his death" (Phil. 3:10), there was a high possibility that some of those who read his letter would literally be killed for simply preaching the Gospel.

But that's not the only way we join Christ in his suffering. Hebrews 4:15-16 tells us that Jesus is *also* "a high priest who is [able] to empathize with our weaknesses, . . . one who has been tempted in every way, just as we are—yet he did not sin. Let us then approach God's throne of grace with confidence, so that we may receive mercy and find grace to help us in our time of need." In pointing out the importance of that work of Christ, Vince Brackett, copastor of Brown Line Church in Chicago, said, "I don't want a God who doesn't know what it's like to suffer. A God who is above suffering or forgets suffering cannot provide the same comfort and help as Jesus who truly understands."[3] We, too, can join with others in their suffering.

Like Jesus or Paul or Bonhoeffer, who voluntarily submitted their lives, we usually have a degree of choice concerning how fully we embrace or stand with someone else in their suffering. The early Christians confounded pagan Roman rulers by their care for the sick. In an article in the National Library of Medicine, Sarah Becker noted,

> While the early Christian Church demonstrates a deep desire to relieve physical suffering, the Greco-Roman world in which it developed lacked the same impetus to respond to human need, especially in the context of epidemic or communicable disease. Christianity's dedication to health care, and its belief that assisting the sick constituted an absolute obligation, distinguished early Christianity from its contemporary cultural milieu which regularly ignored and excluded the sick.[4]

3. Vince Brackett & Hayley Larson, "Suffering & Prayer," Brown Line Church, Feb. 4, 2024, 55, ff. https://www.youtube.com/watch?v=stQHWavwV5E.

4. Sarah Becker, "Awaking to Mutual, Reciprocal Need in Plague and Epidemic Disease: The Origins of Early Christian Health Care," *The Linacre Quarterly*, May 2021, 163-174.

She went on to explain that ironically, "As the sick recovered, their newly acquired immunity also allowed them to serve others without the risk of death, which further improved survival rates." Of course, that is not always the case. There's no promise of a personal reward in this life for the sacrifices we make for others.

Breaking the Bonds Satan Has on Others

At several points in his ministry, Jesus made it clear that the healing he extended to others, even in this life, was part of his direct assault on Satan's realm. It began with his announcement of his mission by reading from the scroll of Isaiah in the synagogue of Nazareth:

"The Spirit of the Lord is on me,
   because he has anointed me
   to proclaim good news to the poor.
He has sent me to proclaim freedom for the prisoners
   and recovery of sight for the blind,
to set the oppressed free,
   to proclaim the year of the Lord's favor" (Luke 4:18, 19).

Jesus accepted that assignment for real, not metaphorically, but for real!

Anytime one of us, as believers, embarks on trying to relieve these conditions for others, we are taking part in Jesus' assault on Satan's strongholds. For instance, when Jesus healed the crippled woman on the Sabbath, he specifically said she was someone "whom Satan has kept bound for eighteen long years" (Luke 13:16). When Jesus healed anyone with mental issues, he spoke of it as casting out demons.[5] Today, "demon possession" is not helpful terminology when speaking of mental or emotional issues, primarily because of the stigma society puts on that term. But whether any of our mental or physical maladies are the direct result of a Satanic attack, a chemical imbalance, a genetic condition, or an

---

5. For example: Matthew 8:28-32; 12:22; 15:21-28; 17:14-21; Mark 1:21-28, 32-34, 39; 16:9; Luke 8:2.

accident, the result in terms of human suffering is the same. *It is not part of God's purpose or will!* In fact, when the seventy-two disciples whom Jesus sent out to proclaim the good news and heal people everywhere—fulfilling the very goals he announced in the synagogue of Nazareth—they returned with glowing reports of their success. Regarding all those reports, Jesus said, "I saw Satan fall like lightning from heaven" (Luke 10:18). In that sense, all healing is an assault on Satan's program of suffering and death.

Our daughter, Rachel, is a therapist who is beloved by her clients, not only because of her skill in helping them get at the roots of their emotional distress, but because of her extraordinary ability to empathize with their suffering. However, she pays a high price in "suffering with" her clients. In that regard, even without articulating it, she is "joining with Jesus" by being with hurting people in their suffering.

The Risks of Failure

In college, I became a certified Red Cross Water Safety Instructor. That enabled me to be a lifeguard at Lake Sammamish Bible Camp in Washington State for two summers. Part of my job was to oversee the waterfront as we tried to keep older kids from doing dangerous things and monitored non-swimmers from getting into deep water. Mostly that meant staying alert, counting heads, and blowing our whistles. Only a couple of times did I have to jump in and help a floundering kid back to safety. But as the WSI, I was also responsible for testing and reviewing our lifesaving techniques with the other lifeguards.

The seriousness of our job exploded one weekend when I was actually off duty and not even at camp. A child went under without anyone noticing and drowned. The trauma gripped the whole camp, especially all of us on the waterfront staff. Our training exercises had focused on the techniques of pulling someone to shore, keeping a panicky person from climbing up on us as they clamored to rise above the water, and how to escape if they pulled us under. In simulations, we'd pushed ourselves to our last breath, but what was needed that day at camp was simply a closer eye on a child who just slipped into the darker depths without anyone noticing.

It had happened over the transition between one week's group of kids leaving while the next week's group were arriving. The waterfront was open, and lifeguards were on duty, but there were too many kids—some of whom had not yet been tested for their water safety or assigned to a counselor, who might have provided an additional pair of eyes on their activity. The parents of the child who drowned were actually still at the camp, but nobody was watching their child. It was not anyone's fault, and yet it was everyone's. Needless to say, policy changes were made, but the horror stuck with us!

I wouldn't claim that our counseling and lifeguarding at that summer camp was embarking on redemptive *suffering*, but it certainly contained the possibility of failure as we so tragically discovered.

The Risk of Misunderstanding

One of the other risks of participating in redemptive suffering is being misunderstood. Certainly, that happened for Jesus, and it can happen for us, too.

In his book, *The Cost of Discipleship*, Dietrich Bonhoeffer made it clear he understood Jesus' example and teachings—particularly the Sermon on the Mount—to call all believers to respond nonviolently when faced with an enemy. Given the probability of being drafted into the German military where he would have undoubtedly had to use deadly weapons, he chose to accept the help of his brother-in-law to join the *Abwehr*, the German military intelligence service. With his many contacts outside Germany, Bonhoeffer was supposed to gather information beneficial to the German military. However, he operated as a double-agent, using his connections and meetings with Allied forces to give *them* information about Hitler's plans and activities. He also used his position to smuggle Jews out of Germany, as described earlier, and to help pastors of the Confessing Church evade military service. It was for these two charges that he was arrested on April 5, 1943, and later hung.

Some people think Bonhoeffer abandoned his pacifist convictions in the face of Nazi brutality and actively participated in an assassination plot, particularly the attempt on July 20, 1944, code-named "Operation Valkyrie."[6] It's true that Bonhoeffer took an early and active stand against the Nazis, and he did have connections with some of the plotters—operatives in Abwehr and even relatives—however, he was not charged with conspiracy and was in prison for fifteen months *prior* to the attempt on Hitler's life where he could not have taken any active role in that attempted assassination. None of his letters from prison published posthumously reveal any knowledge of the plot, and in the one written on July 21, the day after the failed attempt, he said, "I am prepared to stand by what I wrote"[7] in *The Cost of Discipleship* where he articulated the biblical basis for his pacifist commitment.

In their well-researched volume, *Bonhoeffer the Assassin?* Mark Thiessen Nation, Anthony G. Siegrist, and Daniel P. Umbel claim that though Bonhoeffer may have known about some plots to kill Hitler, "There is not a shred of evidence that Bonhoeffer was linked in any way to these attempts on Hitler's life."[8] But the idea made a good Hollywood movie, *Valkyrie* (2008), though Bonhoeffer was not directly named in it.

What Does "Redemptive Suffering" Mean for Us Today?

The Civil Rights Movement of the '60s and '70s gave us a long list of names of men and women who suffered even to the point of death on behalf of others and for a righteous cause. At one point, someone in our church small group joked semi-seriously, "Sure, I'm willing to lay down my life for you, . . . but am I willing to run upstairs to get your sweater?" Small, everyday sacrifices can be the training ground for the redemptive suffering Jesus calls us to.

During the COVID pandemic, we got an urgent email sent out to everyone by a woman in our church who had serious COVID symptoms and felt very sick but didn't have a car to get to the hos-

---

6. Eric Metaxas, *Bonhoeffer, Pastor, Martyr, Prophet, Spy,* (Nashville, Thomas Nelson, 2010), 319.

7. Dietrich Bonhoeffer, *Letters and Papers from Prison,* (London, S.C.M Press, 1953), 124-125.

8. Mark Thiessen Nation, Anthony G. Siegrist, and Daniel P. Umbel, *Bonhoeffer the Assassin?* (Grand Rapids: Baker Academics, 2013), 86.

pital. Could someone give her a ride? Neta and I both hesitated. No one knew very much about the virus yet. Giving a ride could expose us to this deadly virus, which had already claimed the lives of some of our friends. But our conscience wouldn't rest, so we called and said we'd give her a ride. It was what Christ would want us to do. But someone else had immediately offered a ride, so our offer wasn't needed. We were embarrassed by how relieved we were—but also realized we'd been tested. It was important that we came to the point where we were willing.

Discussion Questions

1. How do you respond to the statement, "Redemptive suffering cannot be for the purpose of building up one's personal strength or glory but only to help others"?
2. If Christ's death was the only thing that could pay the ransom to redeem us from Satan, in what other ways can we join with Christ in his suffering?
3. In what ways might adopting a persecution identity be detrimental to the work of Christ in the world?
4. How does Jesus' announcement of his mission in Luke 4:18,19 provide a roadmap for how we might join with Christ in his ministry of breaking the bonds of Satan? What risks do we take in doing so?

Chapter 19
How Should We Then Live?

God is our refuge and strength,
always ready to help in times of trouble.
So we will not fear when earthquakes come
and the mountains crumble into the sea.
Let the oceans roar and foam.
Let the mountains tremble as the waters surge!

—*Psalm 46:1-3* (NTL)

Nᴇᴛᴀ'ꜱ ꜰᴀᴍɪʟʏ ʟɪᴠᴇᴅ ɪɴ Sᴇᴀᴛᴛʟᴇ ꜰᴏʀ ʏᴇᴀʀꜱ where her parents worked in Christian schools—her dad as the principal and her mother as a teacher. But, when they grew up, Neta and her siblings all made their home in the Midwest. Several years after Neta's parents retired, they decided to relocate near the rest of us, and chose an assisted living community in Wheaton, Illinois. Neta volunteered to help by driving them the two-thousand miles cross-country while their belongings came via moving van.

It was a trip we and all the family had made many times for visits, plus they would be going through Montana, where her dad had grown up and other relatives lived. Neta's parents were in good health, in fact, Neta awoke in the motel on the second morning to see her dad doing his usual push-ups. In the afternoon, some thirty miles from Glendive, Montana, on I-74, Neta's dad, eyes closed, started to fall over toward her. Attempting to awaken him or push him back to his side of the seat, she wasn't aware of drifting to the left until her front wheel dropped a couple inches off the main asphalt onto the shoulder. She overcorrected and lost control as the car bounced back onto the highway, fish-tailed across two lanes, rolling over until it came to rest, right-side up in the righthand ditch, facing the opposite direction.

People stopped to help, and neither Neta nor her mother, who'd been in the backseat, seemed to be injured. But her dad, who had only a small scratch on his bald head, remained unconscious. At the nearby hospital, he was pronounced dead of "heart failure." The doctor speculated he'd been having a heart attack before the accident, which probably accounted for him falling over onto Neta.

The trauma of the accident and her dad's death made it very hard for Neta to avoid feeling that she had *killed* her father. If only she hadn't lost control. If only she hadn't tried to push him back into his seat. If only she'd taken a rest stop earlier. If only she hadn't volunteered to drive. If only . . . *There's no end* to the things that might have led to a different conclusion: If only the asphalt-to-shoulder hadn't been uneven. If only one of the siblings had returned to live in Seattle, the folks wouldn't have moved. If only it had been some other day. Why did God let it happen? But it always echoed as: "If only I hadn't *killed* my dad!"

A local pastor came to the hospital and put his arm around Neta. After hearing the story and seeing her anguish, he said, "You can ask God to forgive you." The pastor was not declaring blame; he was simply giving Neta a way to interrupt the blame she was heaping on herself. And it helped. He was being Jesus to her in that moment.

While our experiences of suffering—their severity, nature, and destruction—may be varied and subjective, suffering is unquestionably our human destiny. But if we conclude, based on God's character as revealed in Jesus, that God is rarely—if ever—the *initiator* of human suffering, then let's review the most common sources of that debilitating, exhausting pain that so often crushes us and others.

Causes of Suffering Reviewed

Human Accidents. Human tragedies, such as what happened to Neta and her parents, are accidents. There was no reason to think God caused it. There was no reason to blame Neta—nothing reckless or unwise. There was no one else involved—no malice or fault on anyone's part. In fact, even though Satan does embark on direct attacks on God's children, there's no explicit reason to blame Satan for that accident, even though he always takes glee in suffering and death. We make honest mistakes and have accidents. So do others. There is no value in assigning blame.

Natural Phenomena. As noted in the epigraph at the beginning of this chapter, God is our only refuge from *fear* of destructive earthquakes, roaring seas, or tumbling mountains. We could add solar flares, deadly asteroids, floods, rogue viruses, or tragic genetic anomalies, because the nature of God's creation includes unavoidable dangers that have sadly brought suffering to millions. But those same mechanisms have provided us with a world so uniquely suited to human life it's hard to imagine anything better. This fact is rarely taken into account by those who claim such tragic natural events are God's punishments.

Still, we cannot help but wonder—since Jesus stilled a storm, healed hundreds,[1] and fed thousands—why doesn't God do more miracles today? But maybe he *does* . . . and we don't realize that millions more could have died from COVID without vaccines or that a shift in weather could have resulted in mass starvation had he not brought rain. We also have no idea what other consequences might have resulted from the particular miracle we'd prefer—mysteries we may never know.

Cosmic Warfare. Satan is real. He is at war with God, God's purposes, and God's people . . . that includes you and me and all other humans. There are many places in Scripture where Satan is specifically identified as causing suffering and death. Jesus' earthly ministry regularly included healing people from Satan's oppression and relieving their suffering.

Siding with the Enemy. Our human cooperation with Satan's agenda can range from seemingly insignificant selfish choices to full-blown dedication to evil—violent criminals, ruthless tyrants, abusers, human traffickers, lying politicians, etc. On a personal lev-

---

1. "Jesus did many other things as well. If every one of them were written down, I suppose that even the whole world would not have room for the books that would be written" (John 21:25).

el, Satan relishes seeing humans taking advantage of one another, abusing those who are weaker, trying to move up by pushing someone else down. But the Bible also speaks of the "principalities and powers . . . the rulers of the darkness of this age . . . spiritual hosts of wickedness in the heavenly places" (Eph. 6:12, NKJV). There's reason to believe this refers to Satan's demons in cooperation with human *systems*—oppressive regimes, exploitative economic institutions, ruthless policing and unjust incarceration—all those bigger-than-life enterprises that, while working under "respectable" names and mandates, create great suffering behind the scenes.

Again, we rightly pray that God's "will be done, on earth as in heaven," a vision that should include physically stopping Satan's minions—including evil humans and systems—from the harm they would do. And maybe God stops those evil endeavors more often than we realize, but only God can know the tendrils of consequences from any intervention.

Foolish Choices. Living according to God's revealed wisdom often results in a better life while spurning God's moral laws and the wealth of wise proverbs in the Scriptures often brings pain. This happens not because God delights in punishing us, but because there are natural and often painful consequences for foolish choices. So, when in pain, invite the Holy Spirit to reveal the truth. Do I need to change, make amends, seek help? However, wise maxims aren't promises for an easy life because there are all the other forces we've just enumerated that affect our life experience.

One other thing about "foolish choices": while we often think of them on a personal level in terms of what we need to learn and change, they readily happen on a collective level where masses of people align with the "principalities and powers" in advancing Satan's agenda of pain and destruction. The justification of slavery or the denial of climate change are examples from the past and present of how foolish ideas become widespread beliefs—sometimes claiming religious justifications and loyalty.

Suffering into Joy. Psalm 30:11 says, "You turned my mourning into dancing" (NRSV). This represents God's magnificent work of redemption, retrieving what Satan stole and restoring good back to you. But it should never be mistaken to mean God did evil in the

236

first place so that good could come from it. Because good is never the ultimate result of that transaction. This confusion often shows up in personal testimonies of suffering where people say things like, "I just thank God for taking the life of my baby. Had that not happened, I might never have given my life to Jesus." Well, I can't blame anyone for trying to find a way to cope, but there is better news: God never *caused* the tragedy! But he made himself known at the time of grief, and that *comfort* may have brought the person to Jesus.

Voluntary Suffering. This covers accepting God's discipline so we can grow stronger as well as embracing redemptive suffering, the themes of the previous two chapters. As someone who was well acquainted with suffering,[2] the Apostle Peter was very concerned for how the believers would weather the coming persecution. Preparing them became a repeated theme in his first epistle. Christ set the example of voluntarily suffering—not as a punishment for sin, but in accordance with furthering God's greater purpose. It takes a lot of practice to be prepared for such a sacrifice, and in a church the tone is set by the leaders.

> To the elders among you, I appeal as a fellow elder and a witness of Christ's sufferings who also will share in the glory to be revealed: Be shepherds of God's flock that is under your care, watching over them—not because you must, but because you are willing, as God wants you to be; not pursuing dishonest gain, but eager to serve; not lording it over those entrusted to you, but being examples to the flock. And when the Chief Shepherd appears, you will receive the crown of glory that will never fade away.
>
> In the same way, you who are younger, submit yourselves to your elders. All of you, clothe yourselves with humility toward one another, because,
>
> *"God opposes the proud*
> *but shows favor to the humble."*

---

2. Church tradition says he was crucified upside-down in Rome. https://www.gotquestions.org/apostle-Peter-die.html.

Humble yourselves, therefore, under God's mighty hand, that he may lift you up in due time. Cast all your anxiety on him because he cares for you.

Be alert and of sober mind. Your enemy the devil prowls around like a roaring lion looking for someone to devour. Resist him, standing firm in the faith, because you know that the family of believers throughout the world is undergoing the same kind of sufferings.

And the God of all grace, who called you to his eternal glory in Christ, after you have suffered a little while, will himself restore you and make you strong, firm and steadfast. To him be the power for ever and ever. Amen (1 Pet. 5:1-11).

The noncoercive and nonpunitive tone of this passage is unmistakable. It is the gracious environment and practice we all need to prepare us to stay faithful in voluntary suffering.

Relief from Frightening Stereotypes

I acknowledged at the beginning of this book that I would not be able to answer all the questions. There are still many mysteries I don't understand, and I haven't even experienced severe suffering as so many have, but I trust that in reviewing the above causes for suffering you have found explanations for several kinds of suffering that do not indict God. In so doing, I hope you have been able to set aside some bad theology or at least recognize how overstated the claims are which say . . .

- God micromanages everything, therefore all suffering is from God.
- God's holiness demands our death for sin, therefore we deserve suffering in this life because we're all sinners.
- Permanent harm or even death might be God's discipline.
- If there's a cosmic war between God and Satan, it has little to do with us.
- God is *not* primarily about relationships with people, instead . . .

- God is more like pagan gods: destroying opponents and rewarding obedience.
- If God is good and all powerful, he would and could stop all suffering now.

Most importantly, I hope you embrace the realization that Jesus is the most complete revelation of God's character. This does not mean jettisoning the God of the Old Testament, nor does it mean amalgamating contradictory characteristics of God—a little of this and a little of that. No, it means modifying your *image* of God by the revealed character of Jesus.

So, How Should We Live?

Resist the temptation to be terrified by or to terrify others by the ancient characterization of God as fundamentally violent and retributive, determined to rain suffering on all sinners. Because it is Satan—not God—who comes to steal, kill, and destroy. Satan is the only one to fear. He is our adversary and the would-be deceiver of all God's people, even the saints, when we inadvertently blame God for Satan's work. It is Jesus, by his sacrifice, who redeems us from Satan's claim.

Pray with confidence, knowing that God is not willing for any to perish, that God weeps when anyone suffers, that God is rich in mercy, and by his grace he is so eager to save us from Satan that he sacrificed his Son to Satan's demands.

Fear not. While God calls us to repent of our sin, which can alleviate some suffering for ourselves or others, few if any of us understand all for which we need to repent. In fact, true repentance is more a process of facing our need and turning from justifying ourselves. Remember, God was and is willing to live *with* us sinners while we were and are still unaware of our sin. He does not despise us!

Ask God to show us if there's anything we can learn *in* our suffering—not just to acknowledge how the consequences of our poor choices might have led to suffering, but also in terms of how we may be able to help others, how we can advocate for justice, share the Gospel, and do the work Jesus announced as he began his ministry.

Practice thanking God for *all* good gifts, large and small. It helps us be more aware of his presence, love, and care . . . especially in the middle of our suffering.

Cultivate contentment. In Philippians 4:13 Paul wrote, "I can do all things through Christ who strengthens me" (NKJV). Some health and wealth preachers use that verse like a peptalk from a coach telling us we *really can* run a four-minute mile "if we run with Jesus."[3] What a cruel misapplication of the Scriptures when (baring a miracle) most of us will never run a four-minute mile no matter how much we trust Jesus. They ignore the context of the verse, which comes after Paul's encouragement to "rejoice in the Lord always . . . the Lord is near . . . do not be anxious . . . pray with thanksgiving . . . guard your hearts and minds . . . think on whatever is noble, right, pure, lovely, admirable, excellent, and praiseworthy . . .. And the peace of God will be with you" (vv. 4-9). Focusing on these things will cultivate contentment even in times of trial and suffering (v. 12). The NIV translation (and one or two others) then renders verse 13 as "I can do *all this* through him who gives me strength" (emphasis added). In other words, cultivating *contentment* is important for enduring suffering—a very specific application, not a formula for achieving all our personal goals.

"Wait on the Lord." This encouragement is mentioned often in Scripture[4] and is relevant to the discussion of our myopic conception of time and space back in Chapter 12. The prosperity preachers would say to grab "your best life NOW." But truth is where you find it, even in such unlikely places as The Rolling Stones' song from 1969, "You Can't Always Get What You Want." Within the lyrics themselves, Mick Jagger's caveat varies: "*Sometimes* you'll . . . get what you need;" i.e., life's a crapshoot. Other lines use the singular: "*Sometime* [suggesting, *in time*] you'll find you get what you need, so just wait. But there is far more hope when we

---

3. See Joel Osteen, "Stronger than You Think," https://www.youtube.com/watch?v=MHow0xCAmbY, Sept. 5, 2022, 5:20.
4. Lam. 3:25; Psa. 27:14; 33:20-22; 37:7, 34; 62:5; 130:5; Isa. 40:3.

wait on the Lord because he can transform suffering into a blessing for us and anyone else.

Embrace grace for yourself and others. The patriarchs and even the disciples didn't understand everything. Certainly, we don't either. So, be careful with platitudes. Some reflect a truth that can only be comforting when considered *at the right time.* For instance, Paul made it clear he'd "prefer to be away from the body and at home with the Lord" (1 Cor. 5:8) because he'd then be in a better place. But to tell a bereaved person that their loved one is "in a better place" is rarely comforting at the time. So, give them grace to find comfort in your presence, perhaps your silent presence as Job's friends offered before they began trying to diagnose what was wrong. After all, we may need that grace and time as well before we can cope with suffering.

Live by faith, humbly sharing our peace in ways that encourages rather than condemns others, always remembering that the opposite of faith is not doubt but certainty.

Sing. When we look back over our life without the confusion of bad theology and see that there are various causes of suffering that needn't blame God, we can begin to see how faithful God has been and sing with abandon as Jenn Johnson does about the "Goodness of God," who is so, so good[5] Or, if a classical hymn is more meaningful to you, try "Great Is Thy Faithfulness," by Thomas Chisholm.[6]

> *Great is Thy faithfulness, O God my Father;*
> *there is no shadow of turning with Thee;*
> *Thou changest not, Thy compassions, they fail not;*
> *as Thou hast been, Thou forever wilt be.*

> *Great is Thy faithfulness!*
> *Great is Thy faithfulness!*
> *Morning by morning new mercies I see;*
> *all I have needed Thy hand hath provided:*

---

5. Jenn Johnson, "Goodness of God," Bethel Music, © 2019.
6. Thomas O. Chisholm, "Great Is Thy Faithfulness," 1923.

great is Thy faithfulness, Lord, unto me!

Summer and winter, and springtime and harvest;
sun, moon, and stars in their courses above
join with all nature in manifold witness
to Thy great faithfulness, mercy, and love.

Pardon for sin and a peace that endureth,
Thine own dear presence to cheer and to guide;
strength for today and bright hope for tomorrow:
blessings all mine, with ten thousand beside!

Discussion Questions

1. In the past, which causes of suffering did you think were initiated by God? For each of them have you changed your mind?
2. If many ancient people groups believed their pagan gods destroyed opponents and rewarded obedience, how did your view of God differ? How has your view of God changed after studying this book?
3. Under the subhead, "How Should We Then Live?" which of those resiliency perspectives do you think might be most helpful to you?

Annotated Bibliography

For any of the following books, it's enlightening to go online—Amazon, Goodreads, or any other collection of reader reviews—and take note of who says what and why. Were the positive reviews from people who were struggling and found help? Or were they from contented people who were glad to have their beliefs reinforced? Were the negative reviews from struggling people who went away empty? Or from established people who criticized those who challenged their views?

Boyd, Gregory A. *Is God to Blame? Beyond Pat Answers to the Problem of Suffering,* Downers Grove, IL: InterVarsity Press, 2003.

— *Cross Vision: How the Crucifixion of Jesus Makes Sense of Old Testament Violence,* Minneapolis, MN: Fortress Press, 2017.

— *God of the Possible: A Biblical Introduction to the Open View of God,* Adi, MI: Baker Books, 2000.

Greg's *Is God to Blame?* is about suffering, but you have to add sections from his other books as well as his sermons and "ReKnew" blogs to collect his relevant views on the subject. Also, Greg slips into logical arguments (related to the primary theme of those books) that feel more confounding and complex than illuminating—true though they may be.

Bridges, Jerry. *Trusting God.* Colorado Springs, CO: NavPress, 2008.

The author is so committed to the sovereignty of God over all things, that he ignores the "texts of terror" and other representations of God that seem completely incompatible with the character of Jesus Christ. In essence, Bridges concludes that in spite of that dissonance, we should trust that God is good, essentially gaslighting the experience of many who suffer.

Copan, Paul. *Is God a Vindictive Bully?: Reconciling Portrayals of God in the Old and New Testaments*. Grand Rapids, MI: Baker Academic, 2022.

When I first found Copan's book, I thought there might be no need for my book. However, he takes a very different approach to harmonizing the Old and New Testament portrayals of God. Where he seems to downplay the severity of the "Texts of Terror" by suggesting they are not as bad as they sound, I say, "Yes they are!" It's not just what those passages say, but the implications people have *believed* for millennia concerning God's character. And they've used that model to justify such endeavors as the Crusades, the Doctrine of Discovery, the Inquisition, the genocide of indigenous peoples, slavery of Africans, and the idea of Manifest Destiny.

Copan downplays the seriousness of the Texts of Terror by saying that despite the death penalty for sixteen different crimes,[1] "all of these could be commuted to monetary payment, with one exception. Murder."[2] In practice, that may have frequently happened, but for most of those crimes, the Law does not merely set death as a *maximum* penalty, it mandates capital punishment as *required* with such language as: "*must* be put to death," "*must* be burned with fire," "you *must* . . . stone them to death." And when the Pharisees brought the woman caught in adultery to Jesus, they weren't suggesting she needed to pay a fine. They said, "In the Law Moses *commanded* us to stone such a woman" (John 8:5, emphasis added). Also, being a "false prophet" or a "blasphemer" merited stoning according to Mosaic Law and it, too, was carried out (wrongly) against God's prophets (Matt. 23:37; Acts 7:52). In fact, shortly after Jesus' as-

---

1. Other sources list as many as twenty-eight capital offenses: https://jesusalive.cc/death-penalty-sins-old-testament/.

2. Paul Copan, *Is God a Vindictive Bully?: Reconciling Portrayals of God in the Old and New Testaments* (Grand Rapids, MI: Baker Academic, 2022), Kindle, 72.

cension, the Sanhedrin (the ruling council in Jerusalem) stoned Stephen for what they believed was blasphemy (Acts 7:54-59). So, Copan's argument that the death penalty didn't really paint God as harsh because it was just hyperbole and never meant to be applied (except for murder) is utterly specious.

Concerning the "Old Testament warfare texts," Copan maintains that they, too, "utilize exaggeration or hyperbole and can't in any way be considered 'genocide' or 'ethnic cleansing.'"[3] Really? Genocide is the intent to systematically kill or displace large numbers of people from a particular ethnic group, and God is attributed to giving instructions to do just that, like: "You must destroy them totally. Make no treaty with them, and show them no mercy" (Deut. 7:1-2). It's of no consequence whether Israel fully carried out such commands or not. The text *characterizes God* (not Israel) as ordering that result.

NOTE: Because Copan's conclusions affirm the more traditional wrathful nature of God, some people think Copan bases his ideas on the inerrancy of Scripture while those of us who think the patriarchs got some things wrong do not affirm total inerrancy (which we don't).[4] But when Copan claims the warfare texts are just "exaggeration or hyperbole" and the laws requiring capital punishment weren't so harsh because people could buy their way out (except for murder), he, too, is *not* articulating a literal view of Scriptures, because all those texts identify God as the source.

Ehrman, Bart D. *God's Problem: How the Bible Fails to Answer Our Most Important question — Why We Suffer*. New York: Shakespeare Book House, 2008.

Ehrman has disavowed his faith in Christ. Still, as a renowned Bible scholar, he does not avoid the hard questions, but

---

3. Ibid., 9.
4. "Is God a Vindictive Bully? Interview with Paul Copan," *The Remnant Radio*, Dec. 11, 2023. https://www.youtube.com/watch?v=h1s4agYvAPY. At the end of the show, Michael Rountree praised Copan for supporting the reliability of the Bible and gave a warning: "Be really careful of people who call into question the Scriptures." Despite Rountree's praise, Copan does just that . . . in his own way.

he doesn't give much help, either. The most he can say is, "Our response should be to work to alleviate suffering wherever possible and to live life as well as we can" (p. 278).

Keller, Timothy. *Walking with God through Pain and Suffering*. New York: Penguin Random House, 2013.

Keller divides his book into three sections:

1. The phenomenon of human suffering and the problem of evil and the various ways different cultures, religions, and eras have sought to help people face and get through it.
2. Keller attempts to digest all the Bible says about suffering, but he doesn't deal with the heart of the problem in terms of God's character.
3. Practical help on how we can walk with God in times of suffering, so it changes us for better rather than for worse.

In the end, Keller reminds readers we cannot know the mind of God, but he offers few new breakthroughs.

Kreeft, Peter. *Making Sense Out of Suffering*. Cincinnati, OH: Servant, 1986.

This book doesn't make much sense. Too many rabbit trails, showing off his scholarship regarding cultural responses to suffering while offering too little help. Chapter 7 begins to point us toward Jesus but not in a practical manner.

Lewis, C.S. *The Problem of Pain; Mere Christianity; A Grief Observed*; and *The Lion, the Witch and The Wardrobe*.

These aren't recent, and they don't put together the questions I address, but within them, there are gems of truth relevant to suffering.

Oord, Thomas Jay. *God Can't: How to Believe in God and Love after Tragedy, Abuse, and Other Evils*. Grasmere, ID: SacraSage Press, 2019.

This may be one of the most practical and readable recent books on suffering, making such bold challenges as: "The God who allows evil is guilty," and "Can you imagine Jesus a passive bystander to an evil he could prevent? I can't." Oord argues logically and philosophically but doesn't explain where bad theology comes from. I don't think his use of the concept that "God can't" is helpful or accurate. I believe in miracles, which, if you believe the biblical witness, proves God *can* intervene in natural laws, but there are reasons why he doesn't do so nearly as often as we would like. Also, Oord claims all things have freewill. I disagree. The inanimate universe doesn't have freewill, it operates according to natural laws, some we don't understand, but they still "rule."

Phillips, J.B. *Your God Is Too Small*. New York: Touchstone, a Division of Simon & Schuster, 2004. See the brief discussion of his book in Chapter 10.

Tripp, Paul David. *Suffering: Gospel Hope When Life Doesn't Make Sense*. Wheaton, IL: Crossway, 2018.
    Given the depth of Tripp's personal suffering, this is one of the strongest testaments to God using suffering to strengthen him for ministry: "for my power is made perfect in weakness." Yes, the Potter molds the clay and disciplines his children, but Tripp's suffering was severe, and I have a hard time attributing it to God, even though God used it for good.

Yancey, Philip. *Where Is God When It Hurts?* Grand Rapids, MI: Zondervan, 1977, 2002.
    An excellent book and very accessible without seriously challenging the traditional concepts that God controls everything and might be "disciplining" or punishing us. Philip's recent, *Where the Light Fell* is also relevant and a very personal memoir.

Acknowledgments

Plans fail for lack of counsel,
but with many advisers they succeed.

—*Proverbs 15:22*

When I was helping my friend Nader Sahyouni work on his book, *Anxiety Transformed*, he raised the obvious question about suffering: "God, are you really in control?" He sensed God's answer that he was asking the wrong question. Rather, "The question is not whether I'm in control, it's whether I'm in charge."[1] I told Nader this was great, but he needed to dig much deeper into why we suffer, because there's so much confusion about it. He wisely concluded that would derail the primary purpose of *his* book and focused on learning how to hear and receive God's constant presence and healing in the middle of suffering, regardless of its etymology.

That caused me to review the books on our shelf addressing the problem of pain and to collect newer ones along with scores of articles on the subject. It was a question I'd typically set aside, realizing far greater thinkers than I had answered it to their satisfaction . . . though not mine. Slowly, I began to see a pattern that led to the insights I've suggested in this book. Thank you, Nader.

My wife, Neta, put up with me as I interrupted her so often with, "Hey, listen to this!" or "Would you read this and tell me if it makes any sense?" It was like we'd returned to our college dorms for late-night bull sessions. The further I got into the proj-

---

1. X. Nader Sahyouni, *Anxiety Transformed, Prayer that Brings Enduring Change*, (Skokie, IL: Crossing Place Media, 2022), 128.

ect, the more she picked up my share of household duties, social scheduling, and preparation for the class we co-teach and the reparations committee we're on for African Americans. Thank you, love of my life!

I cannot overlook my gratefulness to those who endorsed the book in the front. I needed a balance of theologians, philosophers, pastors, therapists, and educators. Some may have endorsed my book, realizing their colleagues might not be pleased. But I hope any trouble they get in will be, as John Lewis called it, "good trouble!"

I thank my son, Julian, for designing what I consider is a magnificent cover, and Keri and Michelle for proofreading. Any remaining typos are probably my subsequent additions.

Finally, I give thanks to God. Yeah, I know, that can be a trite phrase offered by athletes and singers when they don't know what else to say, but I say it for a specific reason. I genuinely did have a sense of God's encouragement while working on this, frequently guiding me to the next insight that I'd never considered before and answering my night-time question by the next morning, usually by bringing to mind a scripture passage. But the part that humbles me most is the realization that even though I don't have all the answers, and I may have misrepresented God in some respects, yet God did not strike me down—which is a testament to my conclusion that God is both very good and very forgiving!

www.ingramcontent.com/pod-product-compliance
Lightning Source LLC
Chambersburg PA
CBHW030821090426
42737CB00009B/822